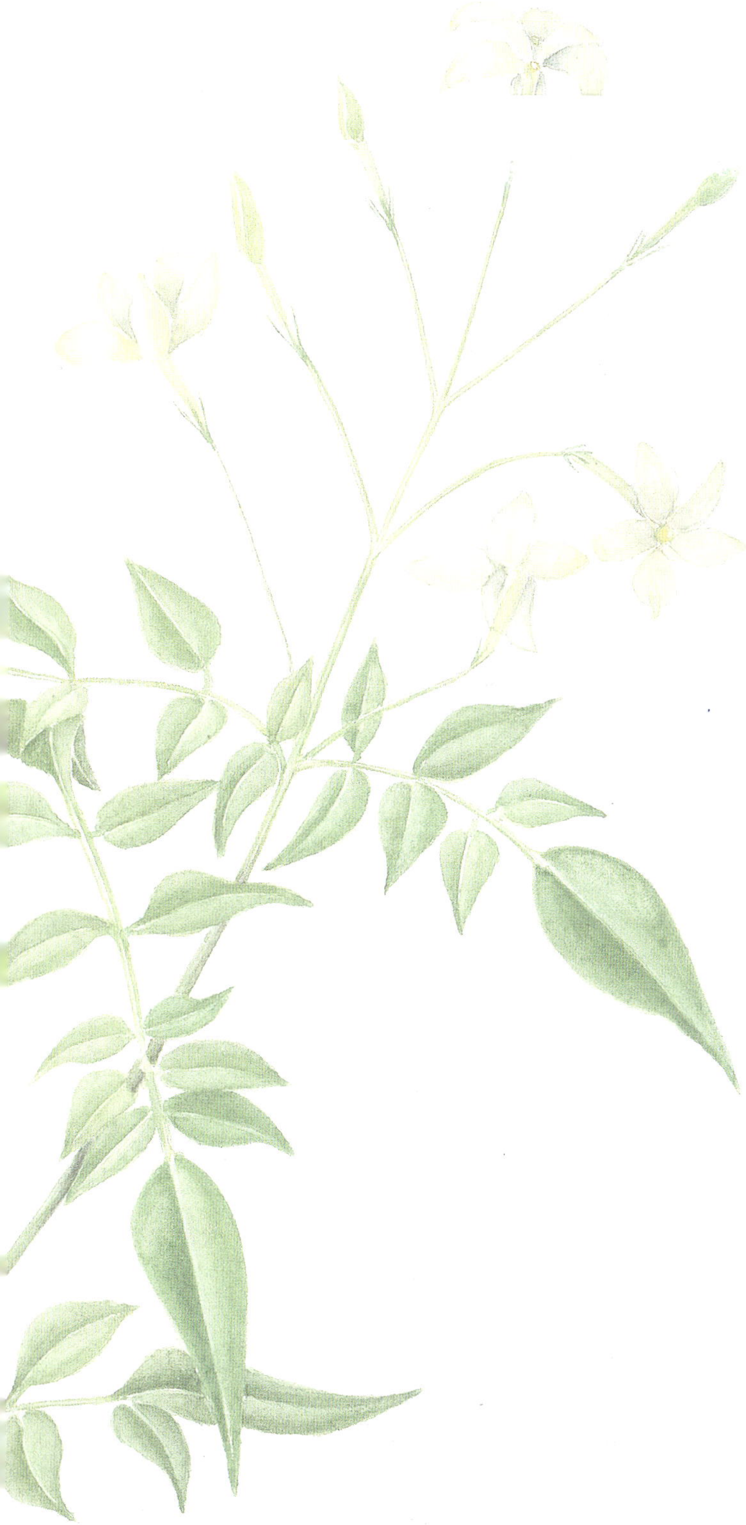

A–Z OF BOTANICAL FLOWERS

IN WATERCOLOUR

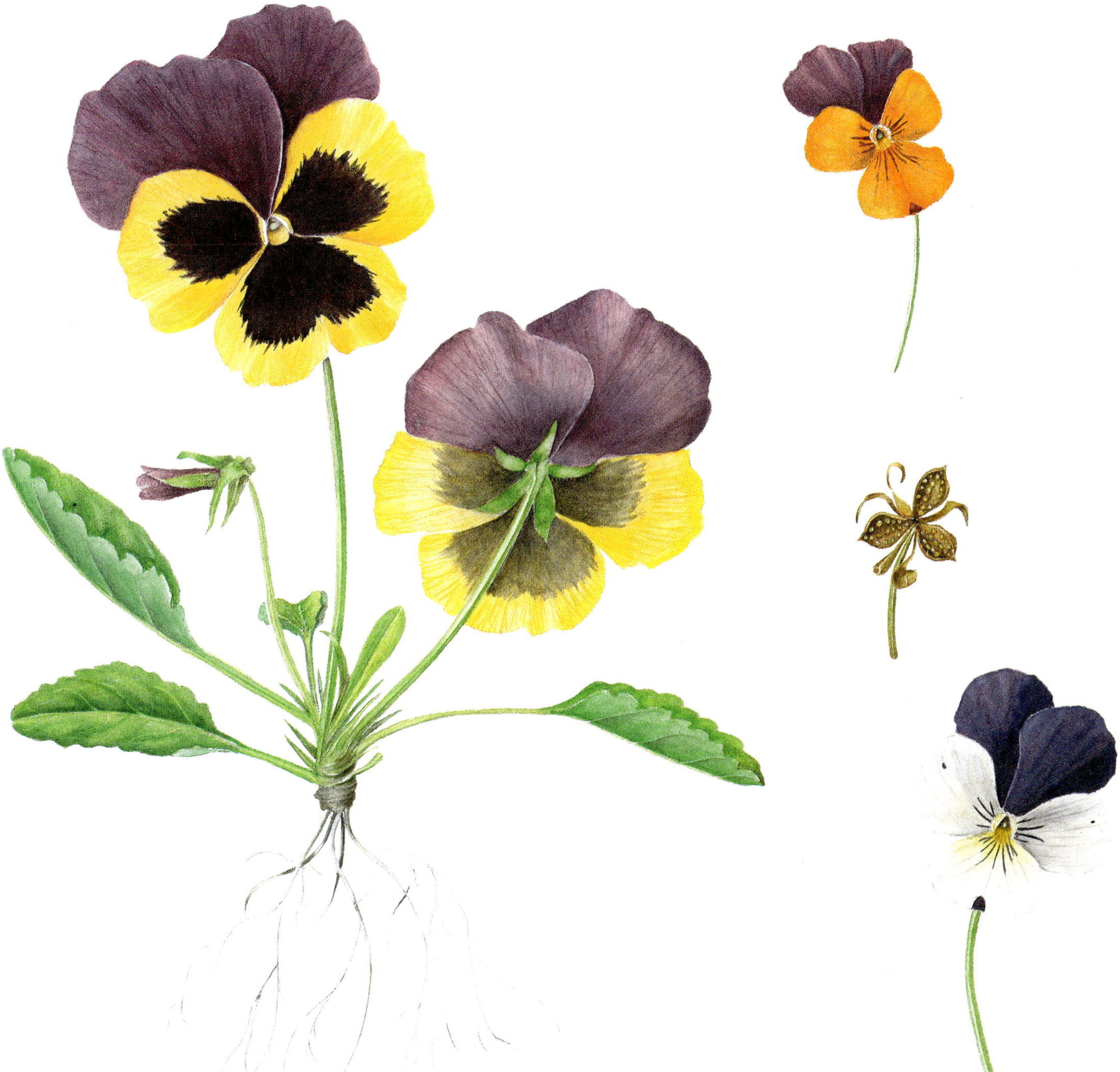

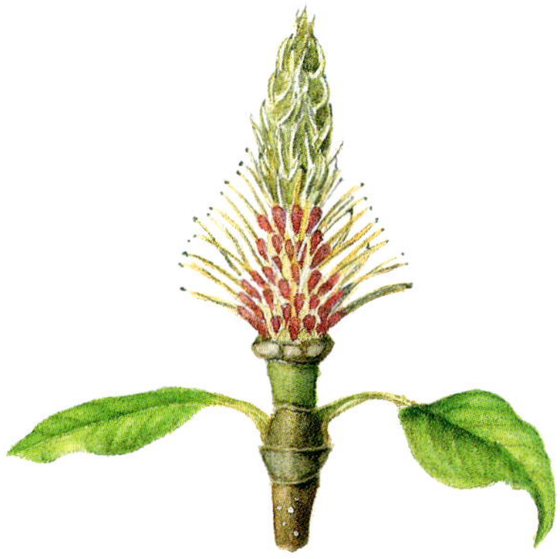

DEDICATION

I would like to dedicate this book to the memory of my late mother and father, Kath and Harry Lakin.

Also to my wife Jane, and son James.

A–Z OF BOTANICAL FLOWERS
IN WATERCOLOUR

MICHAEL LAKIN

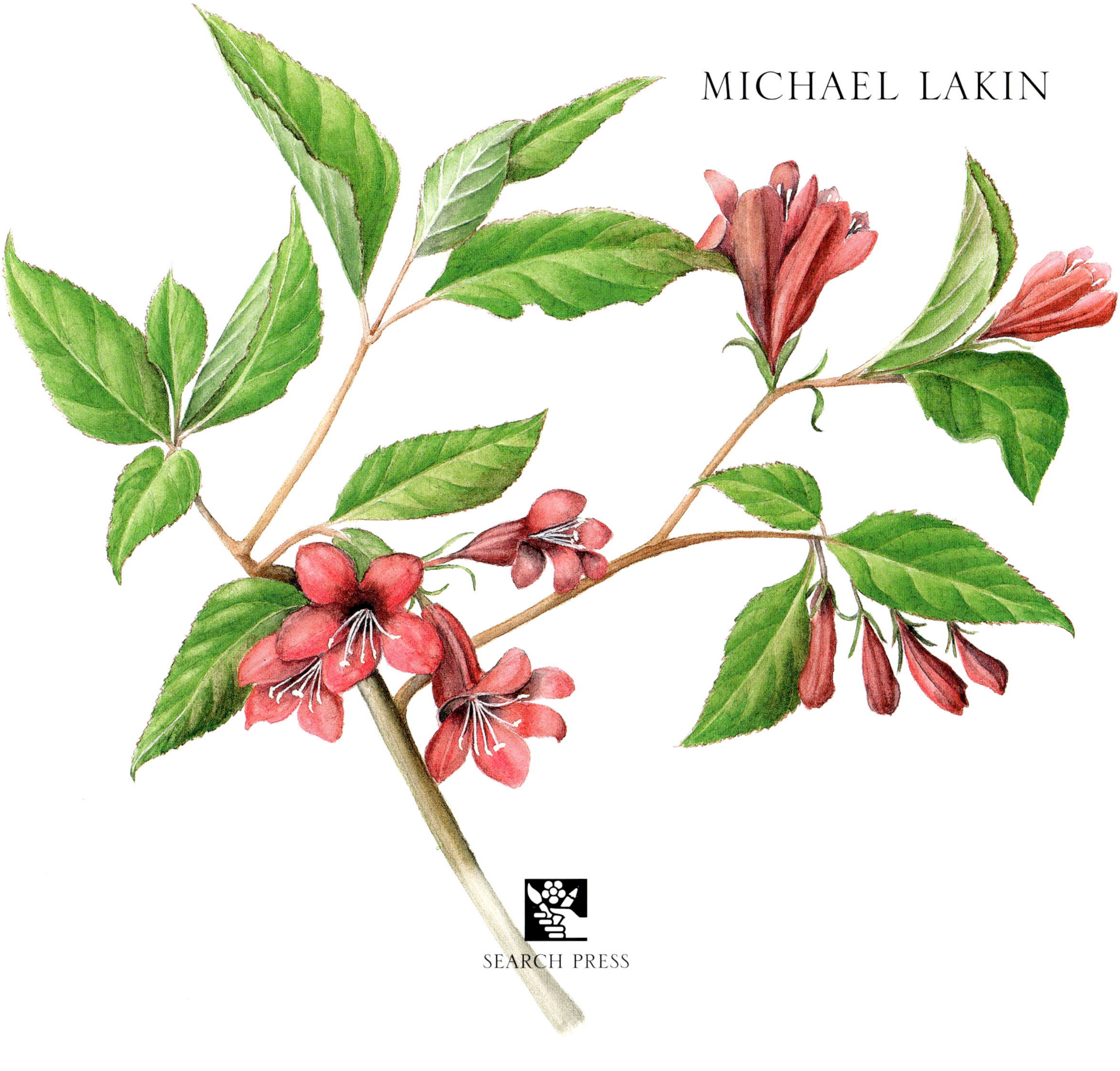

SEARCH PRESS

First published in Great Britain 2012

Search Press Limited
Wellwood, North Farm Road,
Tunbridge Wells, Kent TN2 3DR

Photographs by Roddy Paine Photographic Studios 2012

ISBN: 978-1-84448-562-8

Publisher's note

All the step-by-step photographs in this book feature the author, Michael Lakin, demonstrating his watercolour painting techniques. No models have been used.

Printed in Malaysia

ACKNOWLEDGEMENTS

I would like to thank all of my students for their encouragement in producing this book, especially those who supplied information and plants: Penny Braithwait, Pam Broderick, Julia Blower, Margaret Meagher, Ginni Morrison, Ann Spooner and Janet Stevenson.

Also to all of the staff at Search press, especially Edd Ralph my editor; and to my photographer Roddy Paine.

...And not forgetting my wife Jane, who has had many nights alone while I have been painting in the studio!

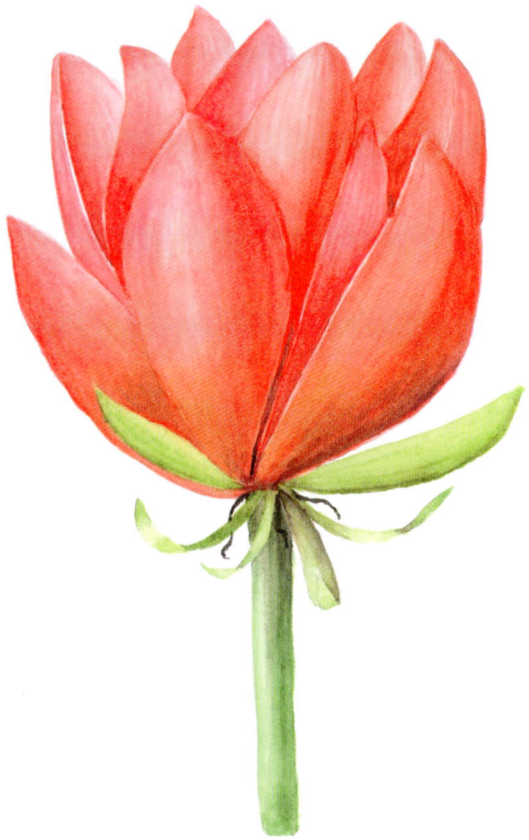

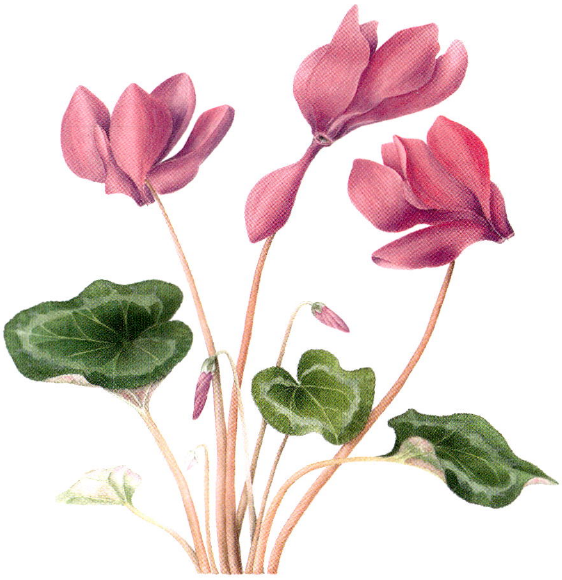

Contents

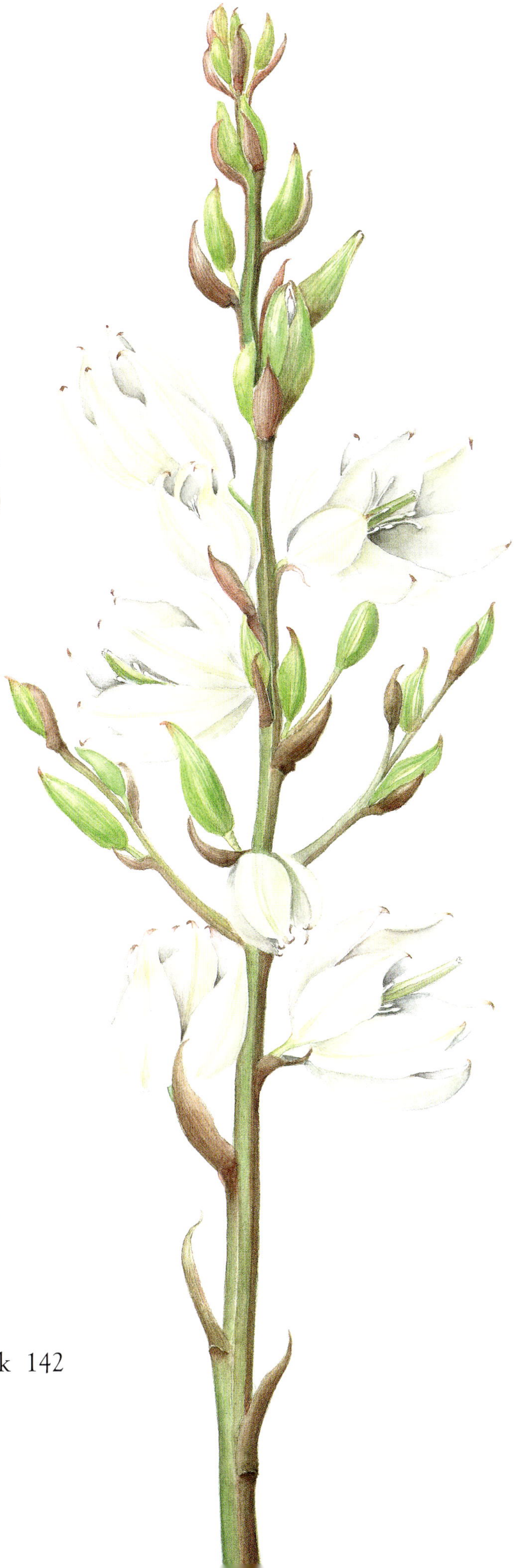

The flowers

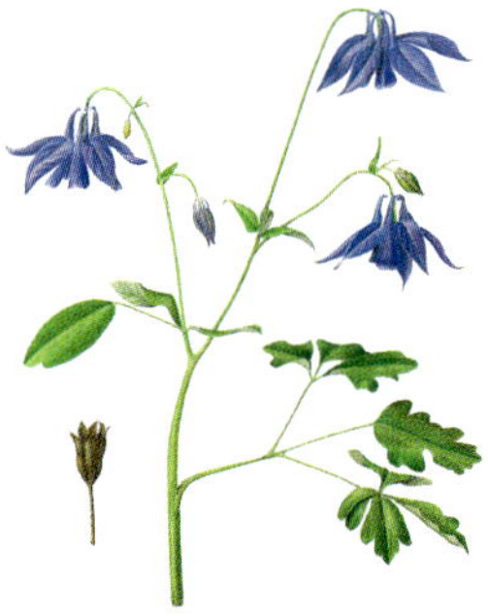

Aquilegia
Pages 38–41

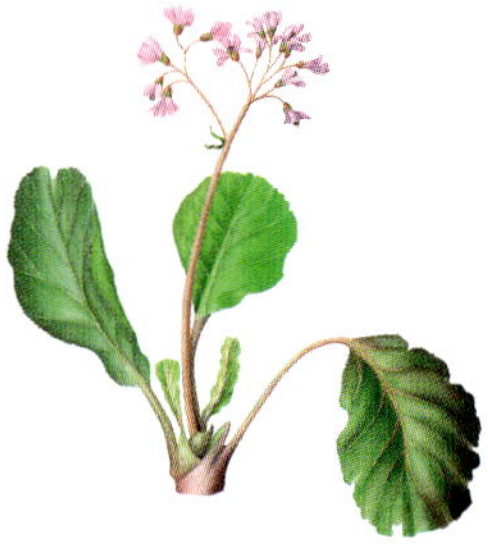

Bergenia
Pages 42–45

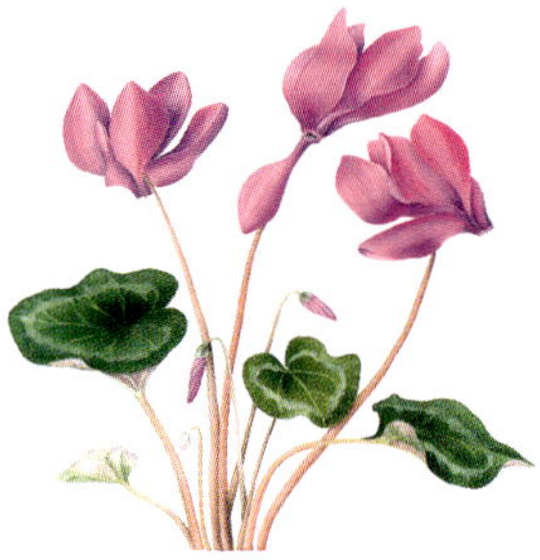

Cyclamen
Pages 46–49

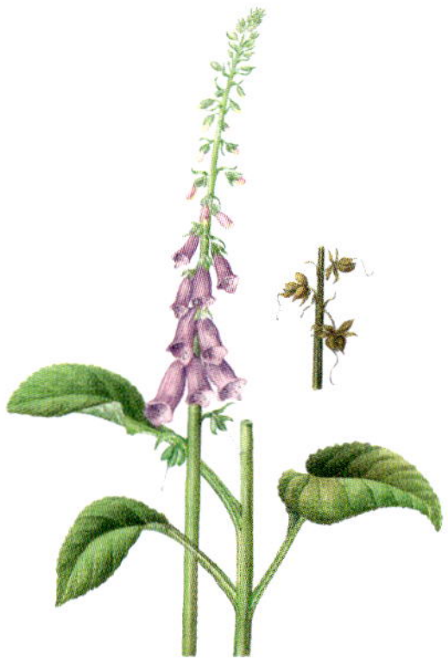

Digitalis
Pages 50–53

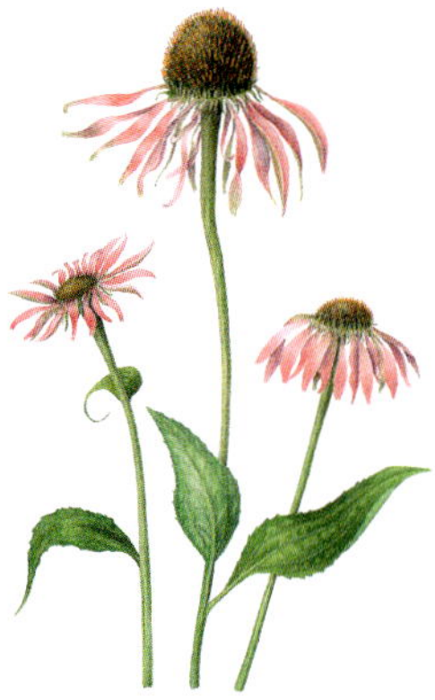

Echinacea
Pages 54–57

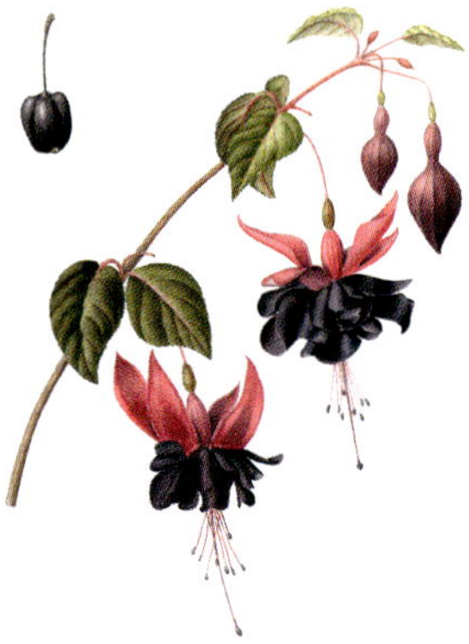

Fuchsia
Pages 58–61

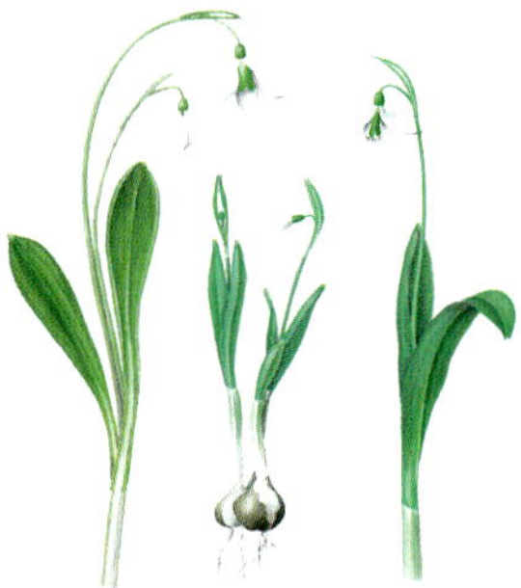

Galanthus
Pages 62–65

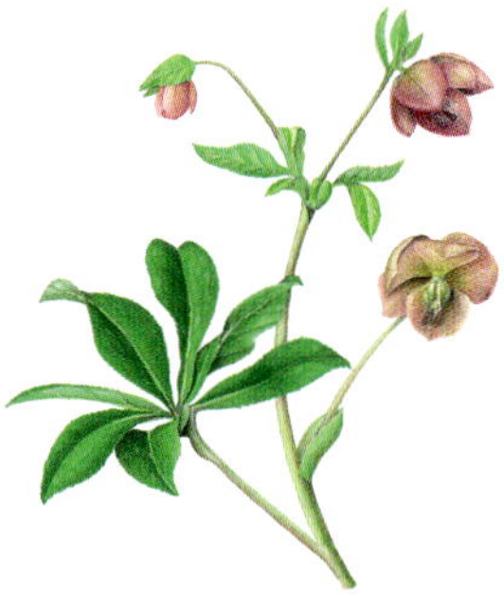

Helleborus
Pages 66–69

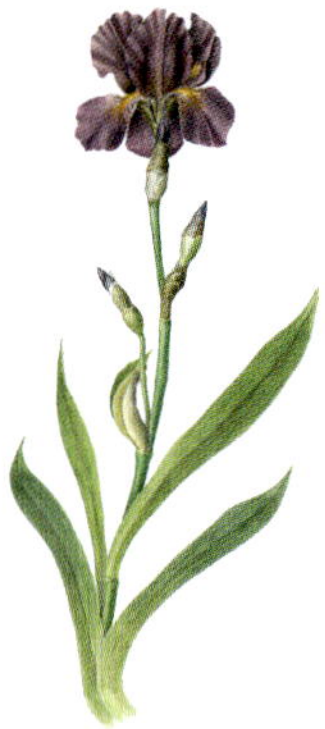

Iris
Pages 70–73

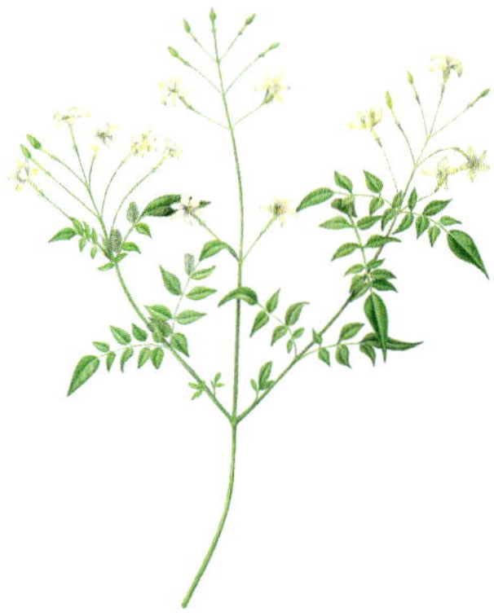

Jasminum
Pages 74–77

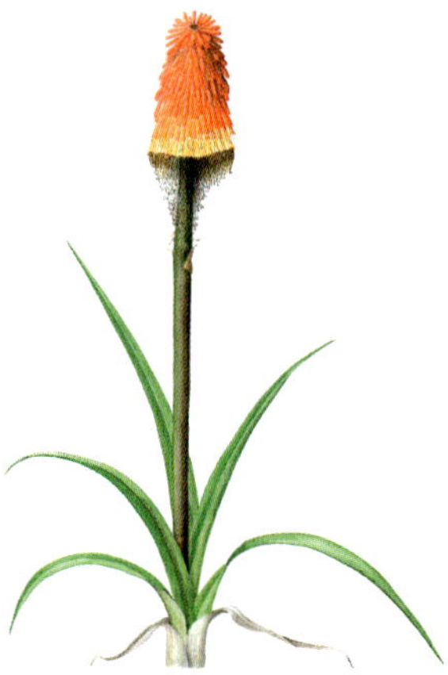

Kniphofia
Pages 78–81

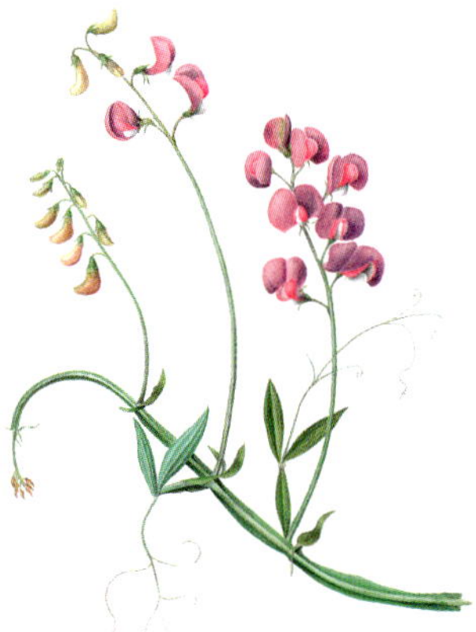

Lathyrus
Pages 82–85

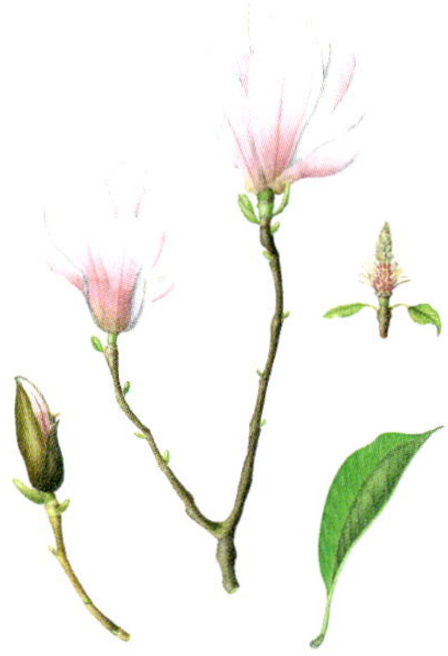

Magnolia
Pages 86–89

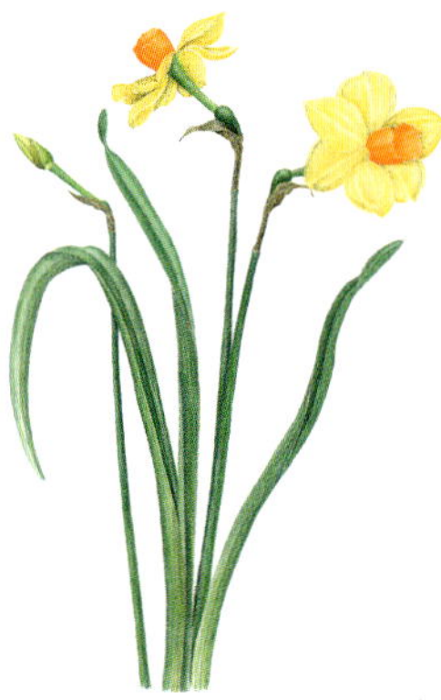

Narcissus
Pages 90–93

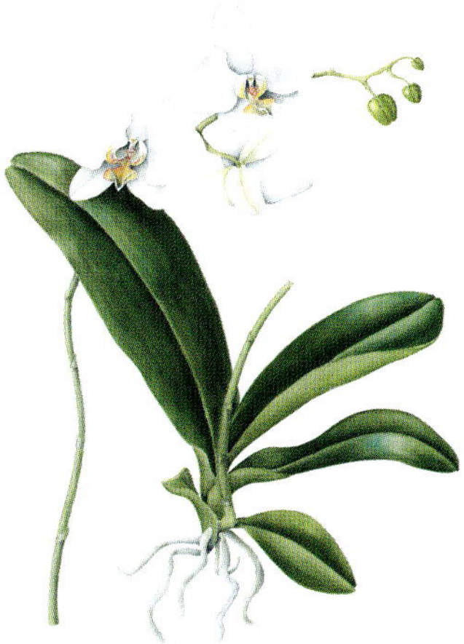

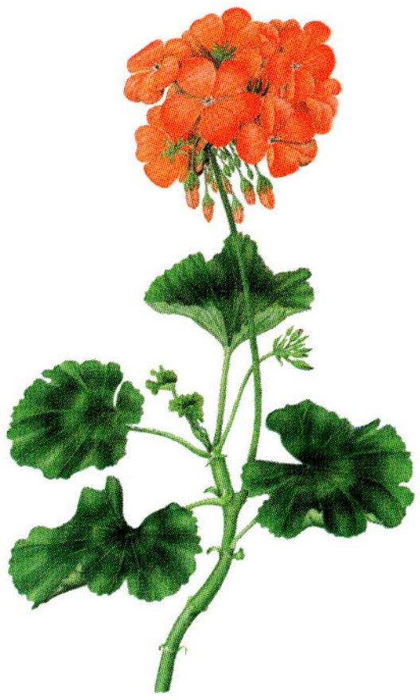

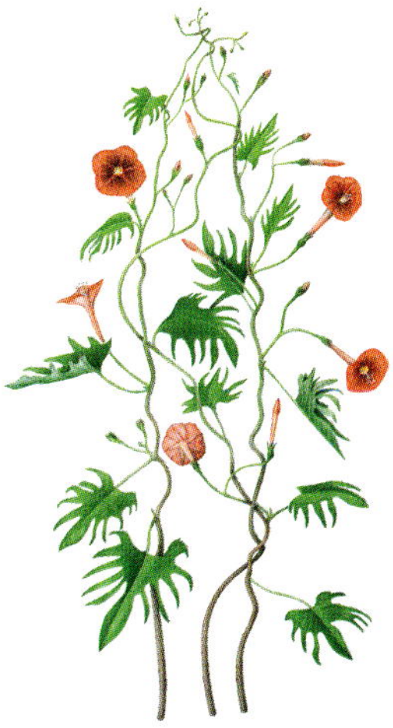

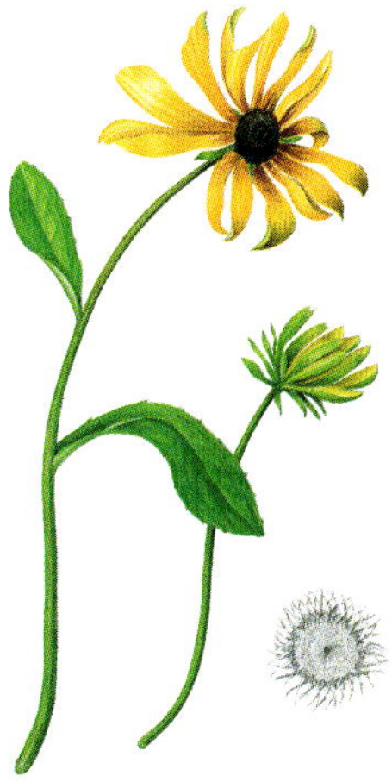

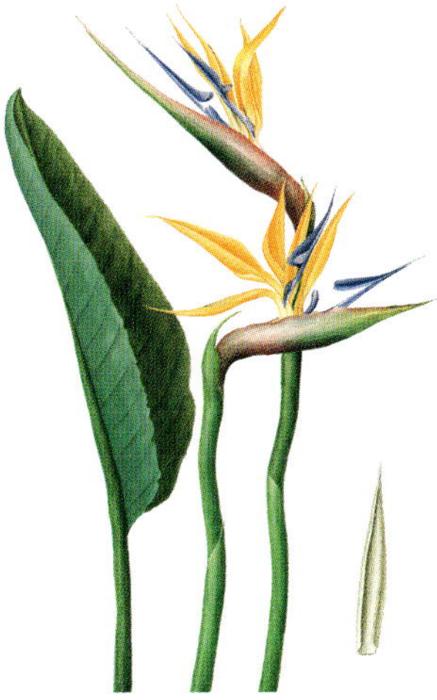

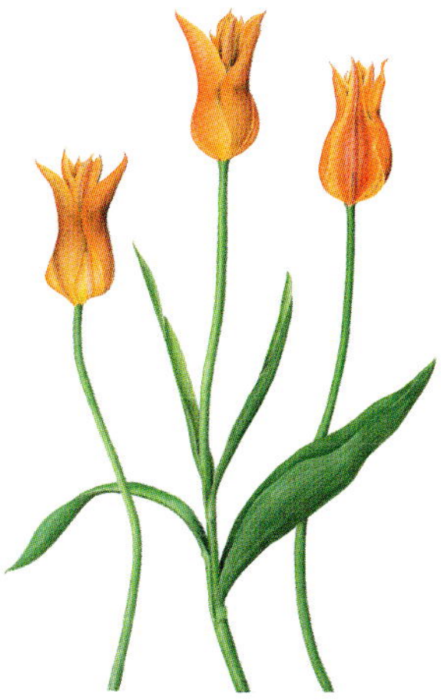

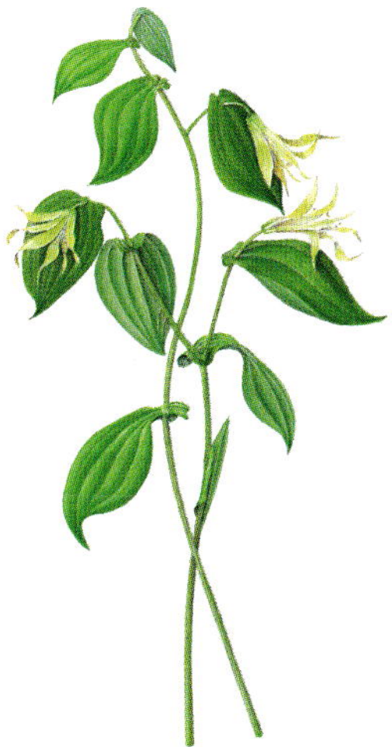

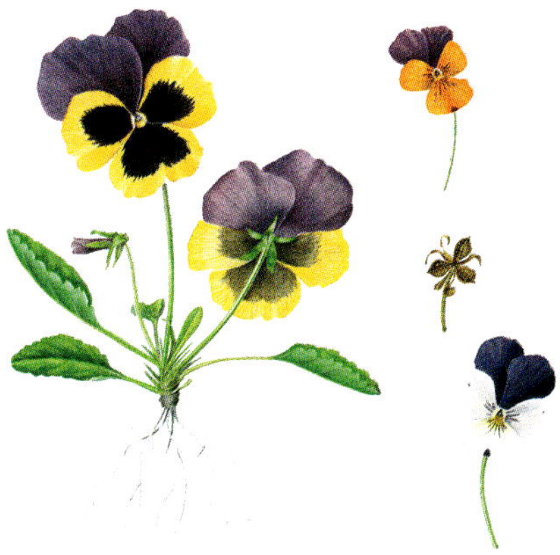

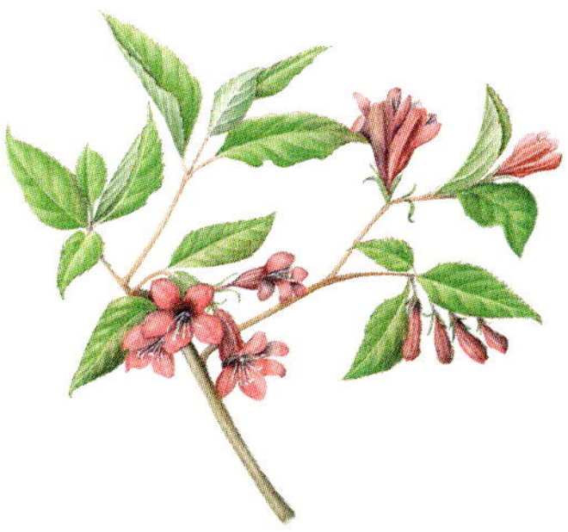

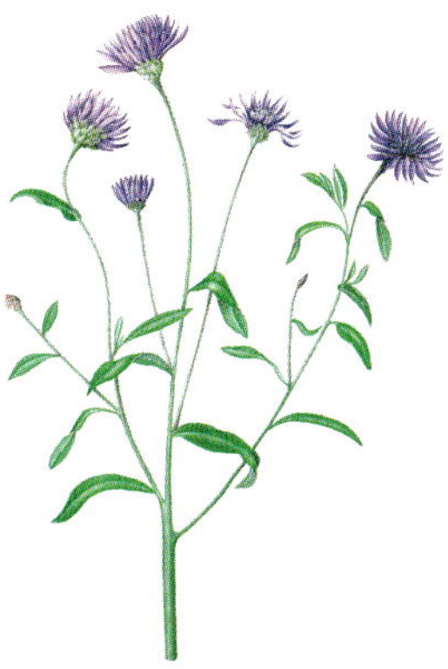

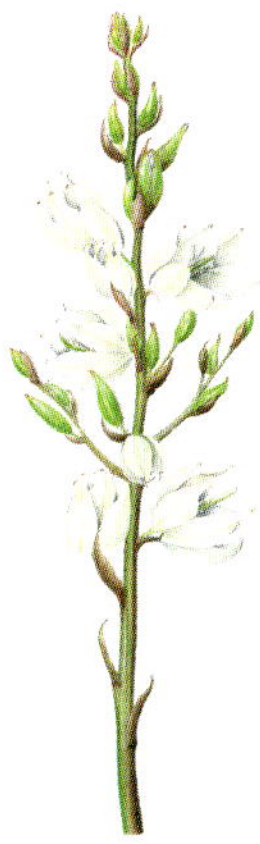

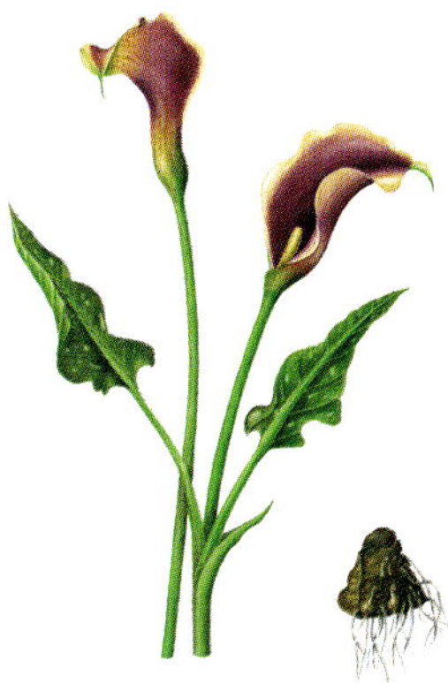

Introduction

Botanical painting can be traced back more than 2,000 years; with illustrations of plants used as aids in medicine or as decoration. Amongst the earliest literature that involved botanical illustration were herbals that contained plant drawings reproduced using woodcuts.

As gardening became a more widely-enjoyed pastime in Europe during the eighteenth and nineteenth centuries, different varieties of plants came into great demand. Plant hunters like Joseph Banks, David Douglas and Robert Fortune brought vast numbers of exotic plants to Europe; and as more plants became available, botanical artists like the Bauer brothers, Georg Ehret, and Pierre-Joseph Redouté began to paint them. These are the artists who have been my inspiration in illustrating flowers and plant life.

Traditional botanical illustration, with its scientific values, makes for an aesthetically pleasing decoration in any home. This book shows you how to produce paintings using the traditional style and methods of the great botanical artists of the past; starting with a drawing and with an organised working system. This method teaches that accuracy is only gained by close study of the plant, and drawing with a pencil. This can be erased if incorrect as many times as is necessary, and the information about the plant gained through this approach is invaluable. Once you are happy with the drawing, this knowledge will help to paint in an organised and confident manner, working for short periods and knowing which steps you have completed and which are yet to be done. Your botanical knowledge will grow and you will begin to look at flowers in a different way, looking for their rich complexities.

Botanical art is addictive, and the satisfaction gained will enrich your life and give you much pleasure. Each plant will give you a new challenge and you will build on the experience gained.

If you aim to exhibit your work, start by visiting botanical art exhibitions in your local area and then progress to the larger ones like the Society of Botanical Artists, Society of Floral Painters or the Northern Botanical Art Society.

I have gained much satisfaction from producing this book, and I hope that it improves your skills and helps you become a successful botanical artist.

Opposite

Orchid phalaenopsis

This is a common houseplant, available in many colours. In this painting, the large dark green leaf is behind the white flower to accentuate the flower. It is also sectioned to reduce the size of the composition.

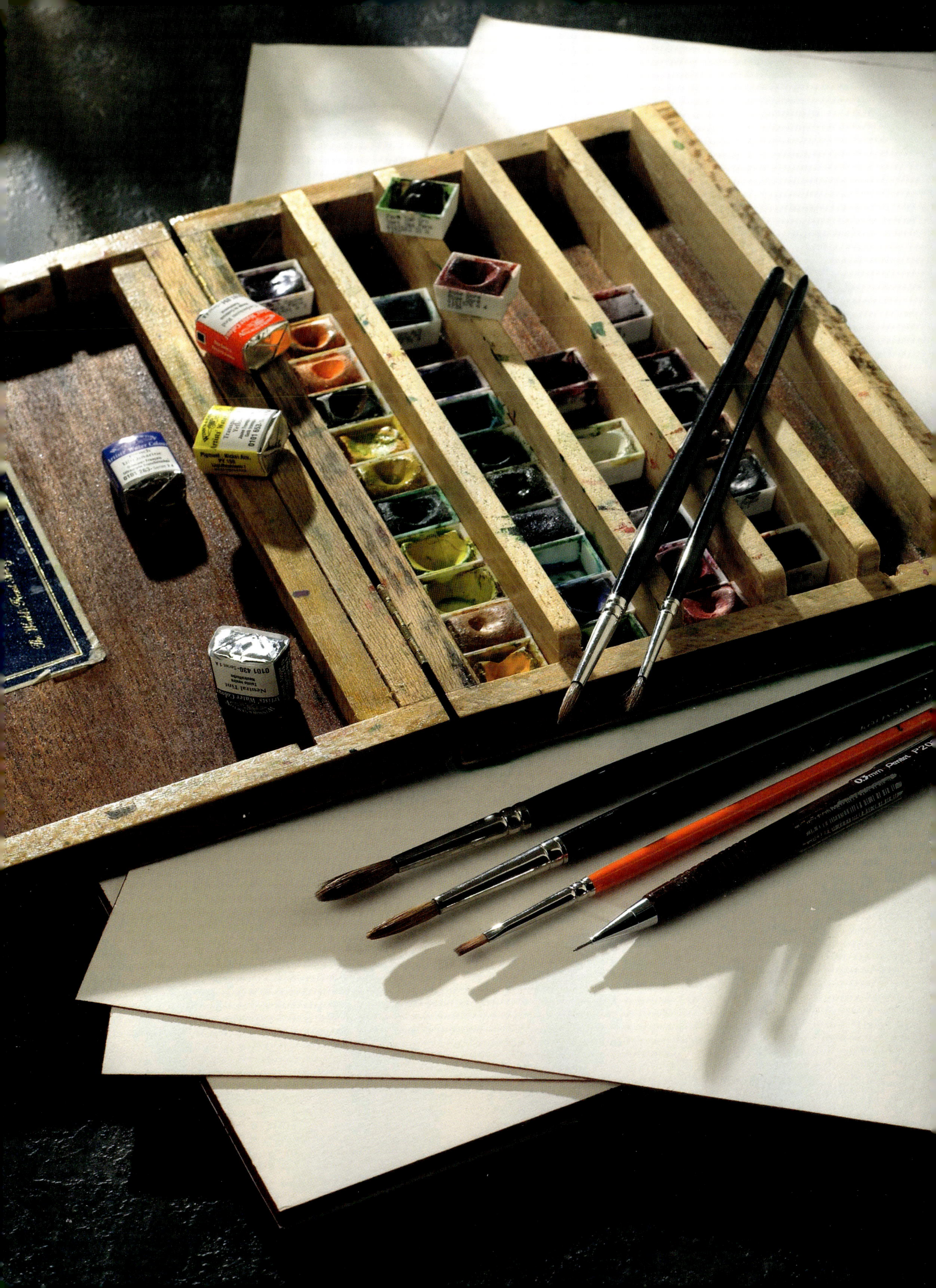

Other equipment

Scalpel This is used for dissecting flowers, seed pods, bulbs and so forth.

Microscope Before drawing small parts of the flower, such as stamens, styles and stigmas, it is useful to use a microscope to better understand their shapes and form.

Scissors A pair of small, sharp embroidery scissors is useful for dissection.

Proportional dividers It is important to measure the components of the subject matter accurately. Dividers are available for scaling up individual parts twofold, threefold or more.

Hair conditioner Because sable brushes are made from animal hair, normal hair conditioner will help to revitalise them and keep them in top condition.

Brush box In order to keep the points of your brushes safe, a brush box should be used.

Masking tape This is used to hold your drawing or painting paper to a drawing slope or board.

Kitchen paper You will find kitchen paper very handy for mopping up excess water from your brush or painting.

Magnifier A handheld magnifier will enable you to see plant material much more closely, while working through a flexible desk-standing magnifier will leave your hands free. Either will allow you to get much more accurate and clean edges to your leaves and petals. Magnifiers with a weighted base and arms that end in crocodile clips are a good alternative. These hold your subject upright while you draw it.

Light box or **tracing paper** You will need one of these to transfer the outline pencil image you produce to Hot-Pressed watercolour paper.

Putty eraser This can also be used for erasing small amounts of pencil work. Unlike a normal eraser, a putty eraser can be rolled and shaped to carefully remove details from watercolour paper.

Soft eraser An eraser is used for general erasing of pencil lines when producing your initial drawing.

Drawing fluid Sometimes you will have areas which need to be left as clean white paper, such as veins, stigmas and stamens. Drawing fluid, also known as masking fluid, can be used to protect these details while you work the surrounding areas.

Mapping pen This is used to apply drawing fluid to the paper.

Cartridge paper This is usually available in pads, and is used to produce the initial drawing.

Tweezers A very useful tool for removing and holding individual components of a flower during dissection, these will help you to get a clearer view of petals, sepals and other small parts of the flower.

Shading pencils HB and H pencils are used with the continuous tone method of shading (see pages 22–23) to create form in your sketchbook. Use a pencil sharpener to keep them sharp.

Water containers Two water pots are needed: one for mixing colours and cleaning your brush, and one kept clean for grading your paint on the paper.

Ceramic palettes Ceramic palettes are useful for mixing your paints to the correct colour.

Drawing slope Drawing and painting should be enjoyable, and a drawing slope or board will ensure that you remain comfortable while you work.

Digital camera An invaluable tool, this allows you to take pictures and review them, in order to quickly get compositional references for your work.

Anglepoise lamp I suggest using a posable lamp with a daylight bulb, as these provide the best, most accurate light.

Fineliner pen A pen with a fine nib (I recommend a 0.3mm nib) is used for outlining your sketch, making it easy to transfer (see pages 24 and 25).

Tip

Water phials hold a small amount of water. While they are not essential equipment, they are useful to ensure your subject does not wilt while it is held upright for drawing.

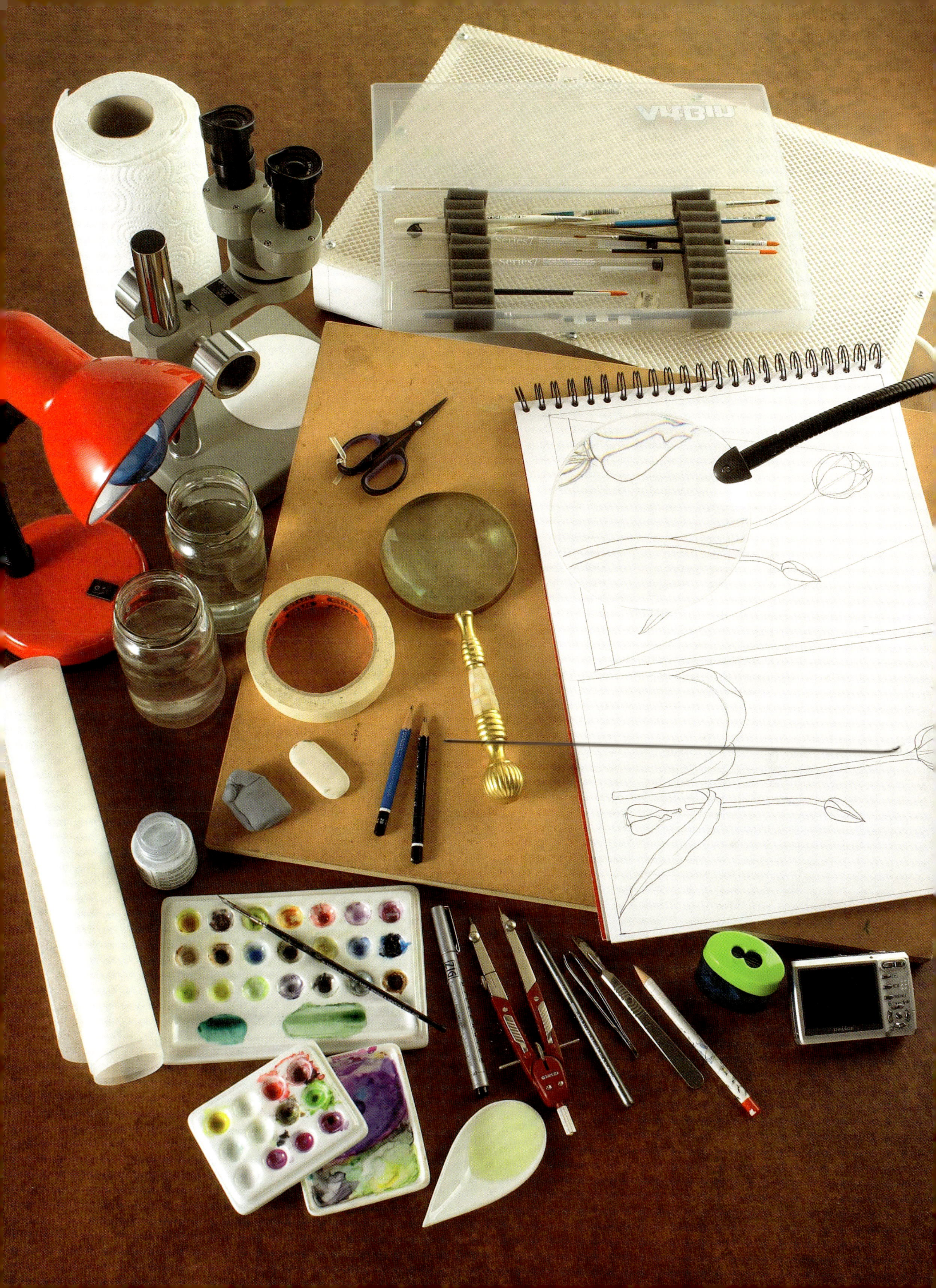
Series7
Series7

Choosing your subject

When choosing your subject it is good practice to have an idea of the composition you would eventually like to produce. Sometimes this can be as nature intended it to be, worked exactly as it appears; and sometimes it can benefit from a few adjustments.

Finding a suitable plant

A traditional botanical illustration should include a full flower, a bud (or buds), the back of the flower, and both the front and underside of the leaves. Overcrowding of the stems should be avoided.

With these considerations in mind, choose a good example of your chosen subject (i.e. healthy, undamaged and representative of the type of plant), cut it carefully, and place it in water.

The flower can be kept in a refrigerator to keep it cool and fresh. You can use a lamp to open a bud or bring a flower further into bloom.

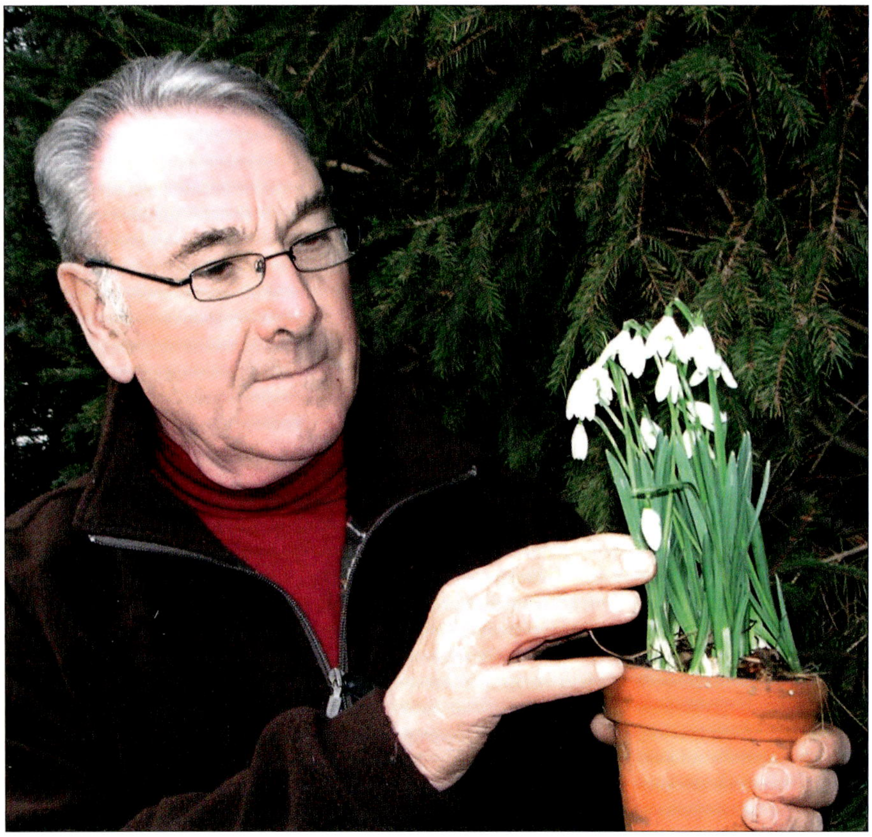

Tip

Wildflowers are protected by the law in many parts of the world. If they are to be drawn and painted, permission from the landowner must first be obtained. In addition, you should check the latest updates concerning wildflowers in your area; do not just pick them. When choosing a subject, pick only a small amount, and replant them when you have finished painting the flower.

Structure of the flower

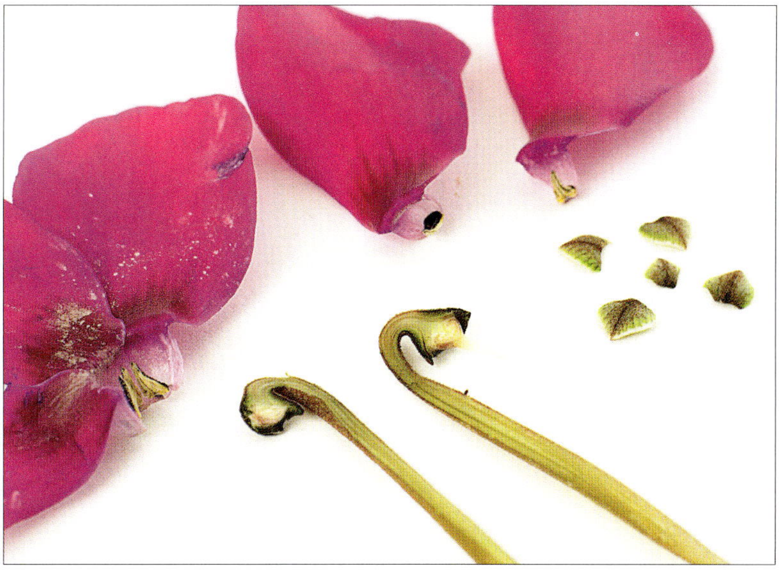

The sepals (the five small green-purple structures on the right of this picture) are slightly tougher petal-like structures which protect the bud before the flower opens. When the flower opens, they are commonly hidden under or behind the larger petals (the large pink-purple parts on the left and top of this picture). Note that the sepals are larger and more colourful than the petals in some flowers. In the example below, the petals are sketched at life size, while the sepals are sketched at twice their actual size.

The stamens are the pollen-producing male part of the flower, and some can be seen on the left-hand side, at the centre of the three petals. Note the scattered dust-like yellow pollen towards the centre of the petals. Because the stamens in this example are markedly different on the inside and outside, I made separate reference sketches.

At the end of the stem is the carpel, the female part of the plant which produces the fruiting body after pollination. Both the stamen and carpel are very small, so I sketched them at five times their actual size.

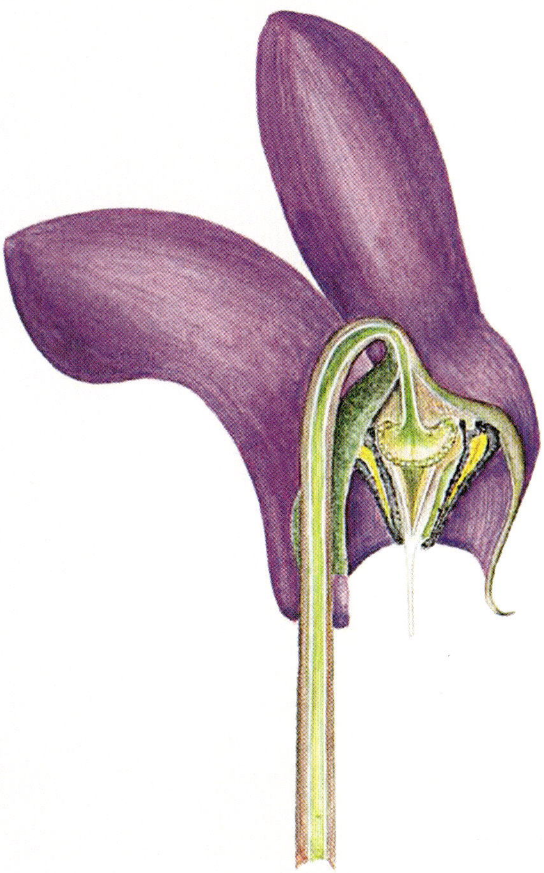

The smaller components were viewed under the microscope and drawn. As I was drawing the parts larger than they actually were, I included a scale (x2; x3 as appropriate) for later reference.

After the dissection, I painted the components individually, but these could be added to the final painting itself if you prefer. Small individual components of a flower are usually arranged neatly at the lower part of the portrait.

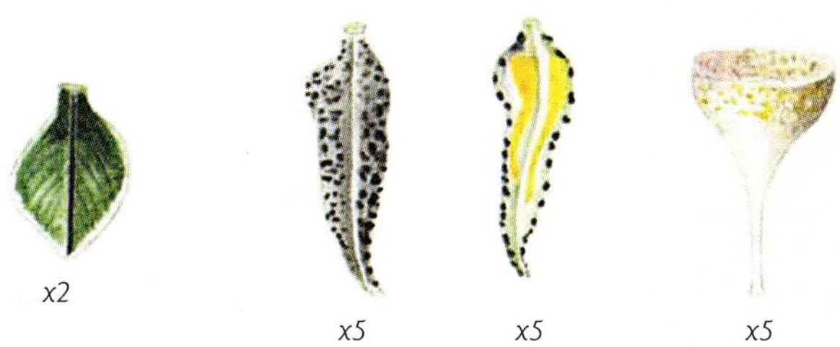

Composition

The basic composition of a painting will usually spring to the artist's mind as soon as the subject matter is seen, but it is worth taking time to think through the specific relationship of the components with each other.

Arranging your work

When you have chosen your subject, place it in water, then look to see the best angle from which to draw the plant. Try moving it around, taking it out of the water and replacing it, and making small adjustments until you are content.

Sitting with the plant at eye level will give you the best all-round view of your subject. Do not place the plant at the side of you – it is much easier to have it directly in front of you, so you do not need to keep turning to look at it.

Source of light

Always organise one light source. Place it above and to the left of the plant if you are right-handed, and above and to the right of the plan if you are left-handed.

What should be in the picture?

Deciding what should go into the final composition is a very broad subject, but to achieve a professional result, it is important that all of the preparation work for the composition of your final painting should be done in your sketchbook before you begin on your watercolour paper.

In addition to the basic elements (a full flower and its back, the front and underside of the leaves and a bud), you may wish to include other interesting or distinctive parts, such as the root system, old leaves or seedpods (see page 61 for a good example).

Decide if the subject is going to be life-sized or scaled to fit the paper you are using. Plants with large leaves, very tall stems or those that are very broad/tall can sometimes go off the page. In these instances, you may wish to have some of the leaves/stem visible in the picture, in order that other parts are shown sufficiently large. Alternatively, you can show separate details in your composition, such as in the foxglove on page 51, where the base of the stem is shown separately to the top.

Leading on from this consideration is whether you wish to include a detail of any dissected parts. This can be very useful to show the inside of the fruiting bodies, roots and other details.

If you decide to include many small components, draw them in the sketchbook individually. These can then be traced separately, which allows you to experiment with different arrangements in your composition before you finalise it.

Finally, I recommend that you ask someone else's opinion of your composition before you transfer it to watercolour paper. An external perspective can offer valuable insights, and prevent any oversights that you have missed by being so closely involved.

Tip

Avoid even numbers in your compositions. Including odd numbers of leaves, flowers, buds and stems is more visually pleasing.

Tip

You will find making a small thumbnail sketch in one corner of the sketchbook is very useful, as this will show whether the basic shapes work well when stripped of the details.

Negative space

Negative spaces are the areas in between the shapes (i.e. the components of the flower; the 'positive shapes') placed on your surface. When the components are placed correctly, the negative shapes of the clean white paper set off the positive shapes of the painted components to form the complete picture.

Remember that the negative spaces you leave bring balance to the composition when you are sketching your image. If you leave too little negative space, the finished painting will look crowded and busy. If you leave too much, it will look lost on the paper.

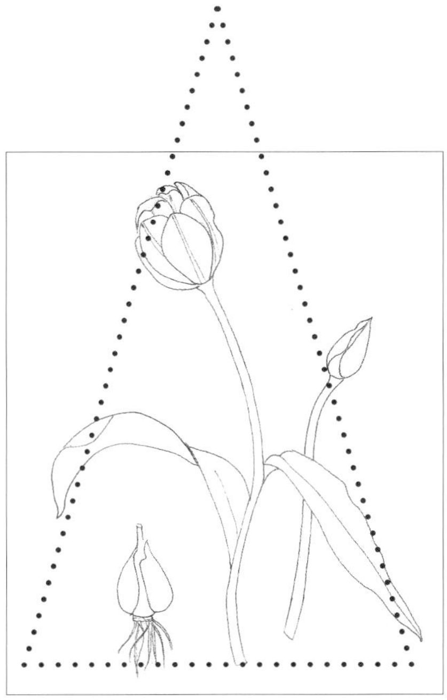

An example of the composition triangle. Note that the top part of the triangle meets outside the frame, and that some important parts of the composition like the bud on the left-hand side sit outside it.

The composition triangle

The composition triangle is a simple method of producing a pleasing composition. Imagine an isosceles triangle on your paper and place the main bulk of the plant within the triangle. The components of the plant subject do not have to fall completely within the triangle lines, merely comply roughly with its shape. The shape of the triangle will vary depending on the plant you choose to paint, and it is only a guideline – do not feel restricted by the triangle. In fact, letting a few parts of the plant escape the triangle adds a sense of natural life to the composition.

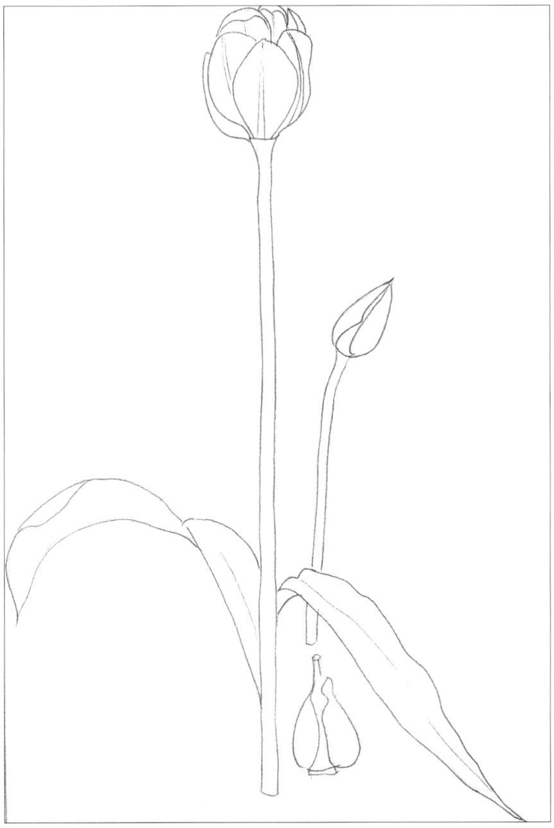

This composition is unsuccessful because the stem is far too tall and straight, leading the eye out of the picture. The main flower is too far away from the rest of the composition, and the bulb is crammed into a small space. Too much negative space has been left, and no margin has been left for framing.

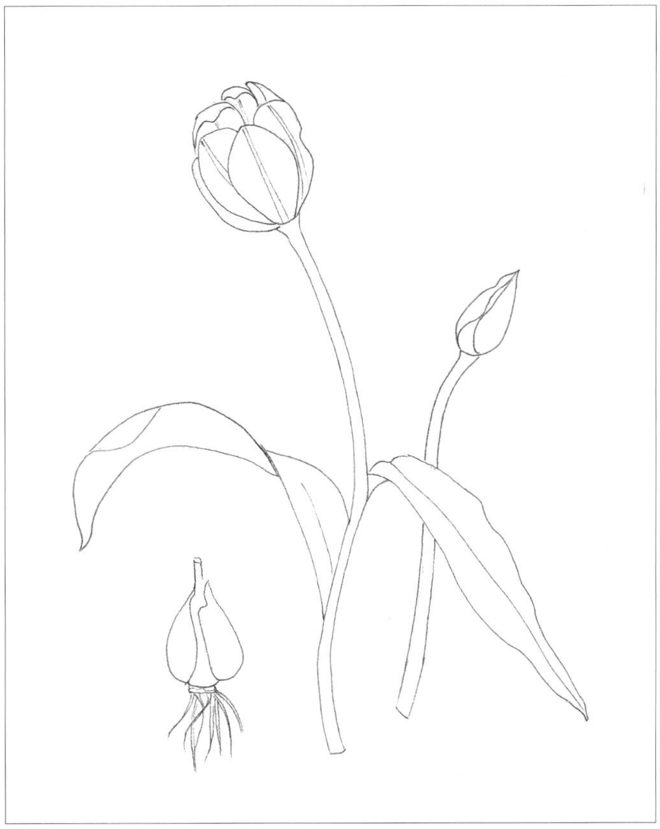

This revised composition is successful because the composition is well balanced. Your eye moves around the image, with equal weight being given to each of the components. The additional bud and stem complement the main flower, mirroring the curve in its stem, and the bulb is in a more pleasing position on the lower left, where it fills a large gap without drawing too much attention from the main flower.

Drawing

Before starting to draw, it is important to have a good understanding of your subject. Observe it well, and relate the shapes of the petals and leaves to each other, as well as the negative shapes between them. Remember, a good drawing is vital to a successful finished painting.

Outlines – the shapes of flowers

Flowers come in a bewildering array of shapes and sizes, which can be intimidating. However, most can be reduced to simple shapes to get the basic size and proportion correct before you develop the details. Geometric shapes are the basic form of many flowers, and these pages explain some approaches to make drawing even complex flowers very simple.

Circle

The circle is the basic shape of many flowerheads, including all the daisy family, dahlias and daffodils. Start by drawing the circle, then simply place the various petal shapes around it.

When viewed from other angles, the circle will become an ellipse: but the principle of placing the petals around it remains the same. Bear in mind that the petals will appear different lengths and shapes from different angles.

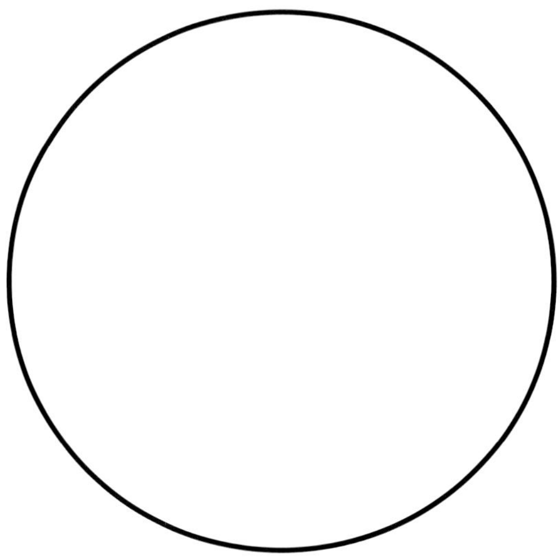

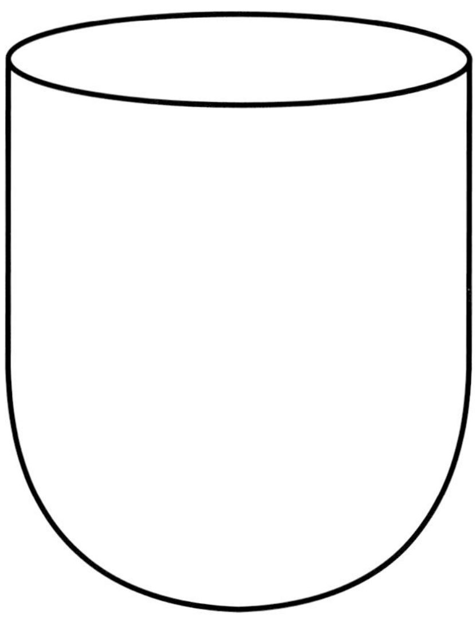

Cup

This drawing shows a simple cup shape, which provides the basic form of flowers like open tulips, roses and many more. Practise drawing cups in various sizes, then try closing in the vertical lines towards the top of the cup and adding some petals. This will allow you to draw cup-shaped flowers in various states of blooming.

Cone

The cone shape shown here is common to the foxglove, penstemen, bluebell and many others. After drawing this basic cone shape, add the stem and petals. Depending on the angle at which you are looking at the cone, the stigma and stamens may be visible, and can also be added.

The basic cone shape is only a little more complex than the circle and cup, but if you pay careful attention to ensuring the basic shapes are correct, accurate flower images will soon follow.

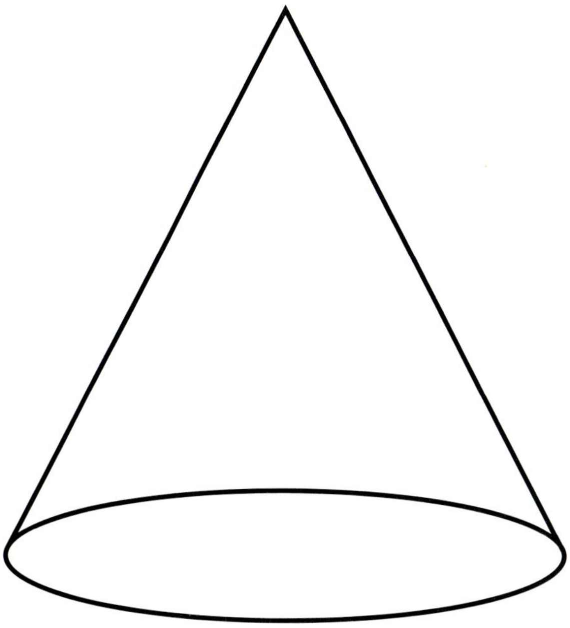

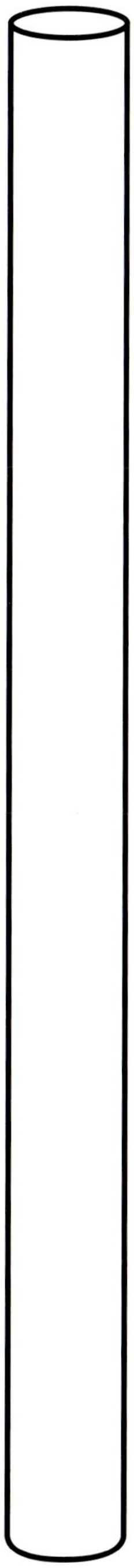

Cylinder

The cylinder, in various lengths and widths, forms the basic shape of stems. Practise drawing them with horizontal and vertical bends and curves in them, as this practice will be invaluable.

When drawing stems of any kind, draw one line first, then draw another line at the side of it. When adding in the second line, ensure that you keep the same distance from the first along the whole length.

Continuous tone

Continuous tone shading is particularly well suited to botanical work as the gradation from dark to light is both gradual and subtle. The lines or dots created by other tonal methods, such as cross-hatching or stippling, could be mistaken for texture on a petal or venation on a leaf that is not present in the specimen.

First and foremost, a tonal drawing is an aid towards your painting. When you identify the form with the tonal work in your sketchbook, then the petals, leaves and stems that make up the image will have a three-dimensional look. This will give you direction and confidence when you come to the painting process.

This band shows a neutral grey tone like that produced with a graphite pencil, from the lightest-toned tints on the left, to the deepest shades on the right. Regardless of the hue of a colour, the tone can be light or dark.

Ellipses

Continuous tone is made up of many small ellipses drawn with your pencil. The movement should originate from the shoulder, not the wrist. After practising for a while you will begin to understand why care should be taken to fill the grain of the paper and not leave empty ellipses.

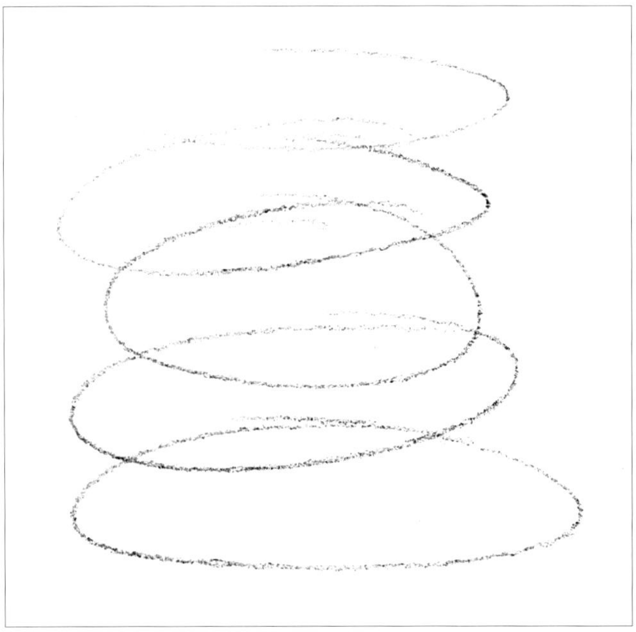

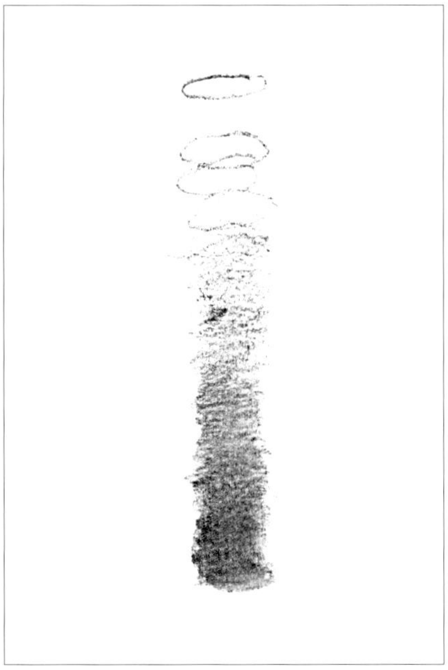

The exaggerated example on the left shows how the ellipses should be overlapped. The right-hand image is enlarged only slightly, and it shows how the individual ellipses blend into one another, covering all of the surface texture of the paper. The tone is altered by changing the pressure you place on the pencil: the more pressure you use, the darker the tone. Note that light-toned areas still have the same number of ellipses: they are just very faint.

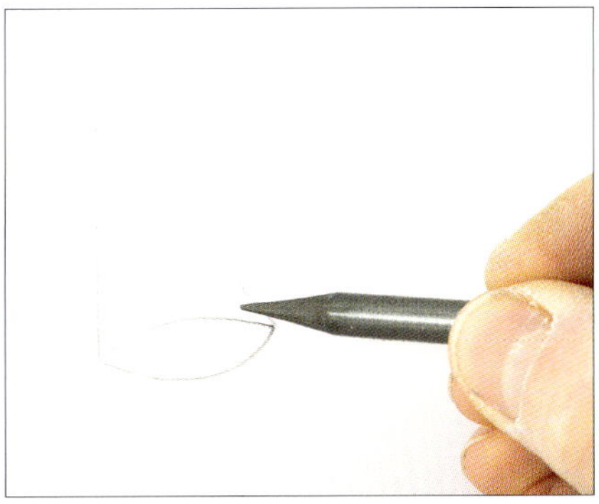

1 With an HB pencil, identify the area furthest from the light source. In this case, it is on the outside of the cone at the bottom left.

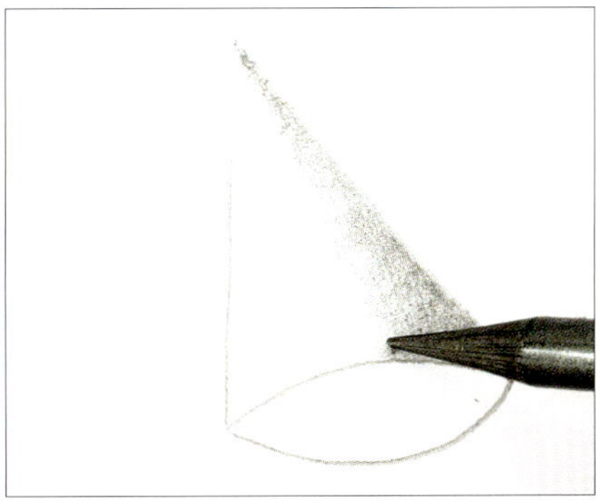

2 Start making tiny overlapping ellipses and gradually reduce the pressure on the pencil as you work towards the lighter areas, paying careful attention to the shape's surface and adjusting the pressure.

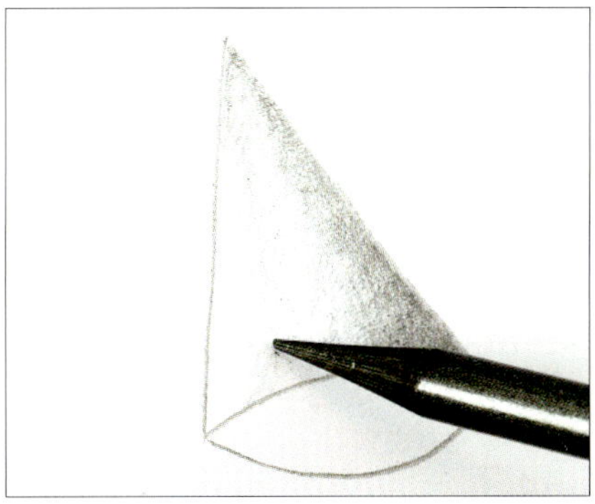

3 Continue working across the shape, reducing the pressure almost to nothing in the lightest areas. Remember that you are still creating the same size ellipses: they are simply so faint as to be nearly unnoticeable.

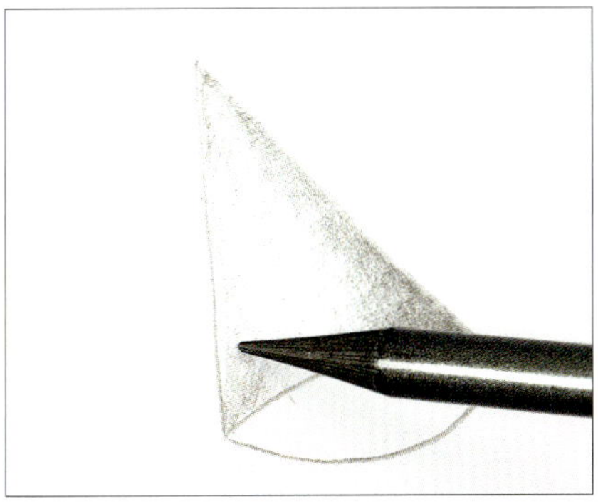

4 As you work past the highlight area, increase the pressure again to darken the tone.

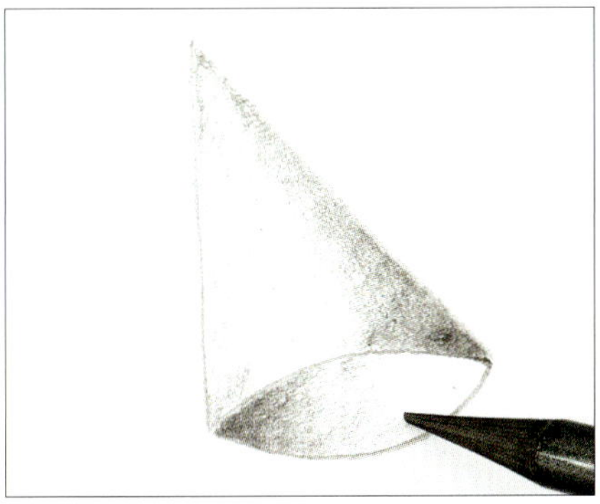

5 Once you have finished one area of the shape, repeat the process on the other areas in turn. In this example, adding shading on the left-hand side of the base suggests the cone is hollow inside.

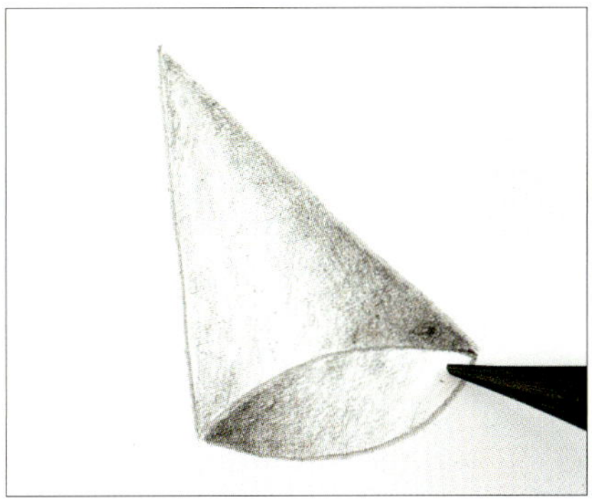

6 Continue creating the overlapped ellipses, altering the pressure to change the tone until you cover the entire surface of the object.

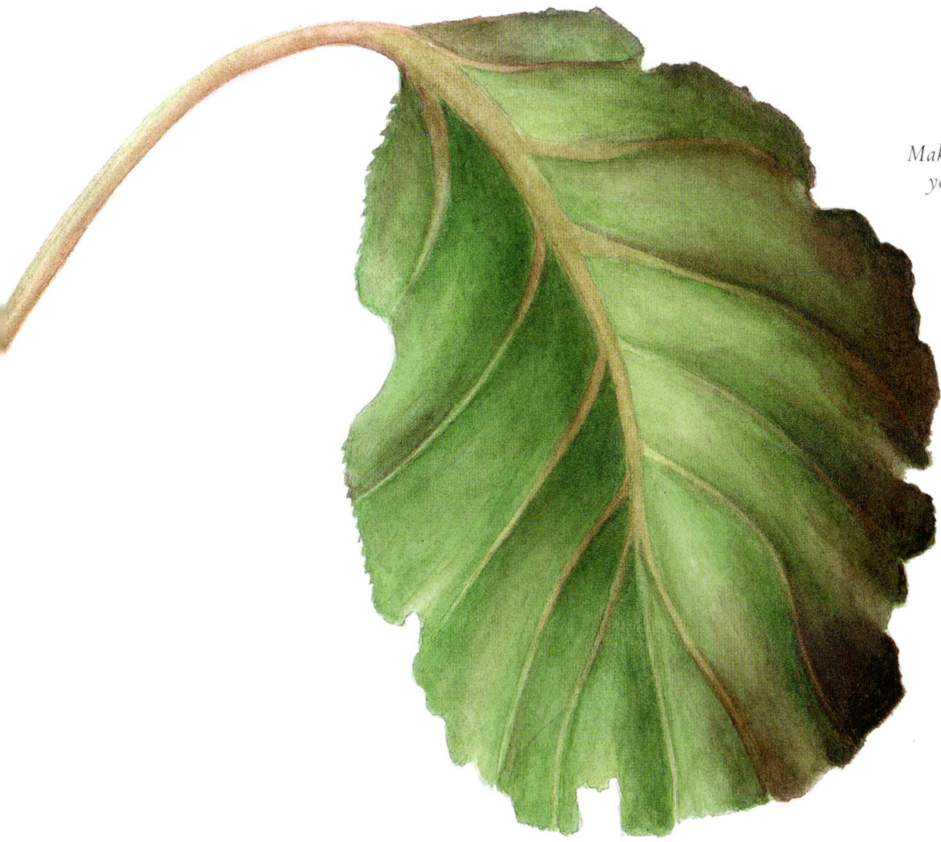

Making a tonal sketch is extremely useful when you come to applying colour. Not only will it help in gaining an understanding of the shapes and form of the plant, but it will also inform your choice of colours when you come to the final painting. Tone and colour are equally important in producing an accurate flower painting.

Transferring the image

When the drawing is completely finished, you will need to transfer the image to watercolour paper, using a light box or tracing paper. The processes for each method are shown below.

Tip
Using a 0.3mm fineliner pen to strengthen the sketch will help you when tracing it through the watercolour paper.

Transferring the image using a light box

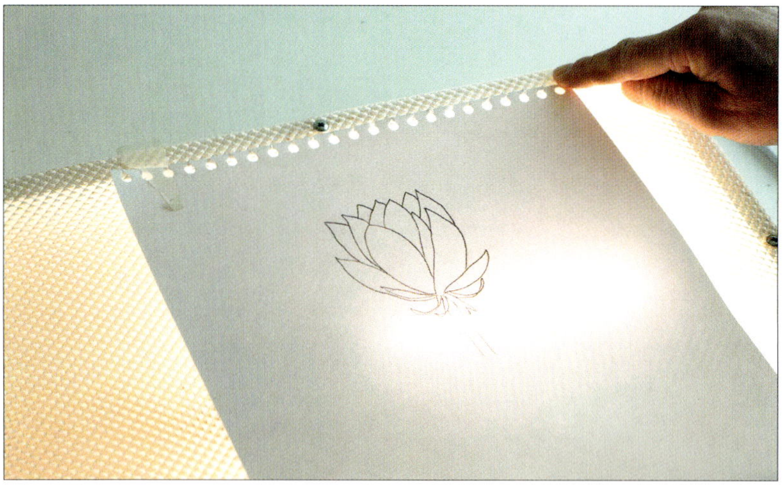

1 Tape your drawing to the light box at the top left- and right-hand corners.

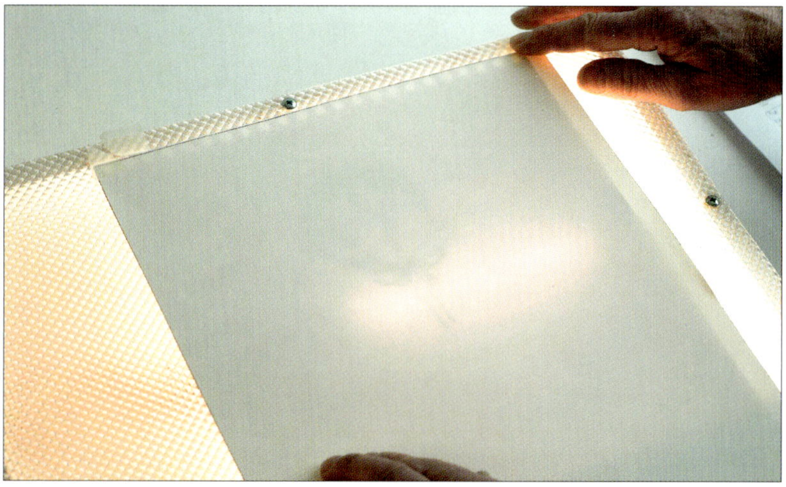

2 Place your watercolour paper on top of the drawing and tape it in place along the top edge.

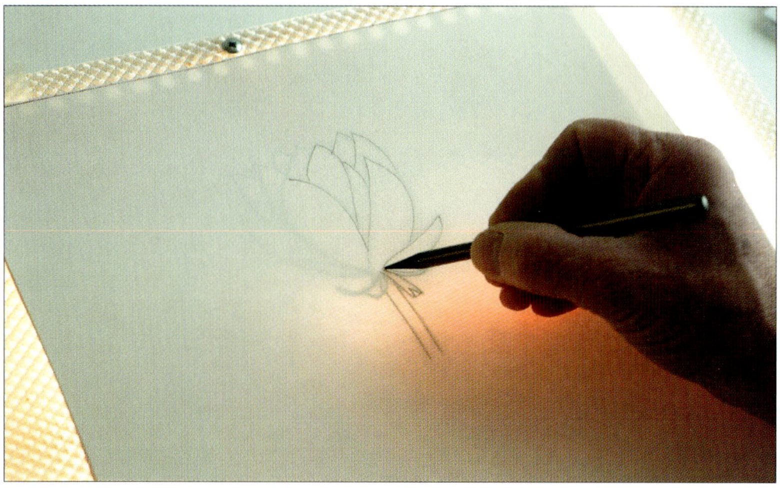

3 Using an H pencil, trace your image through the paper.

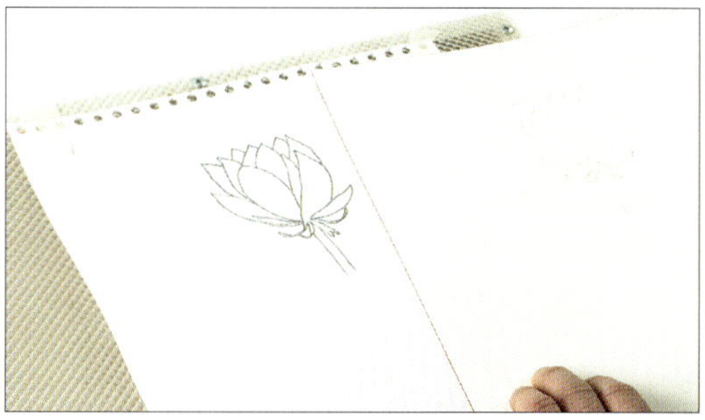

4 Carefully remove the watercolour paper, then compare the transferred image to the original drawing to check you have transferred everything across correctly.

Transferring the image using tracing paper

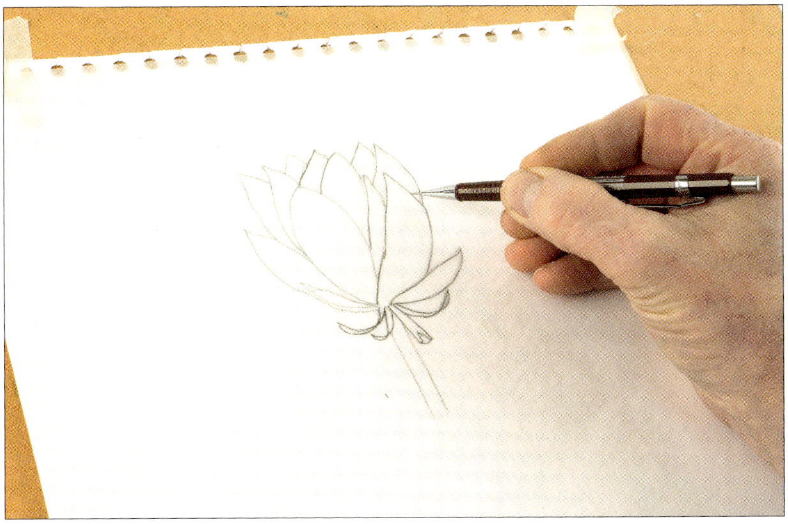

1 Use masking tape to secure your drawing to a drawing board at the top left- and right-hand corners, then tape tracing paper over the top. Use an HB pencil to trace the picture.

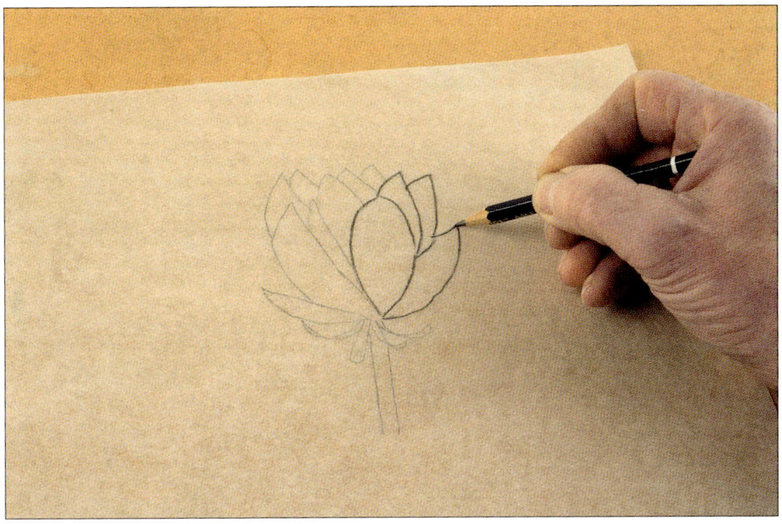

2 Remove the tracing paper and turn it over. Trace the image on the reverse using a 3B pencil.

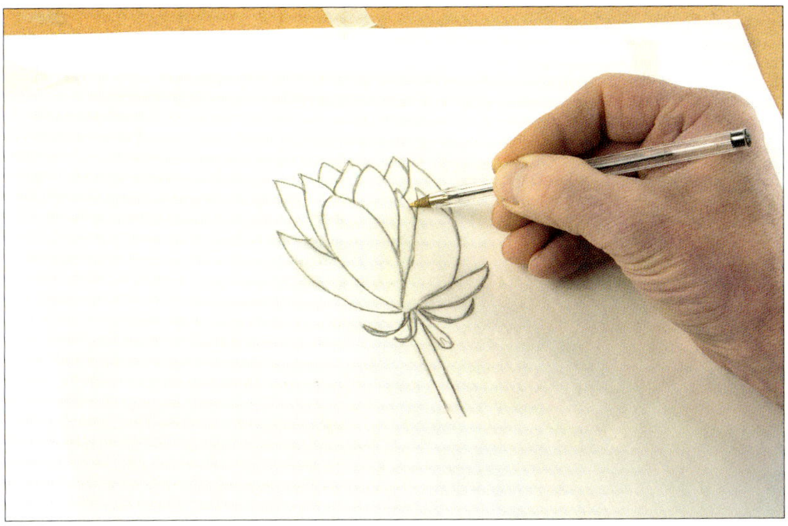

3 Turn the tracing paper over again, secure it to your watercolour paper and go over the lines using a dry ballpoint pen.

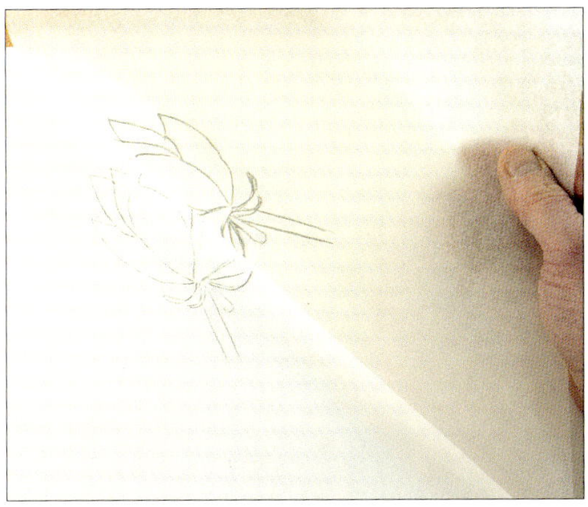

4 Once finished, you should lift the tracing paper to check that you have transferred everything correctly before carefully removing the tracing paper.

Using colour

You must become familiar with your own watercolour box. I prefer to use half pans, which I always place in the same position in the box for easy reference.

Practise mixing colour charts (see page 28) with your colours to familiarise yourself with their properties, and be careful to keep your paints clean. Mix in a white palette in order to keep the colours true.

My palette

The swatches on these pages show the colours in my paint box. Some I use quite often, and others are used less regularly. However, each has its place in my artwork. Even if used only rarely, some colours are perfect for producing the hues of certain flowers.

As well as their unique hue, each paint has qualities that make it more or less useful for certain applications. These are transparency, permanence, temperature and whether it granulates or not. These qualities are noted below each of the paint swatches here.

Transparency Transparent paints allow some of the underlying colour or paper to show through, which creates luminosity and depth of colour. In contrast, opaque colours give flatter washes that cover more solidly.

Permanence Permanent paints are lightfast and will not fade, while others may shift slightly. Bear this in mind when framing and hanging your work.

Temperature Cool colours tend to recede, and warm colours appear to advance towards the viewer. Bear this in mind when composing your picture to create depth. Combining a warm colour with a cool colour will create a less intense mix than two warm or two cool colours.

Granulation When dry, granulating colours will have visible grains of pigment, that can add an interesting texture.

White gouache

Opaque, permanent and neutral. Gouache colours have heavier pigment that makes them more opaque than watercolour paints.

Cadmium yellow

Opaque, permanent and warm.

French ultramarine

Transparent, permanent and warm. Granulating.

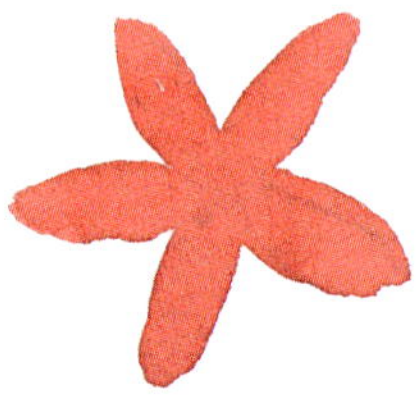

Alizarin crimson

Transparent, moderately durable and cool.

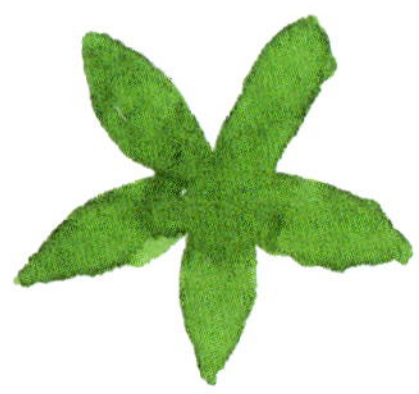

Sap green

Transparent, permanent and cool.

Cadmium orange

Opaque, permanent and warm.

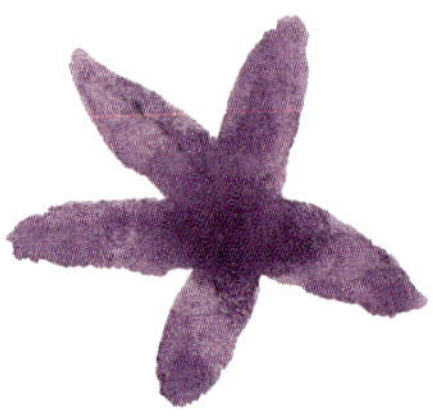

Permanent mauve

Semi-transparent, permanent and warm. Granulating.

Cadmium red

Opaque, permanent and warm. Granulating.

Transparent yellow

Transparent, permanent and cool.

Neutral tint

Opaque, permanent and cool.

Permanent magenta

Transparent, permanent and warm.

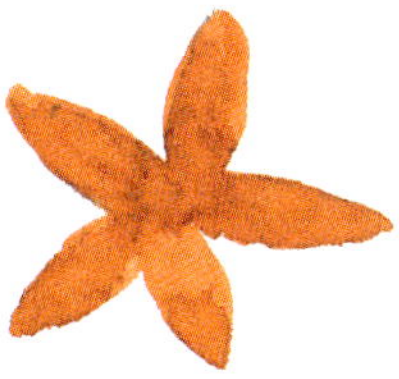

Burnt sienna

Transparent, extremely permanent and warm.

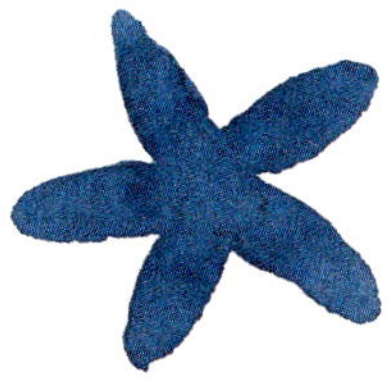

Prussian blue

Transparent, permanent and cool.

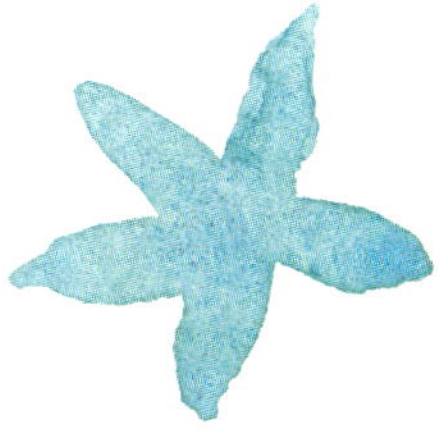

Manganese blue

Semi-opaque, permanent and cool. Granulating.

Raw umber

Transparent, extremely permanent and cool. Granulating.

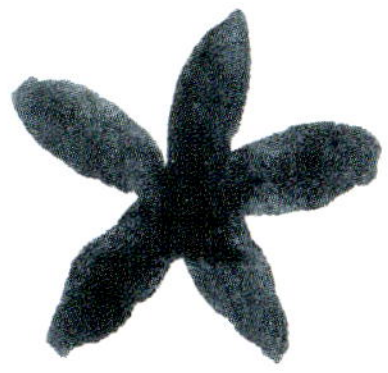

Payne's gray

Semi-opaque, permanent and cool.

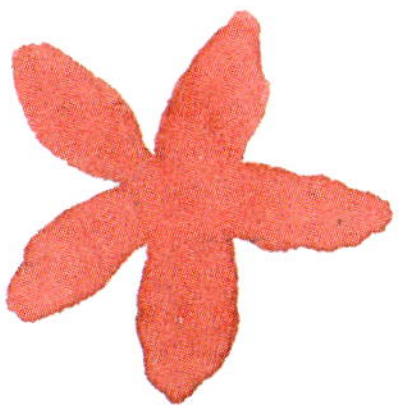

Winsor red deep

Semi-opaque, permanent and warm.

Opera rose

Semi-transparent, permanent and warm.

Winsor violet

Transparent, permanent and warm.

Rose dore

Transparent, permanent and warm.

Winsor blue (green shade)

Transparent, permanent and cool.

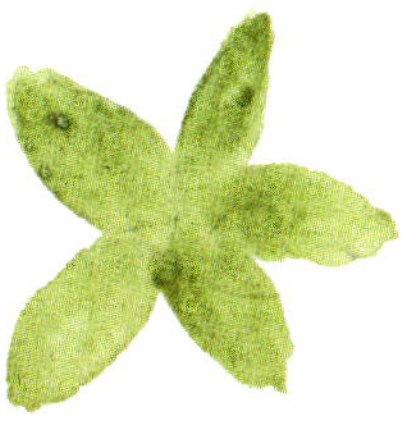

Olive green

Transparent, permanent and cool.

New gamboge yellow

Semi-transparent, permanent and warm.

Yellow ochre

Semi-opaque, extremely permanent and warm.

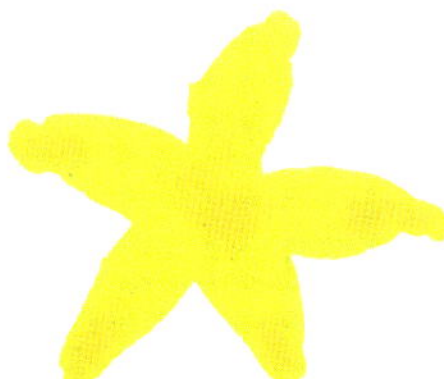

Winsor yellow

Semi-transparent, permanent and warm.

Winsor green (yellow shade)

Transparent, permanent and warm.

Aureolin

Transparent, permanent and warm.

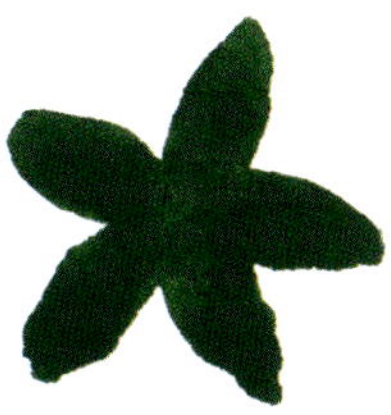

Permanent sap green

Transparent, permanent and cool. This permanent version of sap green is from the Sennelier range.

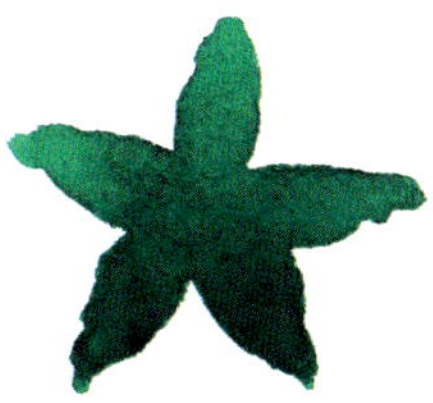

Winsor green (blue shade)

Transparent, permanent and cool.

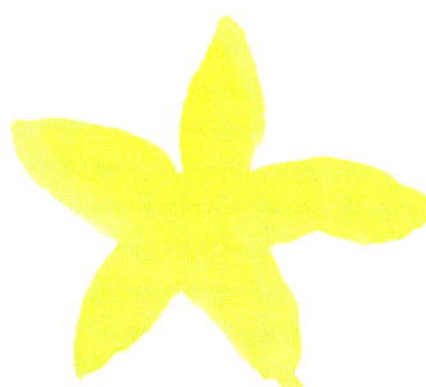

Winsor lemon

Semi-transparent, permanent and cool.

Lemon yellow

Opaque, extremely permanent and cool. Granulating.

Mixing greens

Mixing greens can be a problem for the botanical artist, especially beginners. It is not often that colours straight from the tube or pan match the greens of nature, so you have to mix them in your palette. Practice is paramount to achieve a satisfactory colour.

It is obvious to mix blue and yellow to make a green; but which blue, and which yellow? How much of each?

Colour charts

The best way I have found of producing accurate, lifelike colours is to make colour charts using strips of the same watercolour paper as you use for the final painting. Start with two colours, cadmium yellow and French ultramarine, for example. Make a small square of the first colour (i.e. pure cadmium yellow), then add a little of the second colour while it is wet. Wash your brush, and then repeat with a little more of the second colour each time, making a number of squares with different proportions of the two colours.

Once you have made a range of mixes using the first colour as the base, try reversing the process: making squares of the second colour (French ultramarine) and adding increasing amounts of the first colour (cadmium yellow).

Try mixing different yellows with different blues for a huge range of green hues. You should also try adding a little red to the green mix, to warm the mixture, as this often helps to make a more natural colour for painting leaves.

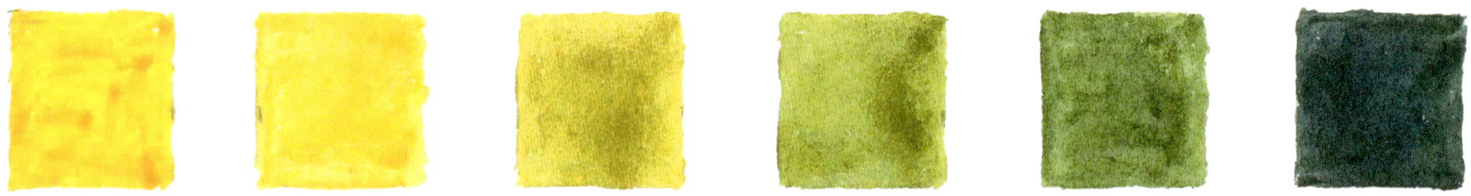

The leftmost square is pure cadmium yellow. Increasing amounts of French ultramarine have been added to the mix to make the squares to the right, resulting in a range of greens.

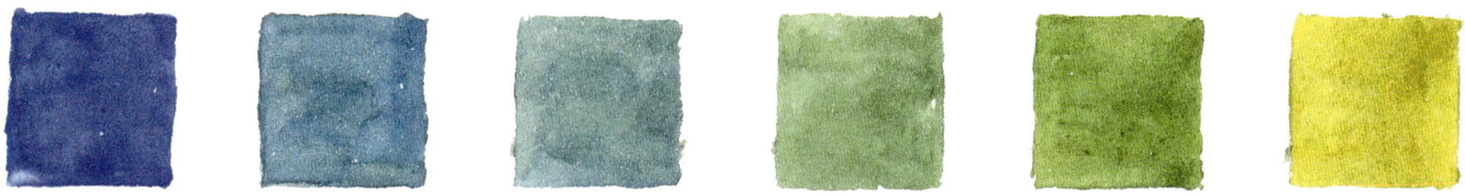

This example uses the same colours, but starts with pure French ultramarine. Again, a range of different greens are created.

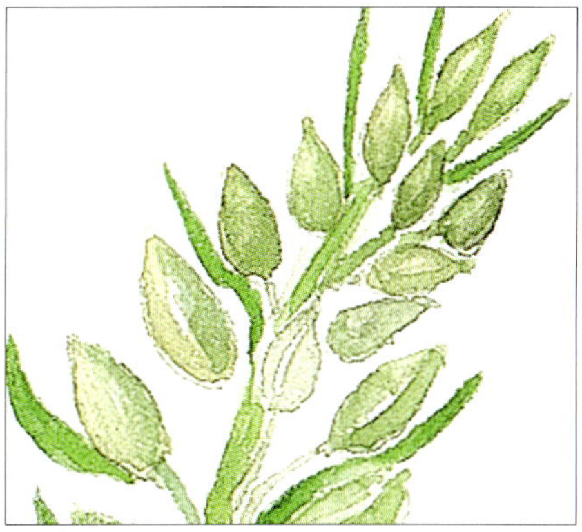

The young and closed buds of the Digitalis (see page 53) *were given several washes of sap green and transparent yellow for a bright fresh green. A little more sap green was added to the same mix for the shadow areas.*

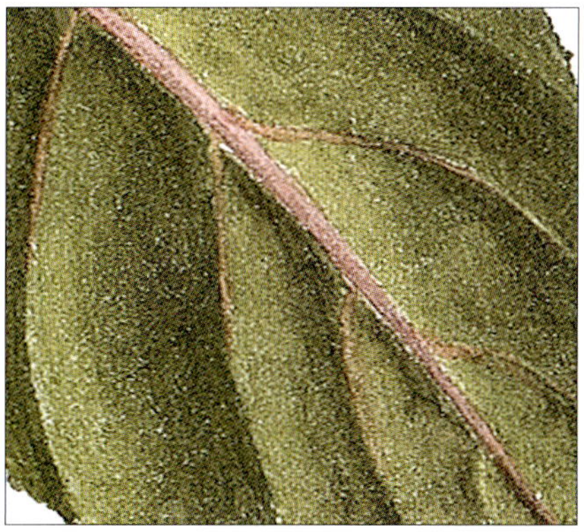

This leaf is taken from the Fuchsia *painting (see page 61). The mix was sap green and alizarin crimson, which produced a muted colour for this older leaf. Several washes were used until the correct tones were achieved.*

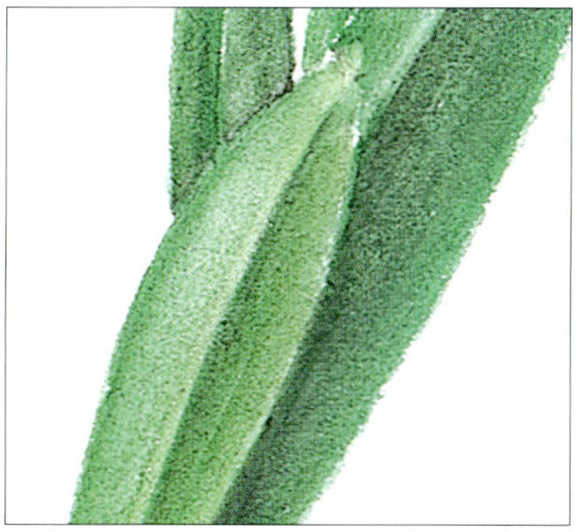

These cool blue-green Galanthus nivalis *(see page 65) leaves were given several washes of a manganese blue and sap green mix. A touch of alizarin crimson was added to the mix for the shadow areas.*

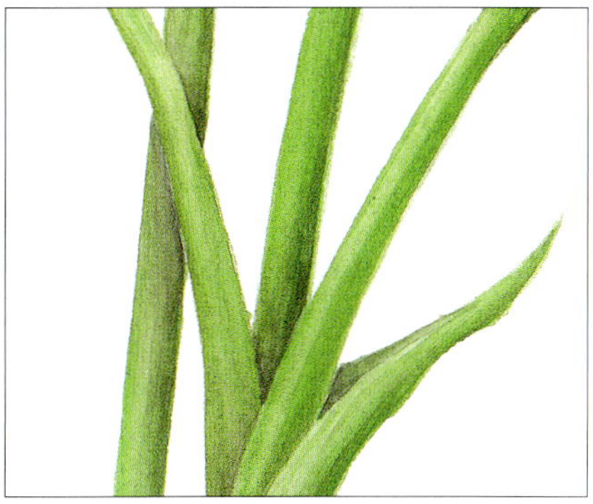

Several washes of permanent sap green, with a little neutral tint added to the mix for the shadows have been used here. This gives a strong green suitable for the stems of this Zantedeschia *(see page 141).*

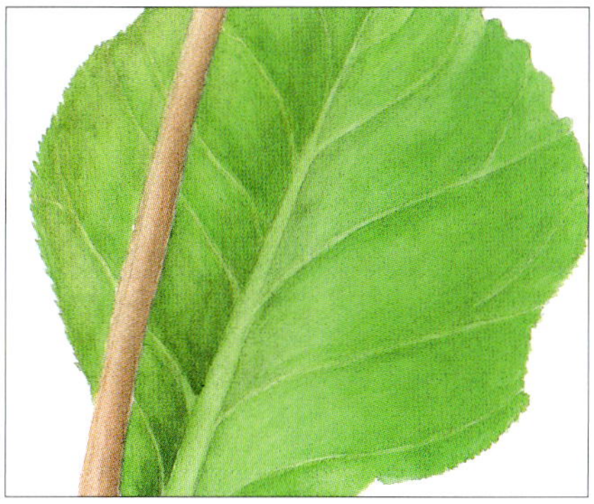

This young leaf, taken from the Bergenia *(see page 45), was given several washes of sap green and Winsor yellow for a rich, vibrant green. The shadow areas were darkened with the addition of a little alizarin crimson.*

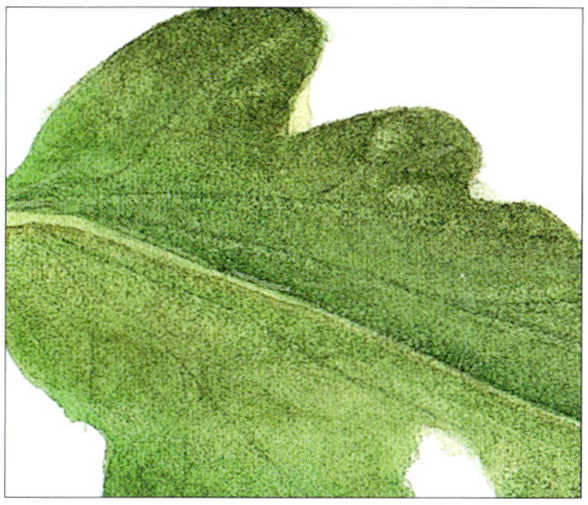

This leaf, taken from the Aquilegia *(see page 41), is one of the older leaves. Several washes of sap green and aureolin make a slightly desaturated green. A small amount of neutral tint was added to the mix for the shadow areas, and a final wash of transparent yellow stopped the colour from looking too muted.*

Relating your palette to the subject

When matching colours to suit your plant, use colour matching strips or a colour mixing chart and match as close as you can. A useful tip it to actually put a small amount of paint on the plant's leaf, stem or flower petal. If the paint blends in with the plant colour, your paint mix is correct. If not, the colour will stand out and you will know that you will need to modify the mix to suit. Always mix in daylight where possible to get the right results.

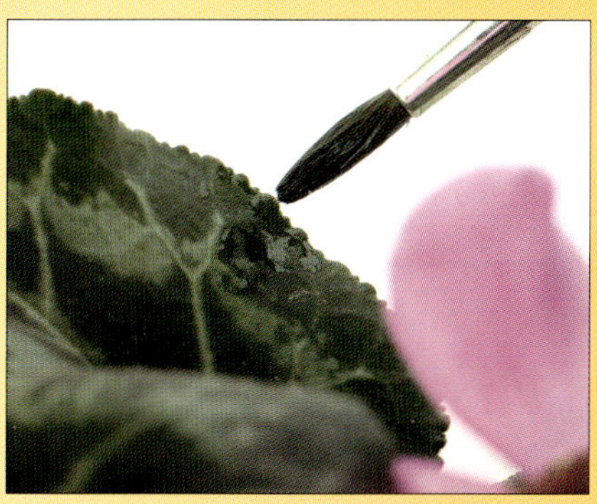

When the paint colour matches the leaf closely, you know that you have the correct hue.

Six stages of painting

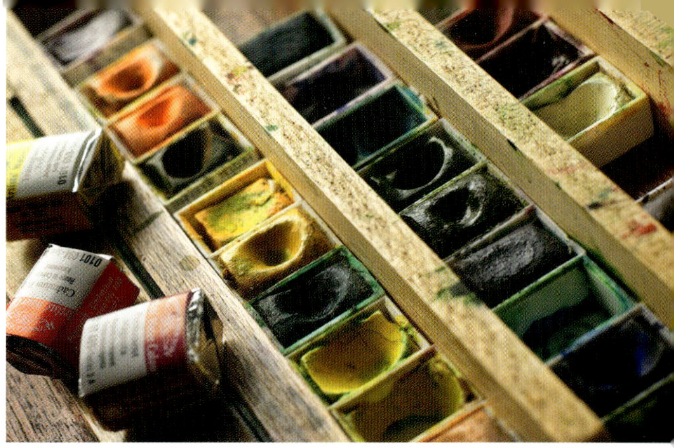

Before you start painting, make sure you are aware of the tonal areas on every part of the plant: from the lightest highlights to the darkest shades. As you paint, bear in mind that every part of the plant has form. Keeping these thoughts in mind at every stage will ensure that the finished painting is as accurate as it can be, and as beautiful as the original flower.

Stage 1 First wash

The first wash is very dilute. It establishes the areas of colour, but in order to produce the depth of hue present in the plant itself, the colour needs to be gradually built up through layers of glazing, allowing each layer to dry completely before continuing.

Preparing your wells

After mixing the appropriate colour to match the area that you will work on (such as a leaf, petal or stem), thin the paint with water to three or four different strengths in small wells, as shown below.

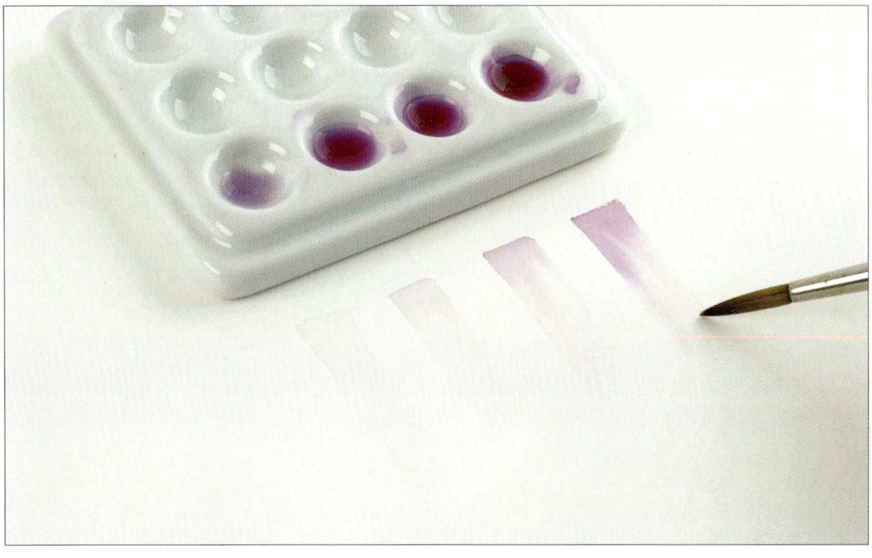

From left to right: well 1 – a very thin mix; well 2 – a slightly stronger mix; well 3 – a stronger mix, only slightly diluted; well 4 – the original mix of the appropriate colour.

Note

Mixes 1 and 2 are mostly used in the first steps, while mixes 3 and 4 are used in the later steps.

Applying the first wash

Once you have your wells prepared, choose the correct size brush for the section (the individual leaf, petal or stem for example) on which you are working, and use clean water to glaze the virgin paper of the area. It is important that you allow the area to dry before beginning.

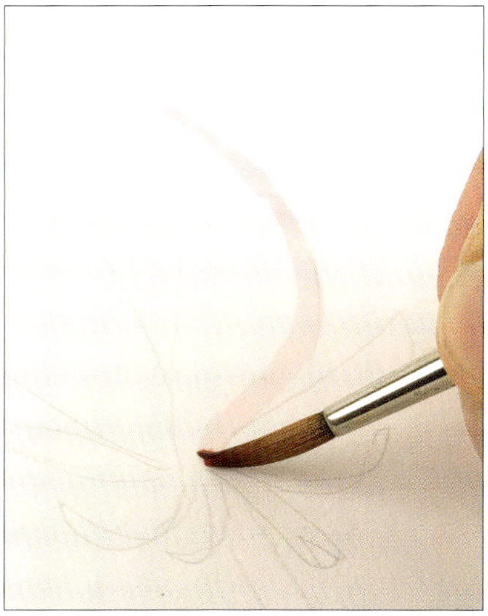

1 Use a single stroke to apply a weak wash (the very thin mix from well 1) of the appropriate colour into the shadow areas.

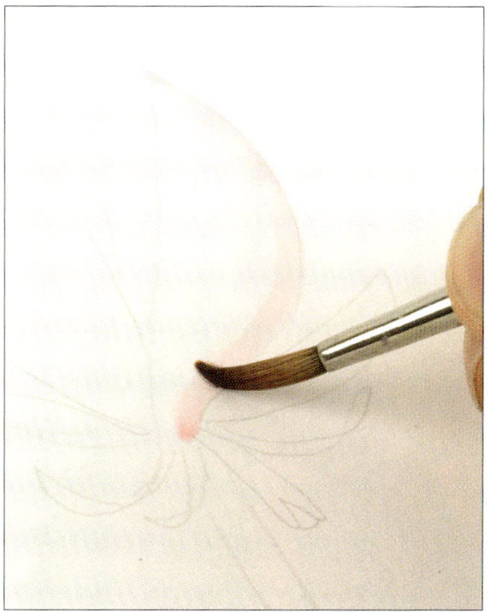

2 While the paint is wet, use your brush to draw the colour towards the highlight area, following the curve of the petal or area you are painting. This is called 'grading' the paint.

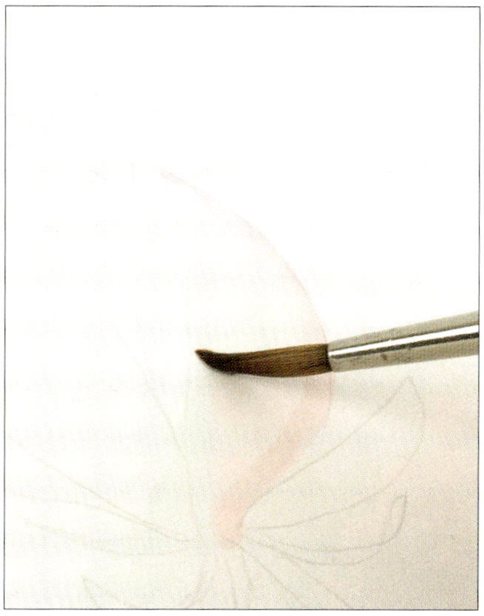

3 Continue grading the paint out towards the lightest part of the petal until you have covered it. The highlights should be left as clean white paper, as the pigment has been drawn out during the grading.

Developing the first wash

The first wash is very pale and subtle, so it is gradually strengthened using a slightly stronger mix and the same method. This layering is repeated until the shape of the area is demarcated, establishing the area and making the shape clear for the late, stronger stages.

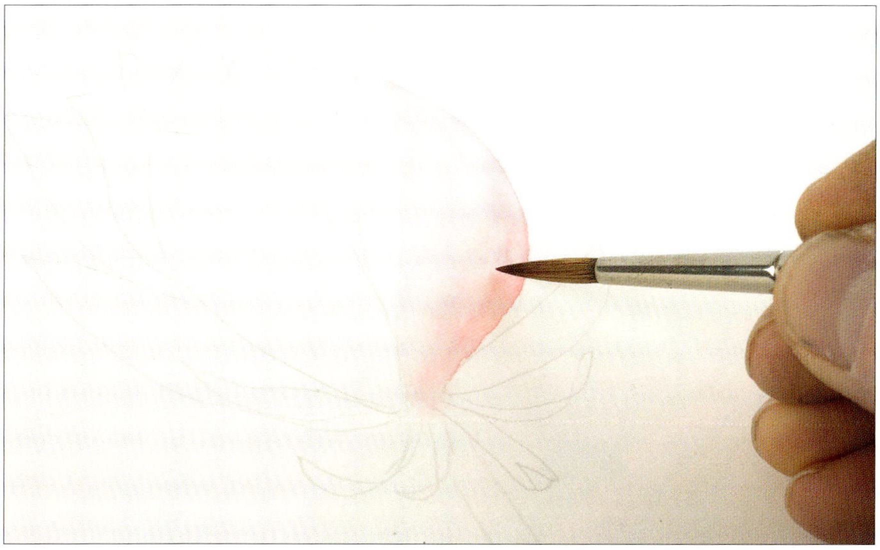

Using the slightly stronger mix in well 2, apply the paint into the shadow areas as before, matching it carefully to where you placed the paint in step 1 above. Grade the colour out as before, then continue until the area is filled. It is important that the paint is still graded out to leave the highlights as pure white paper at this stage. Allow this layer to dry completely before continuing.

Stage 2 Tonal washes

When the first layers are completely dry, you can begin to use the stronger mixes from your palette (wells 3 and 4) to develop the form and give a three-dimensional appearance to the flower. You achieve this by grading the colour into the highlights using clean water. You will need to work quickly to avoid hard edges in your work, which are difficult to grade away.

By the end of this stage, the colour of the painting should match your sketch notes – and more importantly, the original subject.

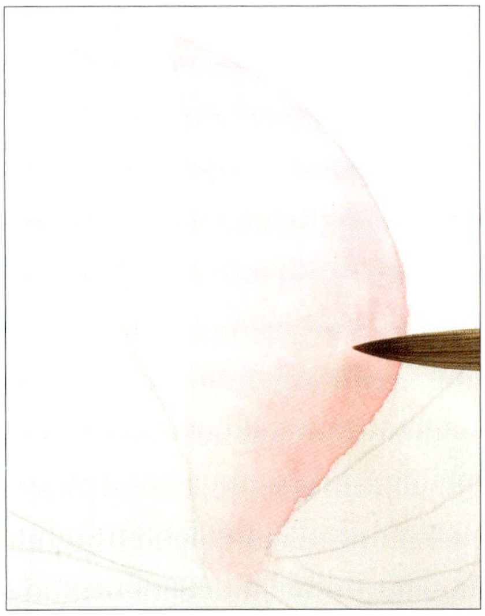

1 Wet the area once again using clean water.

Note

Because these wells have stronger mixes than those used for the first wash stage, you will need slightly less paint on your brush; the colour still needs to grade away to nothing.

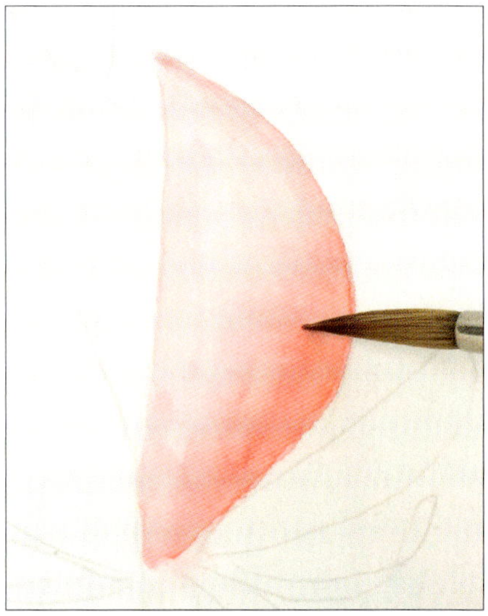

2 Use a single stroke to apply a wash of the stronger mix from well 3 into the shadow areas, grade the colour away towards the highlights and allow to dry.

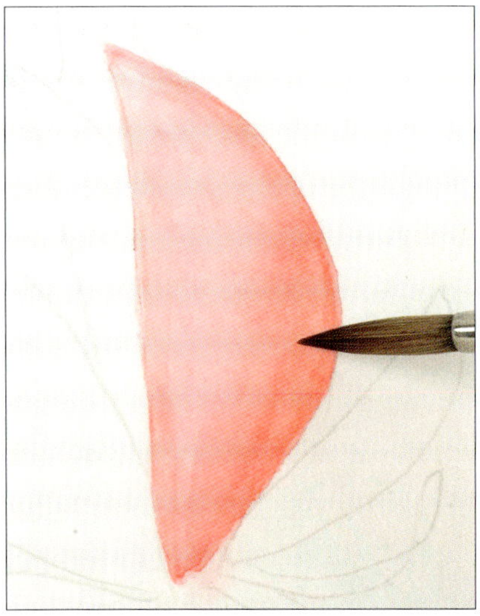

3 Once dry, repeat the process using the strongest colour, from well 4.

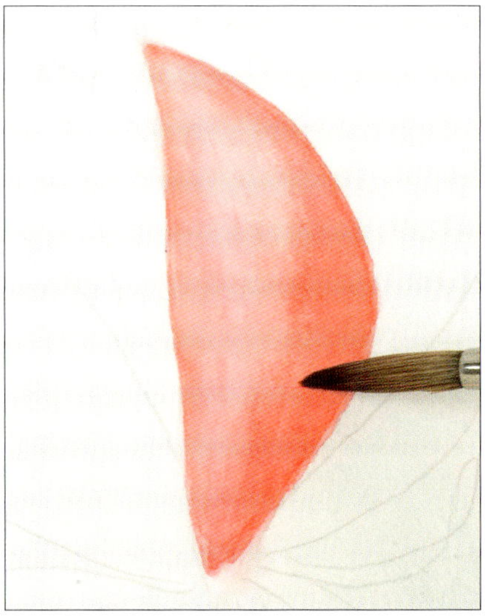

4 Continue repeating the process with the third and fourth wells until the colour of the area matches the original flower.

Order of work

When you start to paint the tonal washes stage, you should organise an order of preference, so that the paint on the areas on which you are working does not run into nearby areas that are still wet – this can create backruns. A good order of work will ensure that you can keep the edges of your work crisp.

Another thing to bear in mind is that you are working from life, and the flower can change quickly. In order to avoid difficulty later, paint the parts that change the fastest first, then move on to the more stable parts: paint buds first, then the open flowers, then the leaves, then the stems. If a root system is to be included, paint this last, as the roots will not change very much.

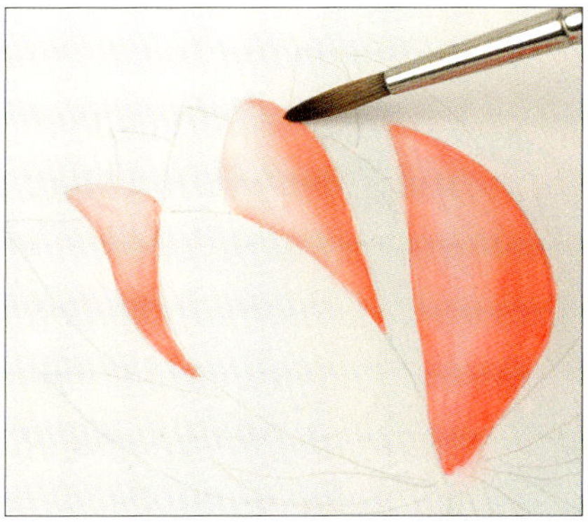

1 When painting flower petals, for example, it is best not to move on to a petal immediately next to the last one worked. Instead, work on one further away from the wet area.

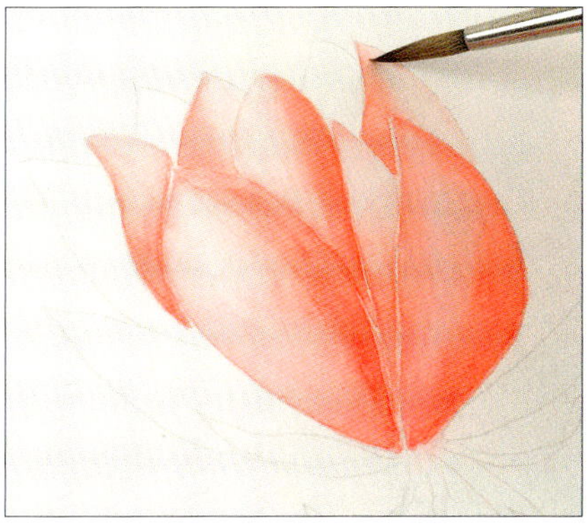

2 Return to the skipped petals or other areas later, once the first areas are dry.

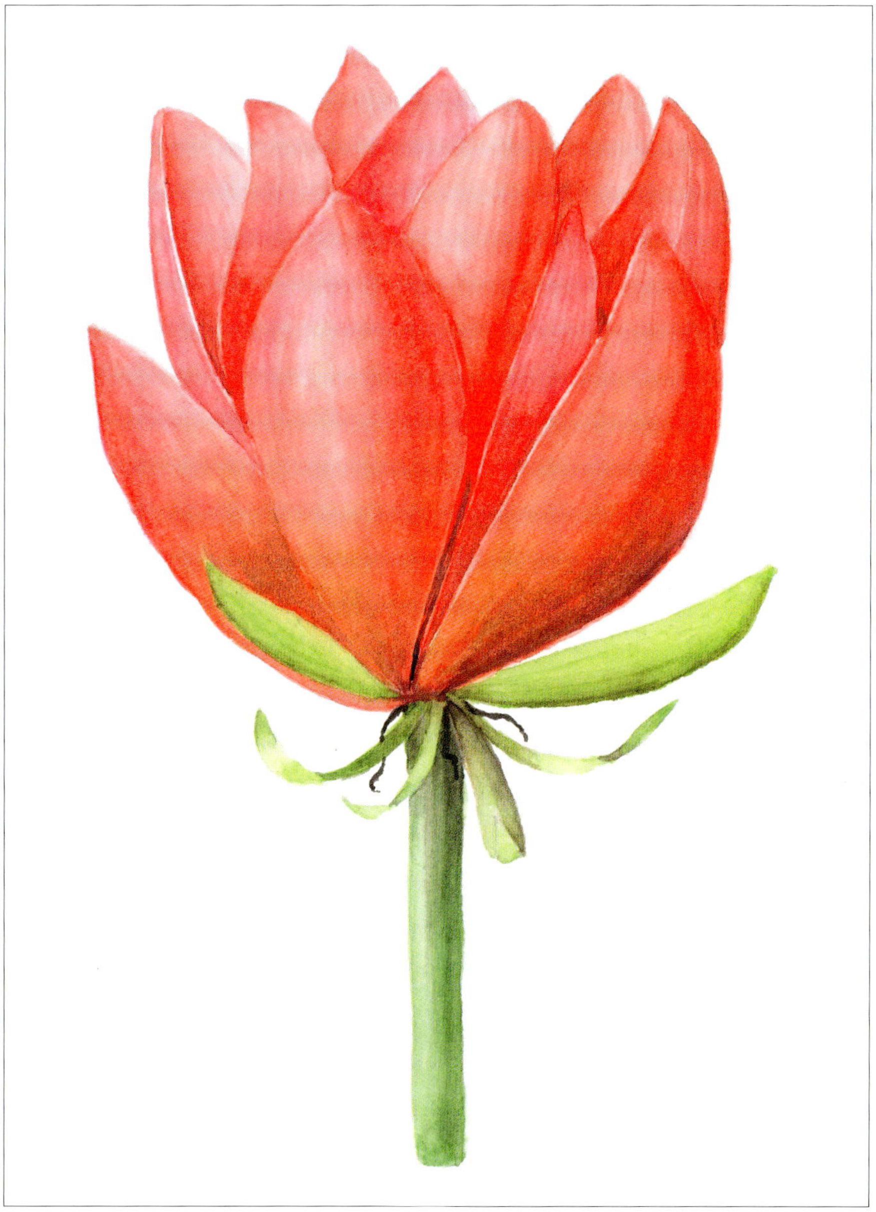

Once the petals were all completed, the stem and sepals were worked in turn. Again, non-adjacent areas were painted, and blank areas were filled in once the first group was dry.

Stage 3 Crossovers

This stage puts the components of the flower into the correct positions, by painting small areas of shadow where areas cross and overlap. This knocks back the parts that are further away, making them appear more distant, rather than physically connected to parts of the plant in the foreground. This can be particularly useful for clarity if the parts to be knocked back are the same colour as those remaining in the foreground.

To add the crossover shading, a darker shade of the same colour can be used, or neutral tint in various strengths: the darkest shade for the greatest distance, working through mid tones to the lightest tint for the areas to be knocked back the smallest distance from the foreground.

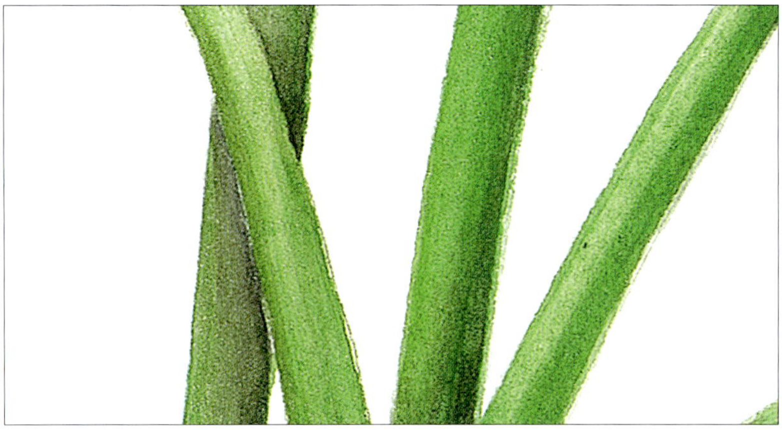

These Zantedeschia *stems cross over each other, so neutral tint has been glazed over the rearmost stem where the foreground stem overlays it. Notice that the effect is subtle: the original colours laid down in stage 1 are tinted, not covered.*

It is not just stems that overlap one another, as this Lathyrus *leaf demonstrates. The process is approached in exactly the same way, but note that you must use either neutral tint (which works well with almost all colours) or a darker shade of the colour used on the background part (in this case, the stem), if it is different to the ovelaying part.*

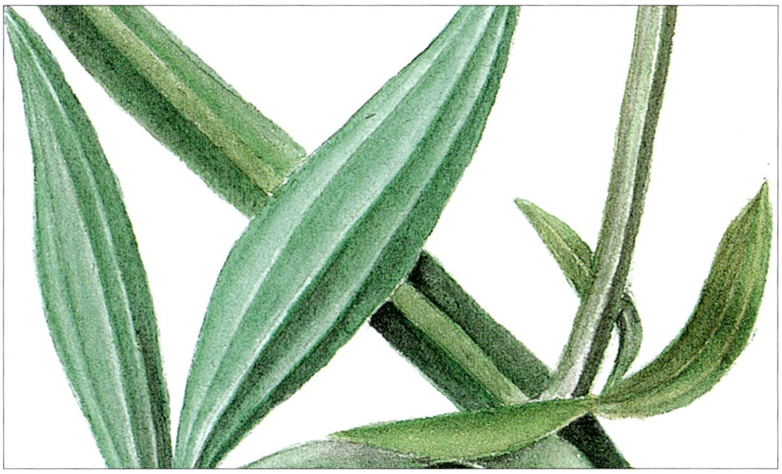

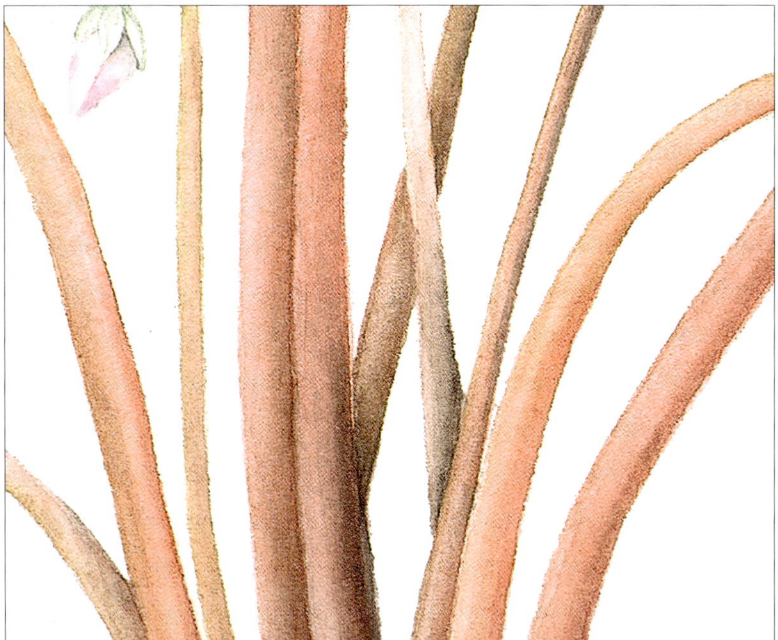

This example, taken from the Cyclamen *project, shows an excellent example of using the darkest shade next to the lightest tint, to suggest a large distance between the two stems.*

Stage 4 Harmonisation

The harmonisation stage can be daunting, especially to the beginner. However, it brings together the colours on the painting and adds a great deal to the realism of the finished painting. As a result, it is well worth a little extra effort.

Light interacts with the colours of the flower. For example, a blue flowerhead juxtaposed with a green leaf will lend a blue hue to the leaf, and in return will have a little green light reflected on to it. This effect is most marked where the light in the painting is strongest.

To represent the effect, a diluted wash of the reflected colour is applied evenly on to the affected part and graded away. Allow the wash to dry, then judge whether a second – or even third – layer should be applied.

This Pelargonium *bud provides a good example of the effect, as the bright red of the surrounding petals is reflected on to the sepals of the bud, and vice versa.*

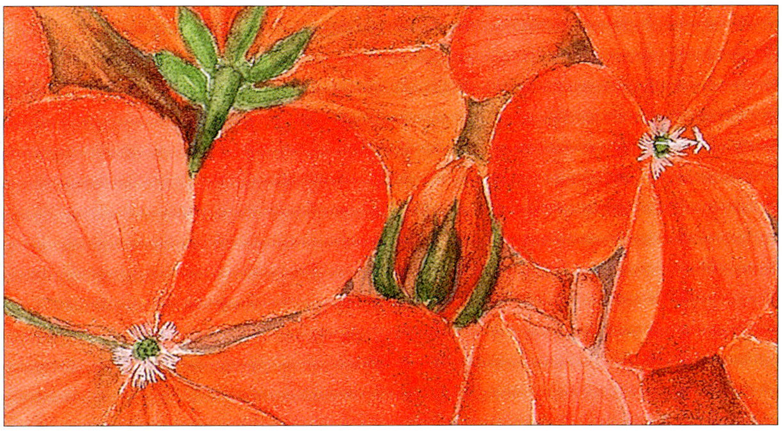

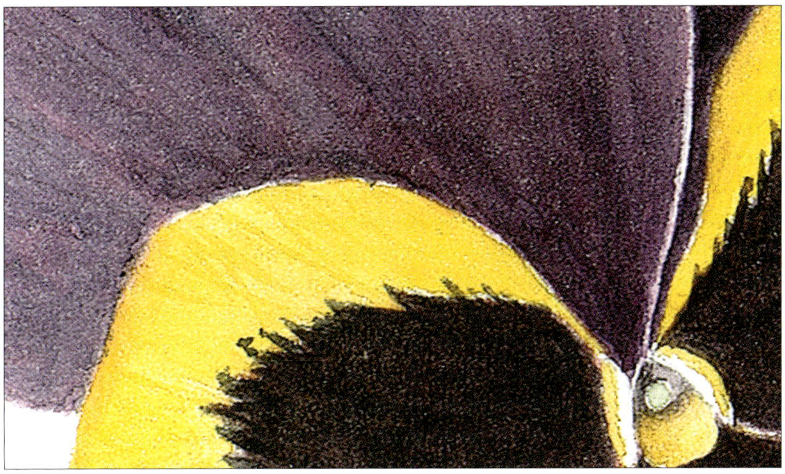

The effect is subtle, but noticeable in the harmonisation between the two petals on this flower.

You should make the harmonisation very subtle when dealing with white petals, as the colour is very sensitive to change.

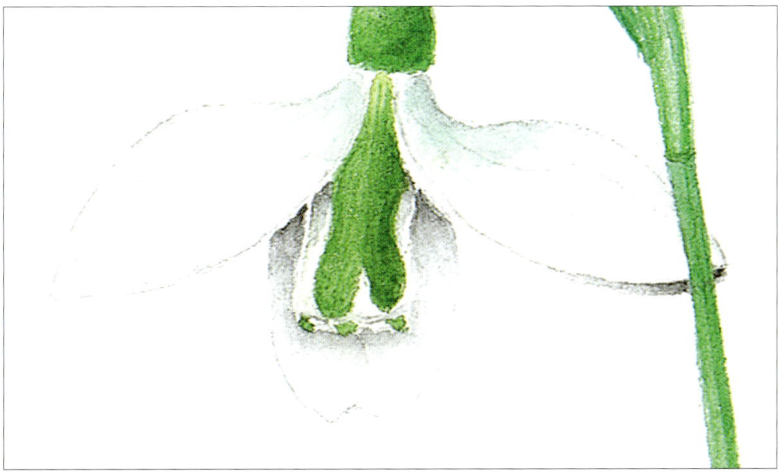

Stage 5 Details

At this stage, the finer details such as barbs, hairs, stigmas and stamens are added along with surface details such as venation, speckles and spots. When applying these details, attention must be paid to their position: hairs that are in shadow should be darker in tone than those in direct light, for example. If this procedure is not adhered to, the painting will take on an unwanted stylised appearance.

Make sure that these details are applied delicately, and remember that even the smallest parts still have a distinct form, so do not paint them with solid blocks of colour.

Tip

White gouache can be used for delicate highlights on even the tiniest parts of a flower.

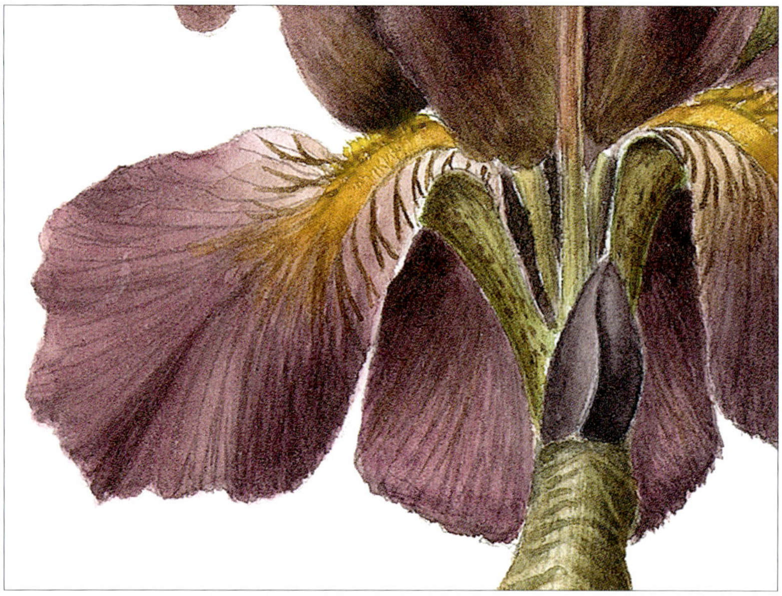

The venation on the petals in this example shows how the tone of paint used varies with the position of the area of detail in relation to the light source.

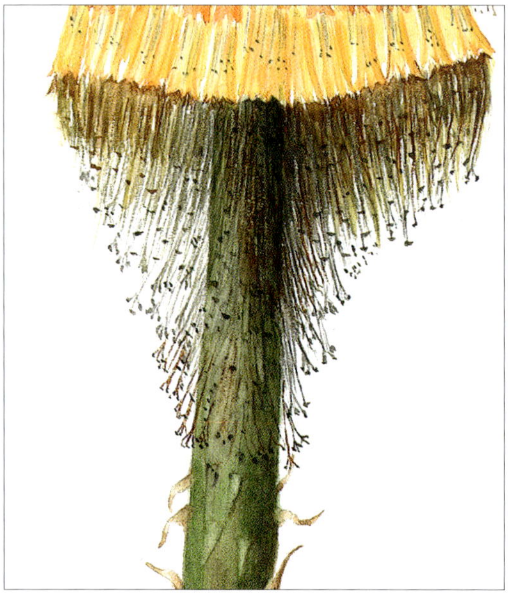

The dozens of tiny parts below the flower spike of this red hot poker require careful brushwork to achieve a realistic finished painting.

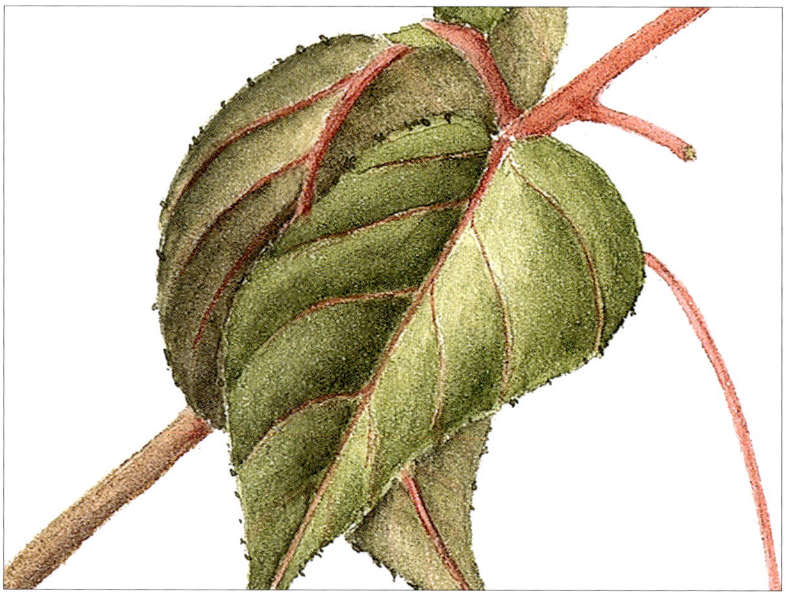

Leaves and stems require just as much attention to detail, as this example demonstrates.

Stage 6 Discretionary washes

Unless you are extremely careful in how you apply the details in stage 5, some detail lines will look too dark and heavy. If this occurs, you can apply a very thin wash of the appropriate colour to the area. This helps to blend the different tones together without destroying the detail work or changing the basic colour of the area too radically.

Some areas benefit from a thin wash of a transparent colour. As an example, a glaze of transparent yellow on a green leaf will give it a lustre. As the name of the stage sugests, these washes are purely optional – if you feel that the painting is finished, then do not change anything.

Tip

Discretionary washes are just that: discretionary. If your work is correct at the end of stage 5, then there is no need to alter any of the elements.

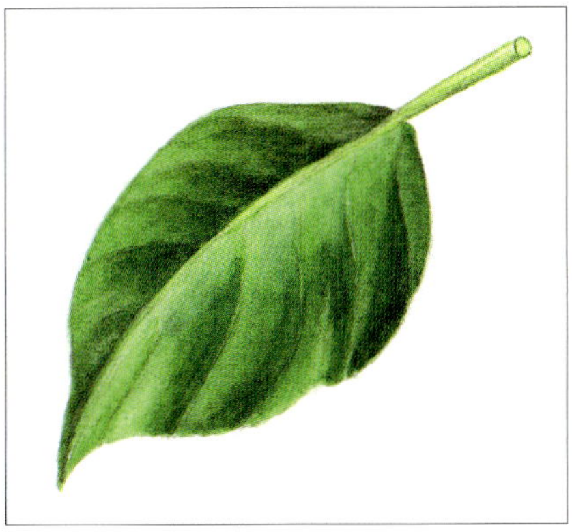

1 Identify whether you consider the area complete. This leaf is essentially finished, with all the tonal washes and detailing complete. However, it may benefit from a subtle wash to help enrich the colours.

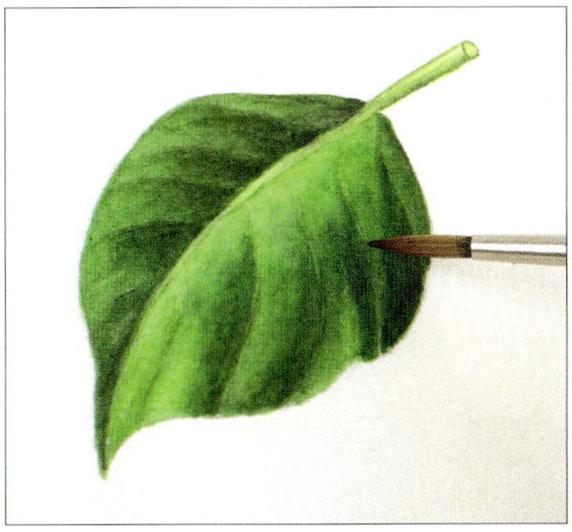

2 Lay in a very thin wash of a colour from well 1 (in this case, transparent yellow) over the whole area and allow to dry.

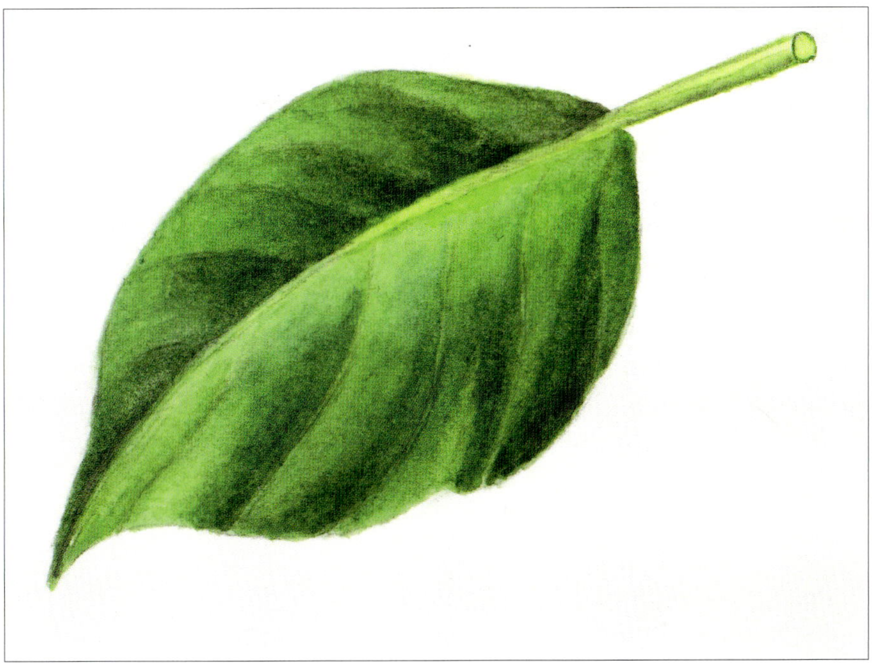

The addition of a subtle transparent yellow wash enriches the colours, helps to merge and blend the different areas and gives the impression of sunlight, adding to the realism of the piece.

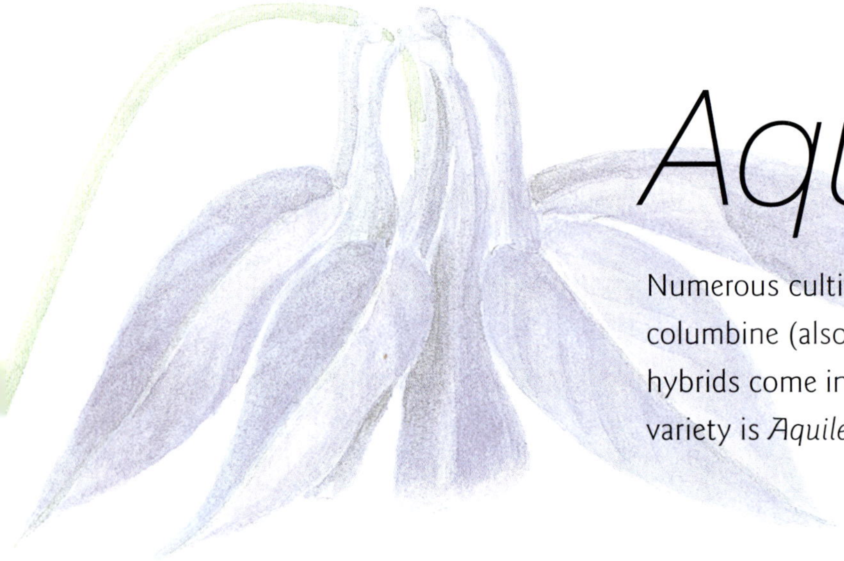

Aquilegia

Numerous cultivars have been developed from the European columbine (also called the common columbine) and these modern hybrids come in many shades, including bi-coloured types. This variety is *Aquilegia vulgaris*.

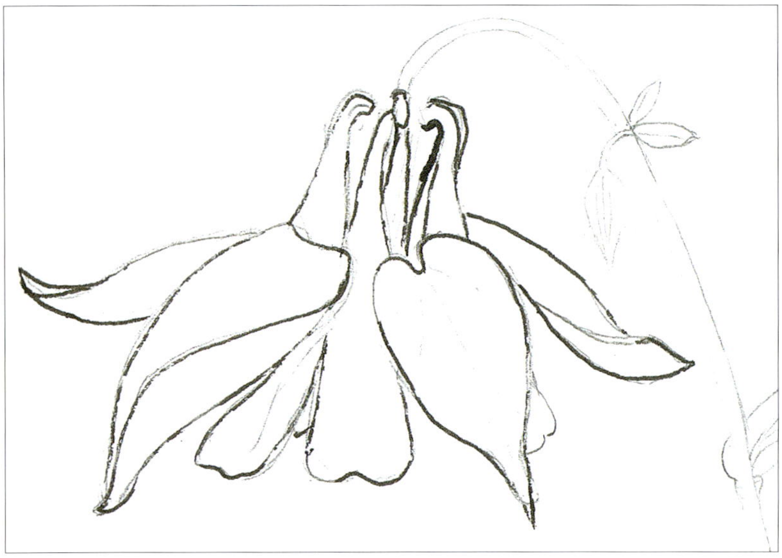

The bell-shaped flowers of Aquilegia vulgaris *have spurs at the top of the petals. Make sure that you can see all of them and that they fit to the petals correctly.*

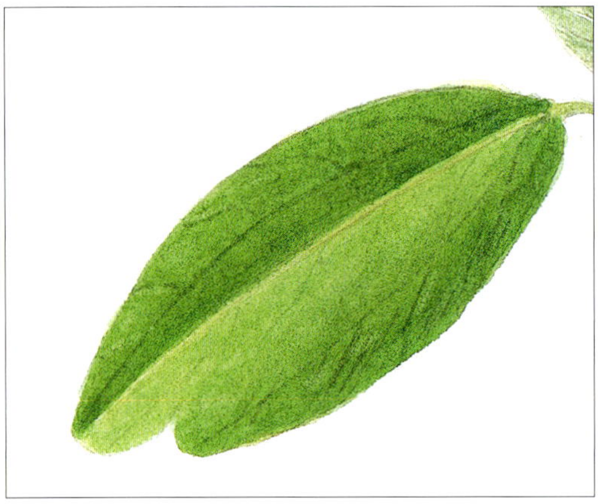

The younger, upper leaves are simpler in shape than the older leaves further down the stem. They are lighter in colour with more yellow added to the mix. The insignificant fine dark veins are added at the detail stage.

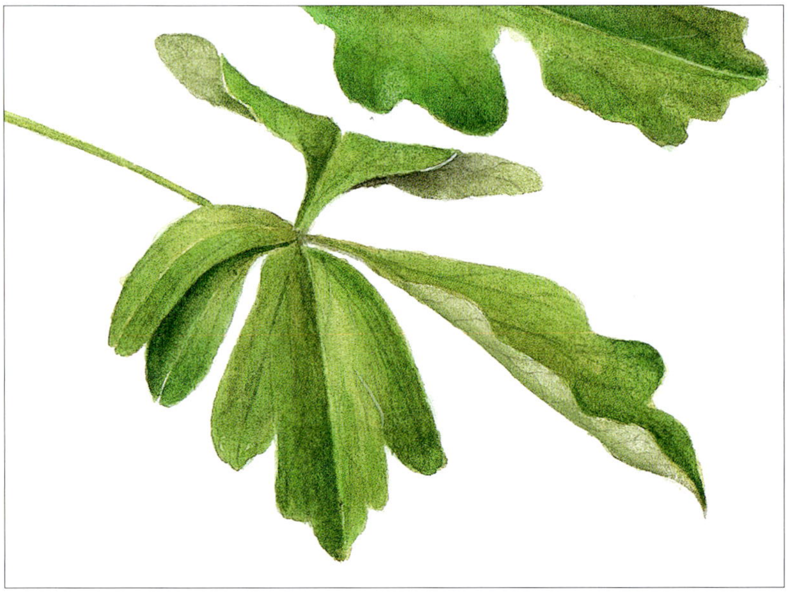

The older, lower leaves are fern-like and divided. The colour is a mid-green, differing in tone to the younger leaves. Adding comparative observations like this to your notes can help your finished painting.

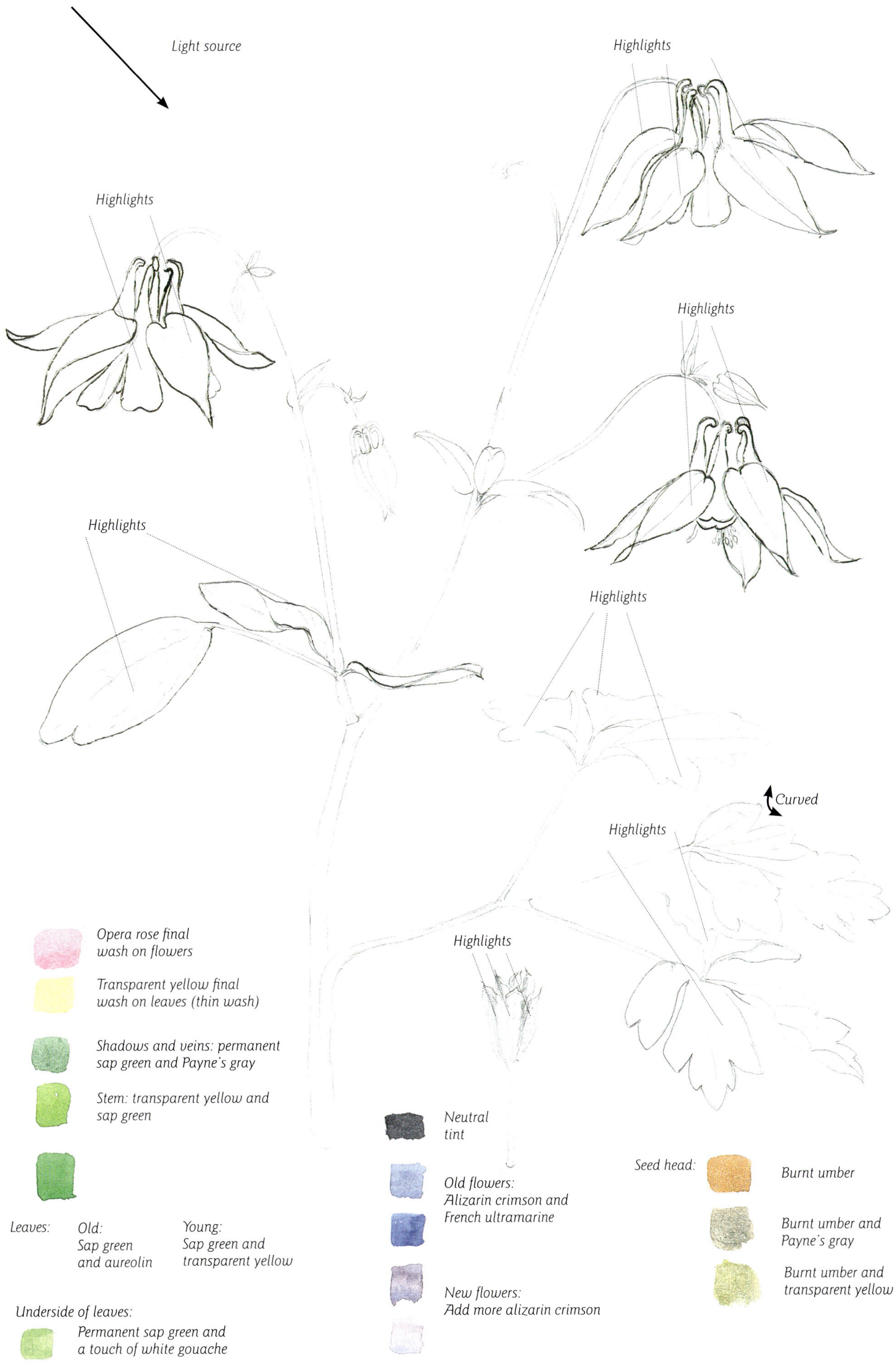
Light source
Highlights
Highlights
Highlights
Highlights
Highlights
Curved
Highlights
Highlights
Opera rose final wash on flowers
Transparent yellow final wash on leaves (thin wash)
Shadows and veins: permanent sap green and Payne's gray
Stem: transparent yellow and sap green
Leaves:
Old: Sap green and aureolin
Young: Sap green and transparent yellow
Underside of leaves:
Permanent sap green and a touch of white gouache
Neutral tint
Old flowers: Alizarin crimson and French ultramarine
New flowers: Add more alizarin crimson
Seed head:
Burnt umber
Burnt umber and Payne's gray
Burnt umber and transparent yellow

Painting the *Aquilegia*

After drawing the *Aquilegia* in your sketchbook and preparing your colours, transfer the drawing to hot-pressed watercolour paper.

First wash

1 Using a size 3 brush, apply a wash of clean water to the petals and leave to dry. Use the mix of French ultramarine and a small amount of alizarin crimson to paint every alternate petal in turn, grading the paint as you work to ensure the highlight areas remain clean.

2 Work on the petals of all three flowers in turn, returning to the first when the wash is completely dry on the first petals. Paint the petals that you missed out earlier, as described above.

3 Glaze the seed head with clean water, then lay in a thin wash of burnt umber, grading it into the highlight areas.

4 Give the leaves and stem the same treatment, using a wash of sap green with a touch of alizarin crimson for the tops of the leaves, and sap green with transparent yellow for the stems.

5 Once the tops are dry, paint the undersides of the leaves (where visible) with a stronger mix of sap green and white gouache.

First wash

Painting alternate petals leaves a dry, clean area that ensures that the paint you use on subsequent petals will not 'rush' into wet paint on previous ones.

Tonal washes

1 Using slightly thicker mixes of the first wash colours, work into the shadow areas of the petals, again leaving the highlight areas clean. This will start to create the form and give shape to your petals.

2 Follow the same procedure for the leaves, seed head and stem.

Crossovers

1 Where the petals overlap one another, add neutral tint to your mix and add the overlap shading.

2 Where the leaves overlap the stem, paint a small triangle with the appropriate darker mix and grade it into the main colour (see right).

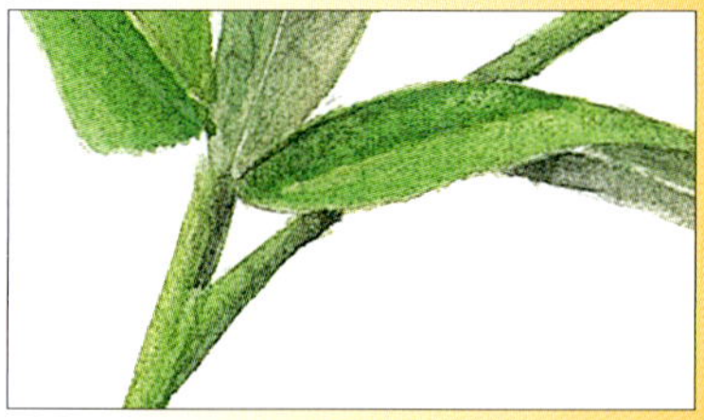

Crossovers

Note how the triangular shape, where the leaf crosses over the stem, has been blended into the main colour of the stem.

Harmonisation

1 Apply the original green wash to the tops of the flower petals, to give a harmonisation between the blue and green.

2 Apply a thin wash of the original blue to the closest leaves.

Details

1 Change to a size 1 round brush and add neutral tint to the original dark green mix. Use this to paint in the veins on the leaves.

2 Add subtle venation to the seed head and petals in turn, using burnt umber and French ultramarine respectively.

Discretionary washes

I mixed a thin wash of opera rose and glazed over each petal to unify the tones. I also painted a thin wash of transparent yellow over the leaves and buds, including the seed head.

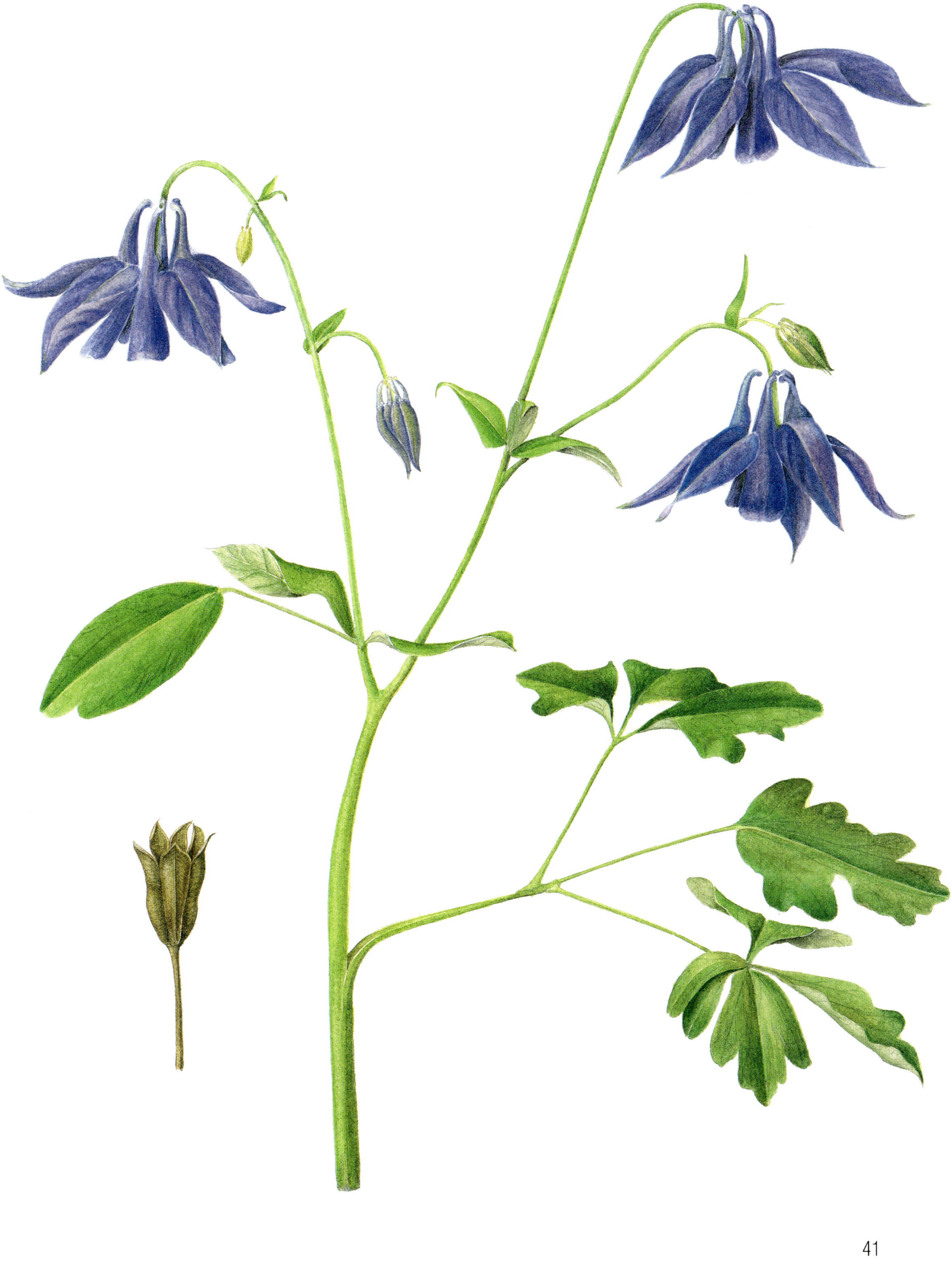

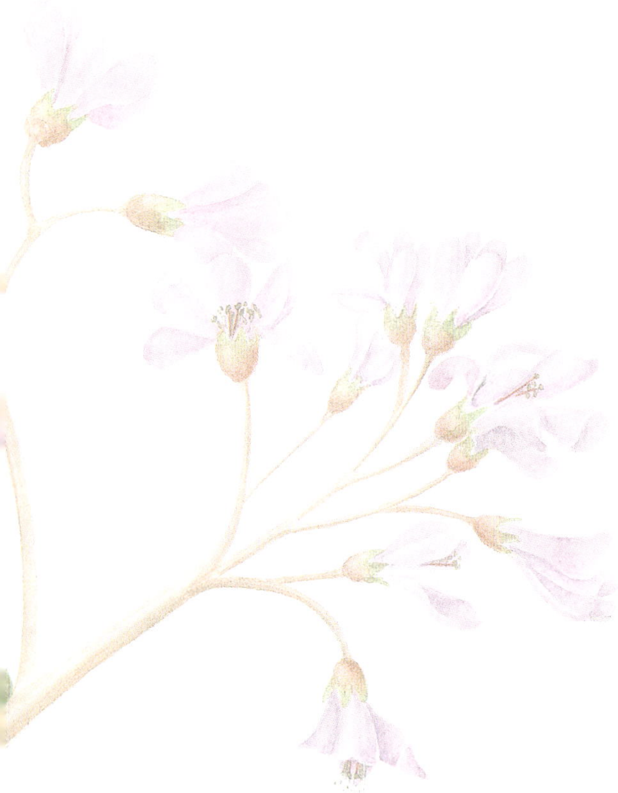

Bergenia

This hardy herbaceous perennial, *Bergenia crassifolia*, was formerly known as *Saxifraga*. The pink flowers emerge on long stems from the large leathery leaves, which turn to shades of red in autumn.

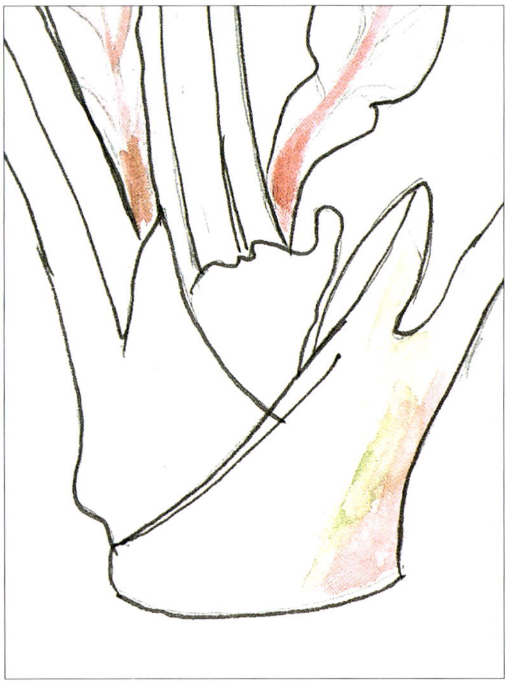

With complex areas, like the base of this Bergenia, *care must be taken to grade the colours individually and leave them to dry before applying washes to adjacent areas, otherwise the separate components will be lost.*

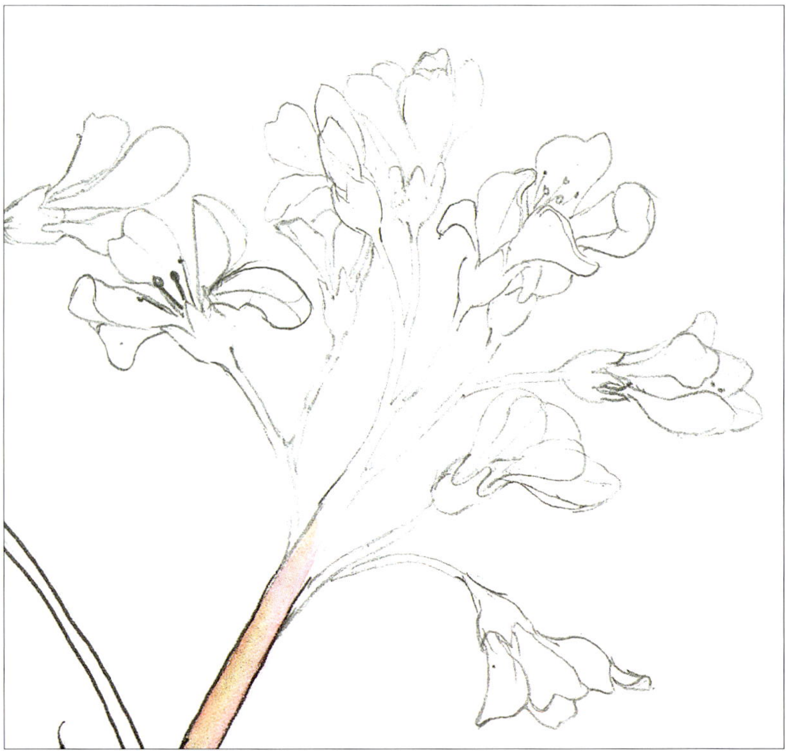

Each floret of the composite flowerhead contains two stigmas, ten stamens and five petals. When painting small flowers, it is easy to apply too strong a mix too soon. This will make the delicate flowers too heavy – ensure that they appear fresh and crisp with pale washes, and make sure the delicate stems are treated in the same way.

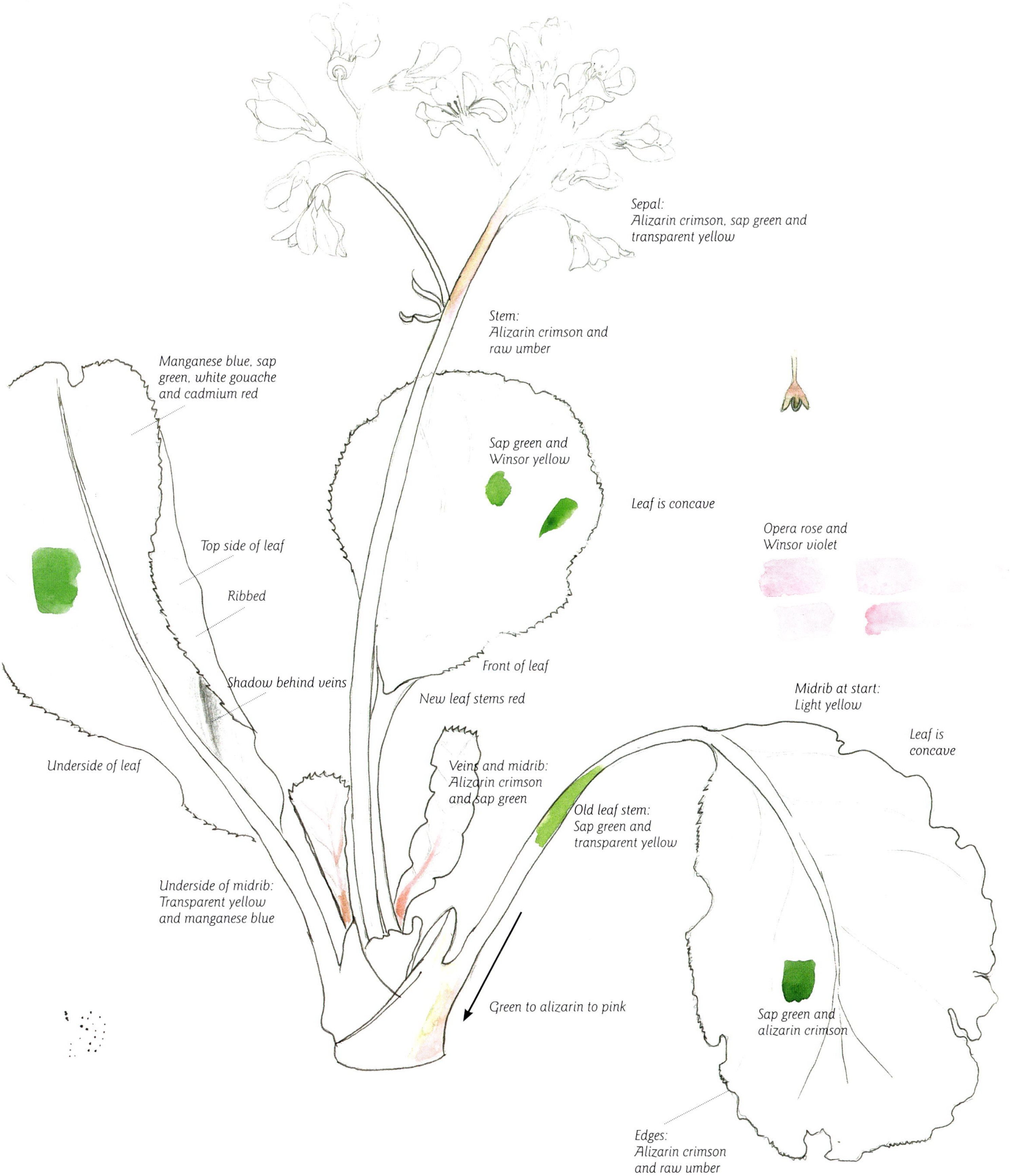
Sepal:
Alizarin crimson, sap green and transparent yellow
Stem:
Alizarin crimson and raw umber
Manganese blue, sap green, white gouache and cadmium red
Sap green and Winsor yellow
Leaf is concave
Opera rose and Winsor violet
Top side of leaf
Ribbed
Shadow behind veins
Front of leaf
New leaf stems red
Midrib at start:
Light yellow
Leaf is concave
Underside of leaf
Veins and midrib:
Alizarin crimson and sap green
Old leaf stem:
Sap green and transparent yellow
Underside of midrib:
Transparent yellow and manganese blue
Green to alizarin to pink
Sap green and alizarin crimson
Edges:
Alizarin crimson and raw umber

Painting the *Bergenia*

Prepare your colours, transfer the drawing to hot-pressed watercolour paper, and have your sketch nearby for reference.

First wash

1 Using a size 5 brush, glaze all of the leaves with clean water and let them dry. Use the same brush and a dilute mix of sap green and alizarin crimson to apply the first wash to the right-hand outer leaf, leaving the midrib and veins unpainted. Grade the paint towards the highlights but leave the highlights unpainted.

2 With a dilute mix of sap green and Winsor yellow, paint the younger centre leaf, leaving the midrib and veins unpainted and graded into the highlights.

3 Paint the underside of the left-hand leaf with a mix of sap green and manganese blue with touches of white gouache and cadmium red. Leave the midrib and veins unpainted and let the illustration dry. Still using the size 5 brush, paint in the leaf curl on the same leaf with a dilute mix of sap green and alizarin crimson.

4 Use a size 2 brush to glaze all of the flowers and stems with clean water and leave them to dry. With a dilute mix of opera rose and Winsor violet, paint the flower petals, grading into the highlights to create form. Use the same brush with a dilute mix of alizarin crimson and raw umber to paint in the lower stem, grading from the right-hand side into the highlights.

5 Use the same brush with a mix of transparent yellow and sap green to paint in the midribs and veins. Add alizarin crimson to the mix towards the base of the leaf stems, finishing with a weak pink mix.

6 Still using the size 2 brush, glaze the small young leaves and new shoots then allow them to dry. Use a dilute mix of sap green and transparent yellow to paint in the leaves, leaving the midrib and veins unpainted.

Tonal washes

1 Using the size 2 brush and stronger mixes of the colours listed above, build up the tone and form with more washes, still grading the paint into the highlights.

2 At this stage, use neutral tint to add the shadows on the right-hand sides of the veins on the underside of the left-hand leaf.

Crossovers

1 Using a size 1 brush and the petal mix (opera rose and Winsor violet) with a little neutral tint, add shadows to the small areas where the petals overlap to distinguish them from one another.

2 Use the same brush with neutral tint to paint in the small shadow where the stems overlap the leaves and where the leaves overlap the stems at the base of the plant.

3 Repeat this process until the required depth between the components had been achieved.

Harmonisation

1 Very little harmonisation is needed in this portrait. Apply a dilute mix of sap green and transparent yellow to the lower petals with a size 2 brush.

2 Use the same brush with a dilute mix of alizarin crimson and raw umber to paint the shadow from the main flower stem to the centre leaf.

Details

1 Using a size 1 brush and a dilute mix of alizarin crimson, paint the base of the sepals, grading the colour to suggest form and changing to sap green and transparent yellow towards the small fingers near the base of the petals.

2 Repeat this process until the correct tone has been reached. Use the same size brush with a mix of alizarin crimson and raw umber to paint the serration on the leaf margins. With a size 0 brush, paint in the stigmas with a little sap green.

3 When dry, paint in the stamens with alizarin crimson.

Discretionary washes

I used a size 5 brush with a dilute mix of sap green and transparent yellow to wash over all of the leaves, being careful to paint accurately around the margins. I then applied the same wash to the flower stem.

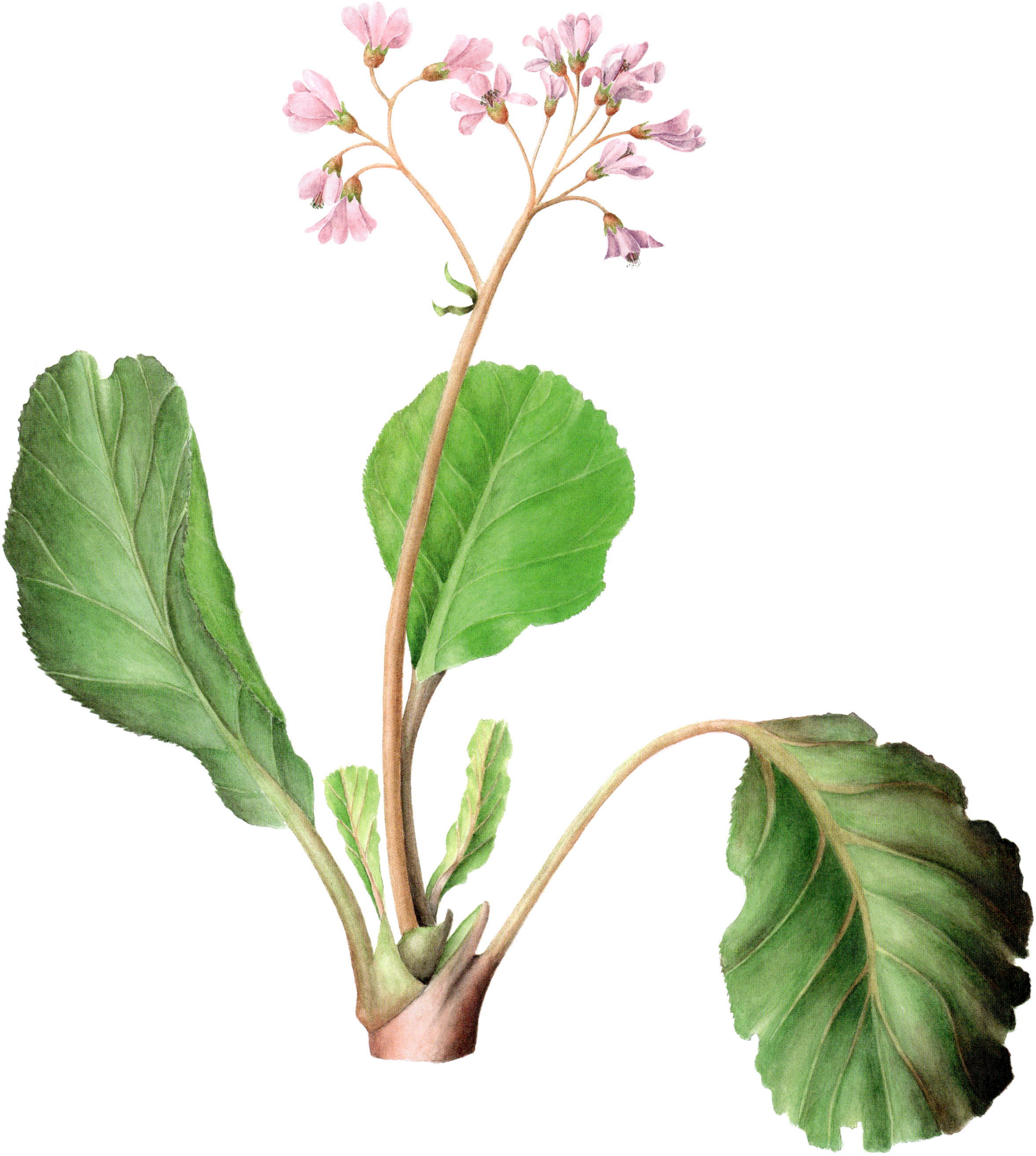

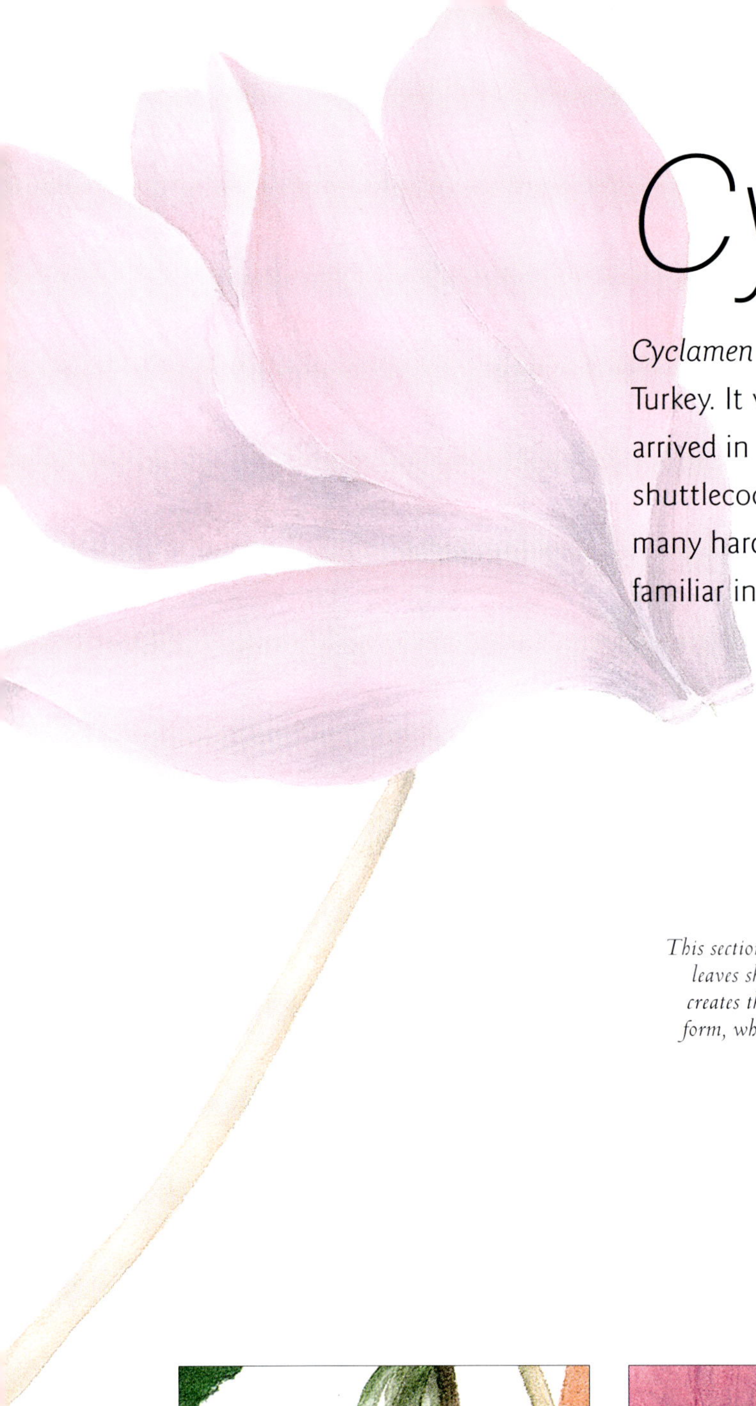

Cyclamen

Cyclamen concerto, known as 'Violet Improver', is originally from Turkey. It was first recorded on woodcuts dated from 1460, and arrived in Western Europe in the 1750s. A tuberous plant with shuttlecock-shaped flowerheads and various leaf patterns, it has many hardy varieties as well as the many pink-red shades of the familiar indoor specimens.

This section of one of the Cyclamen's main leaves shows some tonal pencil work. This creates the impression of three-dimensional form, which helps to develop understanding of the shape before painting.

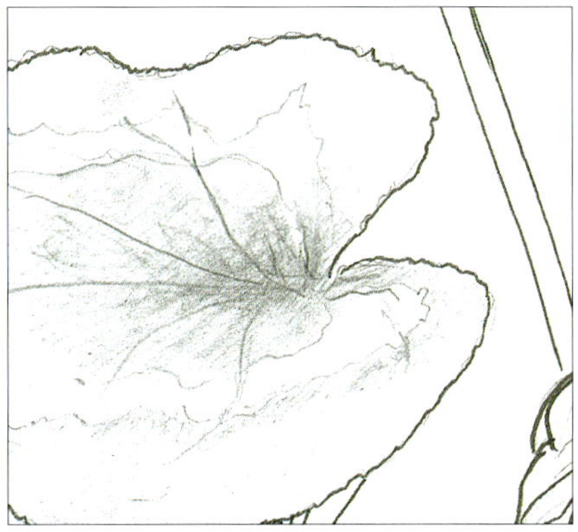

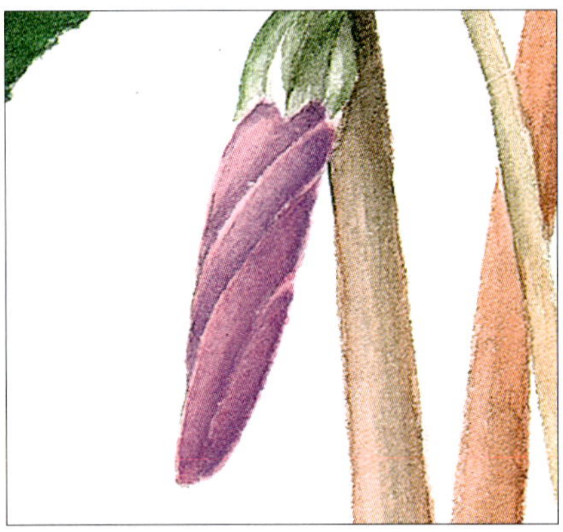

The twisted buds are a delight to paint. Each ridge is shaded from right to left to create form.

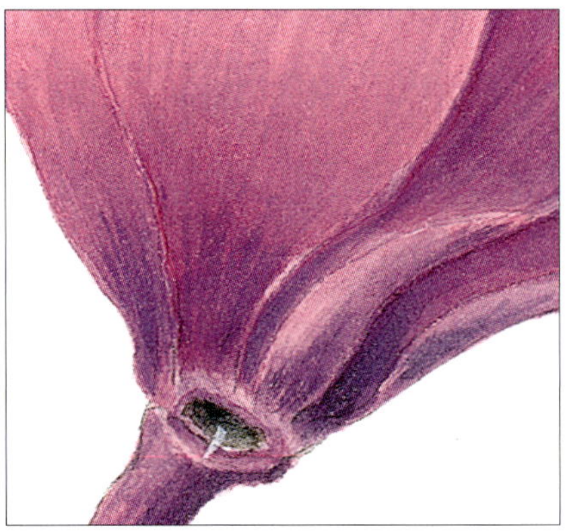

At the base of the petals, a small round lip is visible. This must show on your painting.

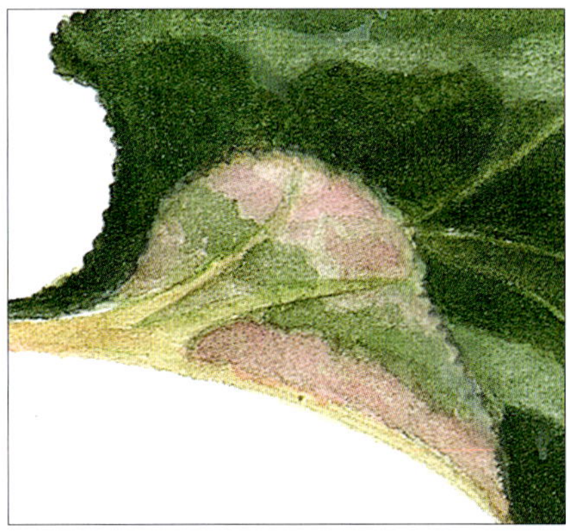

Note the different shades of colour on the underside of the leaves. The veins cast shadows which help to make them stand proud.

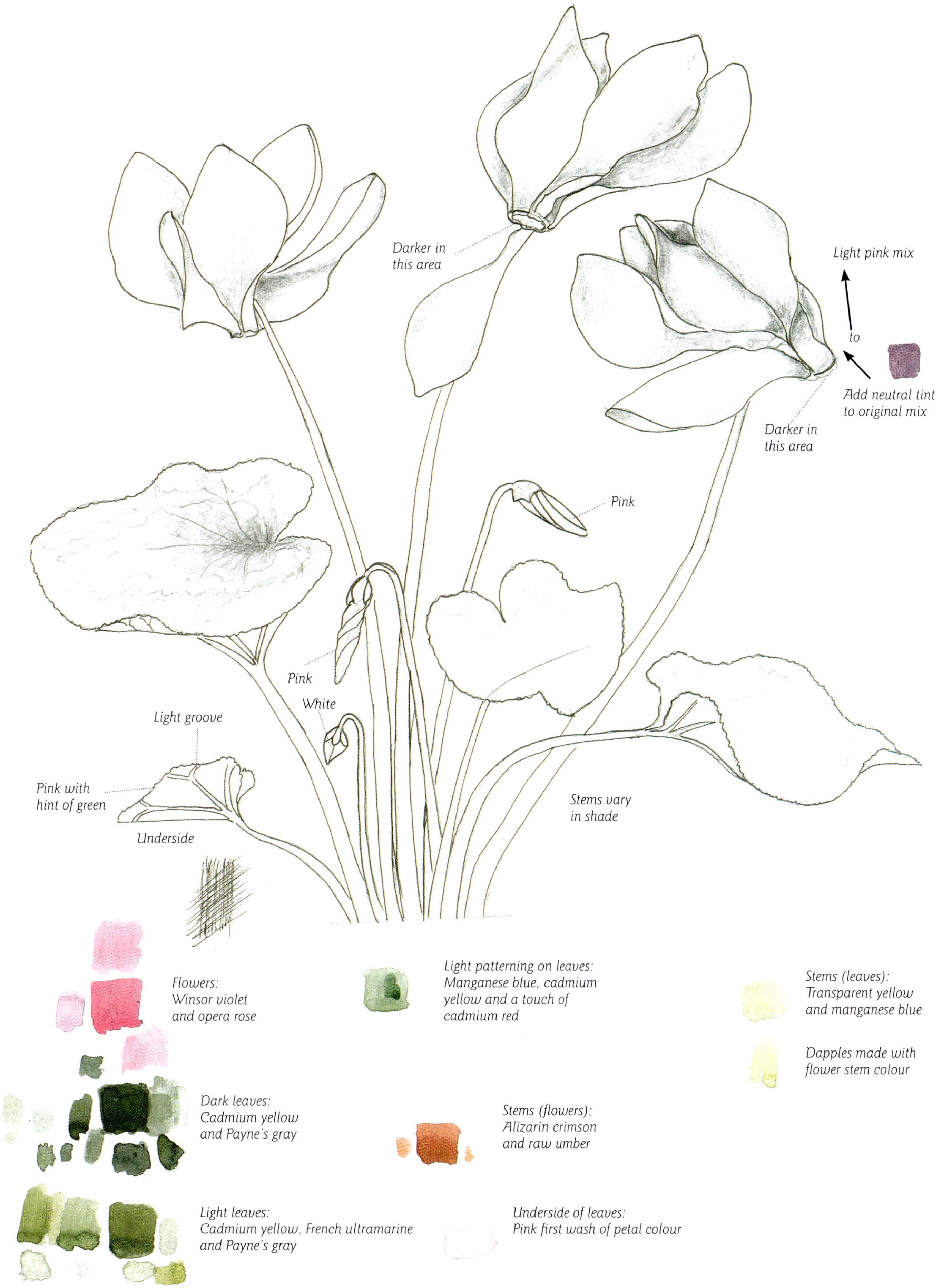

Darker in this area
Light pink mix
to
Add neutral tint to original mix
Darker in this area
Pink
Pink
White
Light groove
Pink with hint of green
Underside
Stems vary in shade
Flowers: Winsor violet and opera rose
Light patterning on leaves: Manganese blue, cadmium yellow and a touch of cadmium red
Stems (leaves): Transparent yellow and manganese blue
Dapples made with flower stem colour
Dark leaves: Cadmium yellow and Payne's gray
Stems (flowers): Alizarin crimson and raw umber
Light leaves: Cadmium yellow, French ultramarine and Payne's gray
Underside of leaves: Pink first wash of petal colour

Painting the *Cyclamen*

Transfer your drawing to hot-pressed watercolour paper and prepare the wells of colour.

First wash

1 Firstly, glaze over all of the petals with clean water using a size 3 brush and leave them to dry. Once dry, apply the first diluted wash of opera rose and Winsor violet to the petals, leaving the highlights unpainted but grading the wash into them, taking note of the highlights from the tonal drawing.

2 Glaze the leaves with clean water and allow them to dry. The older leaves are darker, so apply a dilute wash of cadmium yellow and Payne's gray leaving the lighter pattern areas unpainted. Add more cadmium yellow and a little French ultramarine to the mix and apply a dilute wash to the younger leaves.

3 Glaze all of the stems with clean water using a size 3 brush and leave to dry, before applying a dilute mix of transparent yellow and manganese blue to the leaf stems. Apply a mix of alizarin crimson and raw umber to the flower stems.

4 Paint the undersides of the leaves with a dilute wash of the petal colour.

5 Glaze the two larger buds with water, then apply the flower mix, leaving the highlights clean. Paint the lighter patterns on the leaves with a dilute wash of cadmium yellow, manganese blue and a little cadmium red.

Tonal washes

1 Using the same colours and brush sizes, but with slightly stronger mixes, apply second washes, replicating what you did earlier by leaving the highlights unpainted but graded into. Repeat this process until you have a three-dimensional image.

Crossovers

1 Using neutral tint added to the flower colour mix, paint into the shadow areas, making them darker on the petal at the base and lighter towards the point of each flower.

2 Apply shadows behind the crossing stems by adding neutral tint to the original mix of the stems.

Harmonisation

1 Using a size 3 brush and the original dilute wash of pink, wash over the leaf closest to the flower.

2 With a dilute green wash, paint over the lower part of the flower petals.

Details

1 Leave the small bud as white paper, but put in shadows to create form with neutral tint.

2 Give the sepals a wash of manganese blue, cadmium yellow and a touch of cadmium red, repeating the layers until the depth of colour is correct.

3 Paint the faint lines on the petals with a size 1 brush and a slightly darker mix of the petal colour with French ultramarine added.

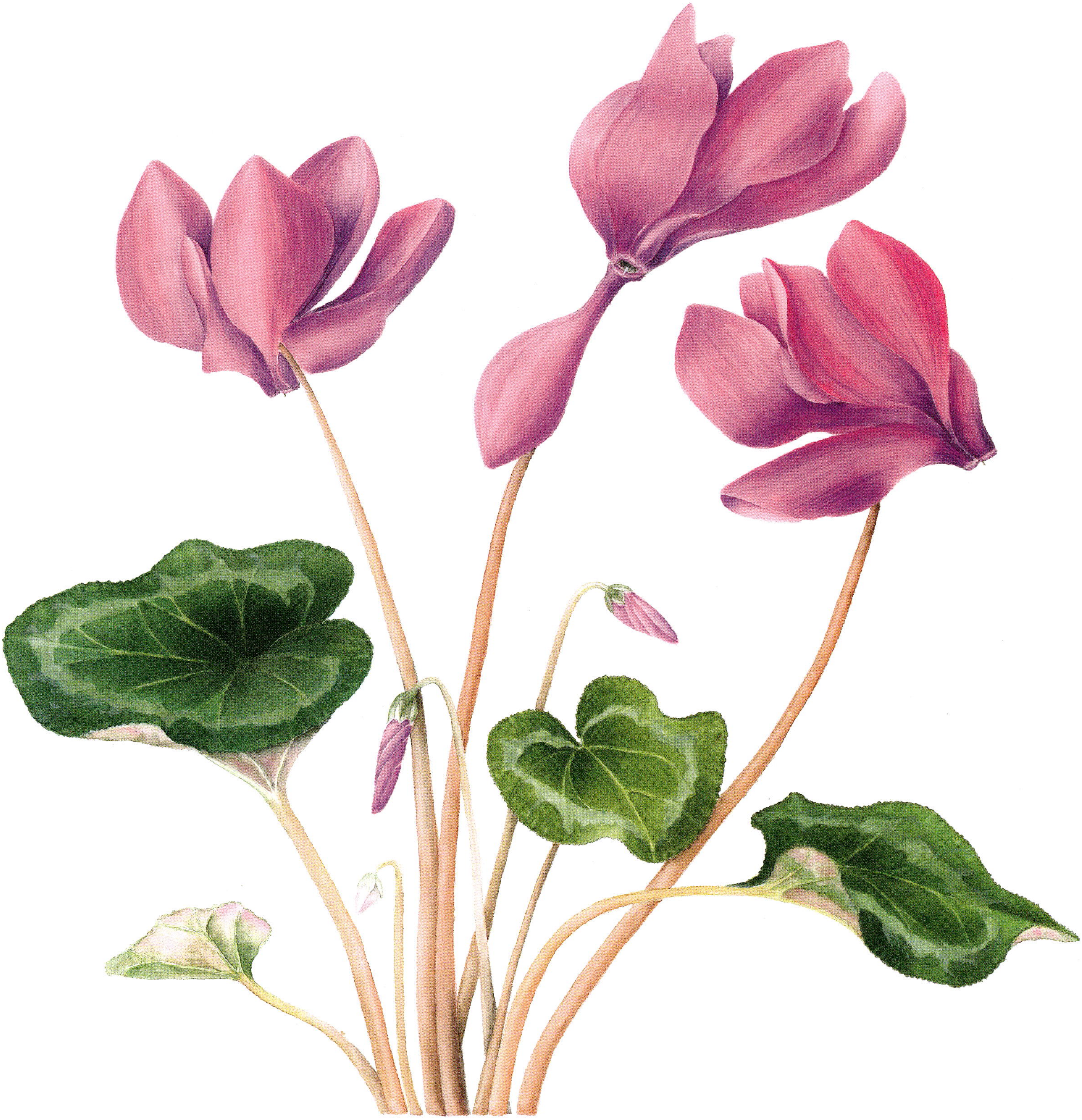

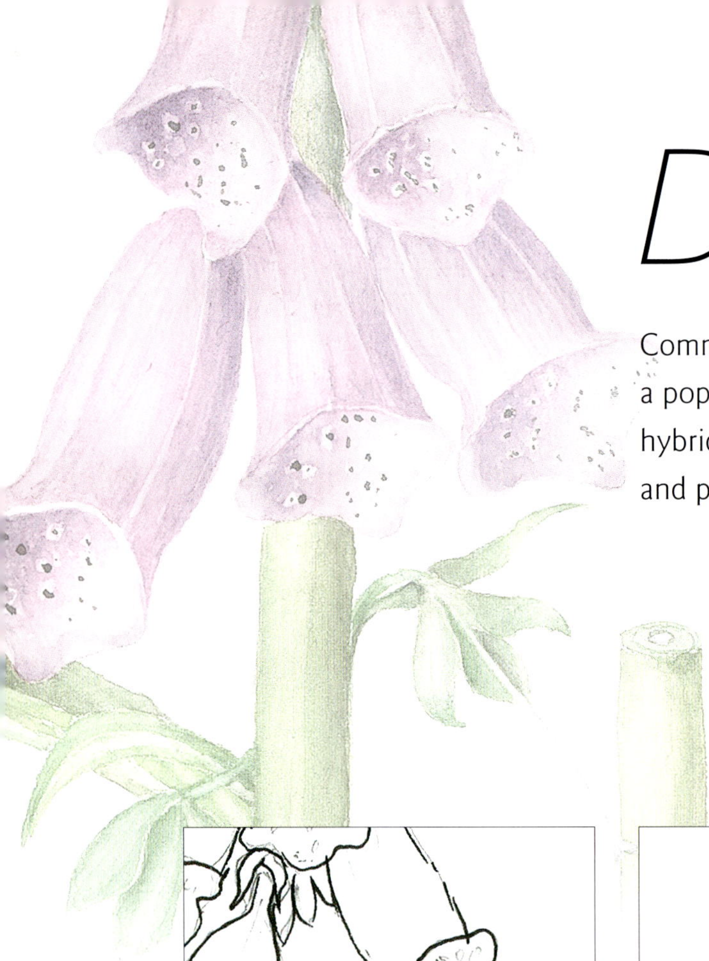

Digitalis

Commonly known as the foxglove, *Digitalis purpurea* has long been a popular garden flower. It has also been used as a medicine. Many hybrid varieties exist in various colours, including whites, yellows and purples.

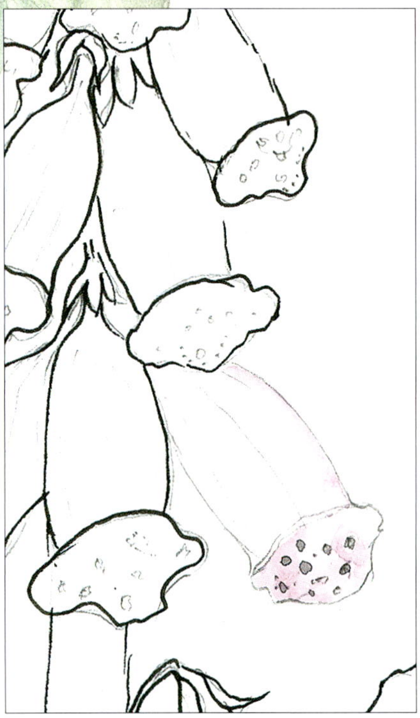

After drawing the foxglove flower, a little paint was applied to one of them to get a feel of the form. Do not feel restricted to line and tone alone in your sketches: using them for colour notes is sensible.

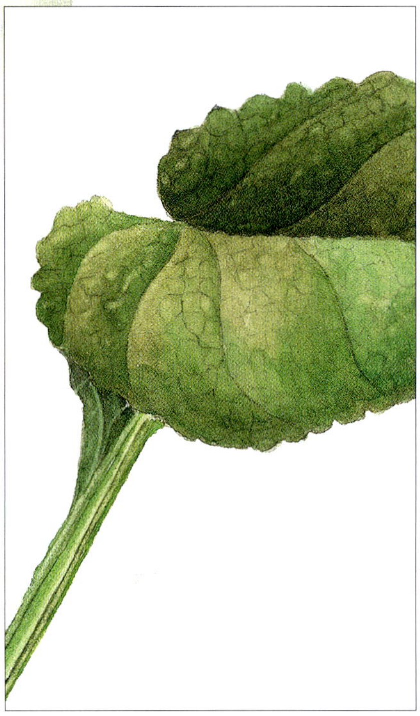

The main leaf shows the subtle change in the tones of the different greens. This is only achieved by using many thin overlaying washes of colour.

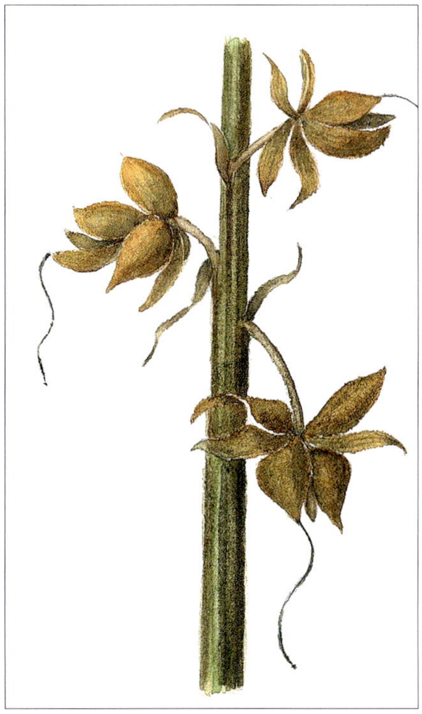

The seed pods form an interesting part of the portrait. Note the form on each of the outer pods: they will differ markedly from each other.

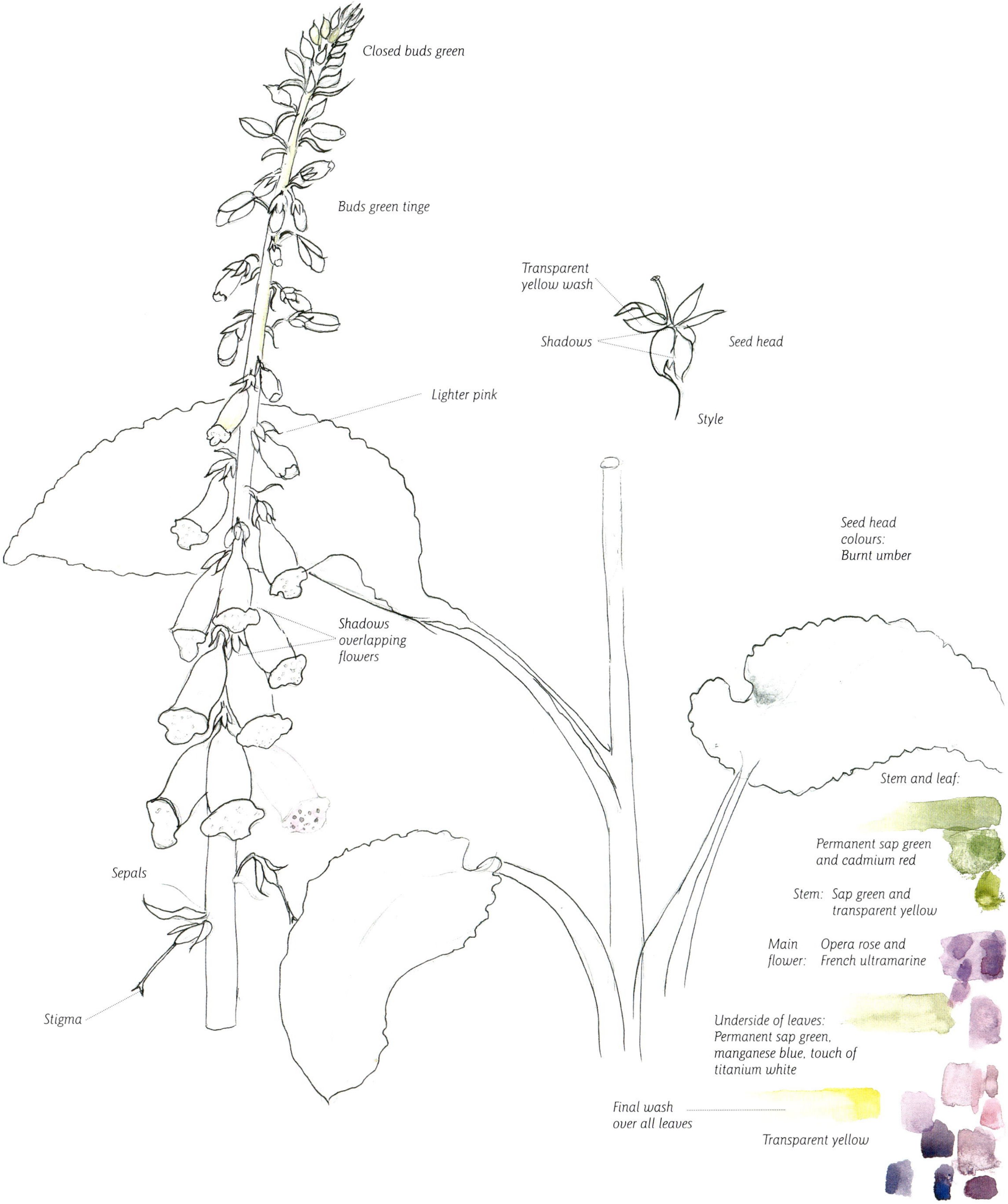
Closed buds green
Buds green tinge
Transparent yellow wash
Shadows
Seed head
Style
Lighter pink
Seed head colours: Burnt umber
Shadows overlapping flowers
Stem and leaf:
Permanent sap green and cadmium red
Stem: Sap green and transparent yellow
Main flower: Opera rose and French ultramarine
Sepals
Stigma
Underside of leaves: Permanent sap green, manganese blue, touch of titanium white
Final wash over all leaves
Transparent yellow

Painting the *Digitalis*

With your sketch to hand and your colours ready, transfer the drawing to hot-pressed watercolour paper.

First wash

1 Using a size 3 brush, glaze all of the petals with clear water and leave them to dry. Then, using a dilute wash of opera rose and French ultramarine; and starting from the shadow areas, grade the wash, leaving the highlights and the spotted areas white.

2 Glaze the stem and leaves with clean water and leave them to dry. Grade a wash of sap green and transparent yellow from the right-hand side (the darkest area) to the centre of the stem (the lightest highlight). Next, grade the paint from the left-hand side back to the centre highlight to give the stem a three-dimensional round look.

3 Give the leaf and leaf stems a wash of permanent sap green with a little cadmium red grading from dark to light to create form.

4 Apply a graded wash of permanent sap green and cadmium red to the small flower buds.

5 Give the undersides of the leaves a wash of permanent sap green, manganese blue, cadmium red and a little titanium white. Leave everything to dry fully.

6 Apply a dilute mix of burnt umber to the seed heads.

Tonal washes

1 Use the same colours and brush sizes with slightly stronger mixes of the same colours to replicate what you have done, making sure to leave the highlights unpainted but grading into them. This produces a three-dimensional image.

Crossovers

1 Add a little neutral tint to the flower mix and paint into the throats of the flowers to give more depth, using a size 1 brush. Make sure you do not paint over the white spots. Repeat this on all of the flowerheads until the required depth has been achieved.

2 Apply shadows where the flowers overlap, then shadow the left-hand side behind the main flowers and stem.

3 Add shadows to the seed head using a brown mix with neutral tint added.

Harmonisation

1 Using a size 3 brush and a dilute wash of the leaf colour, wash the flowers directly in front of the leaf. Use a dilute wash of the original flower mix to wash a small area of the leaf, grading it out with water until no lines are left.

Details

1 With a size 1 brush, add dark circles around the white spots on the flower mouths using neutral tint.

2 Paint the filament, style and stigma on the two spent flowers at the bottom of the flower stem in the same way as the seed head.

Discretionary washes

I used a size 5 brush with a dilute mix of transparent yellow to wash over all of the leaves, making sure I kept to the margins, and also used the same mix on the left-hand side of the seed head to harmonise the whole portrait.

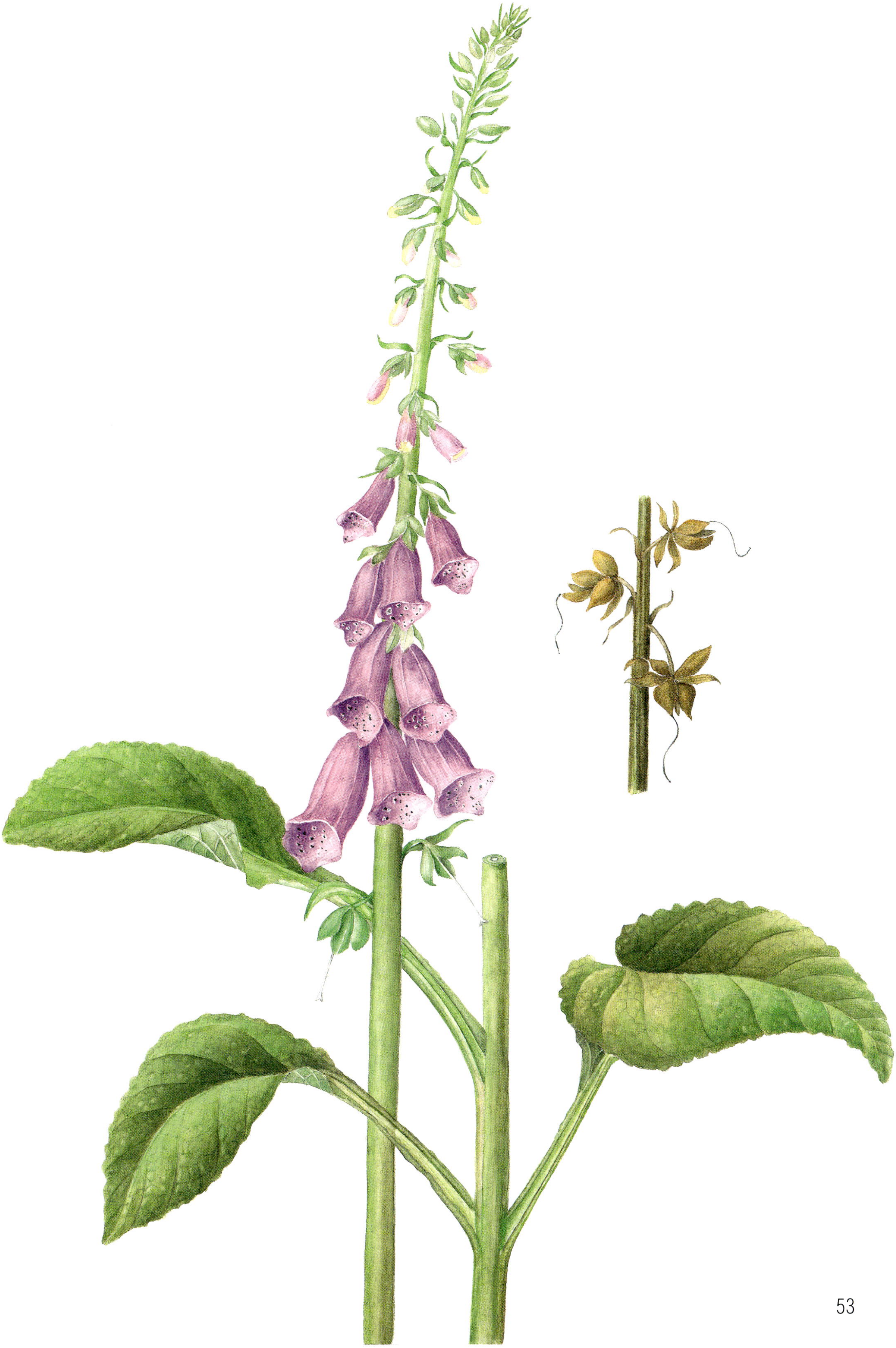

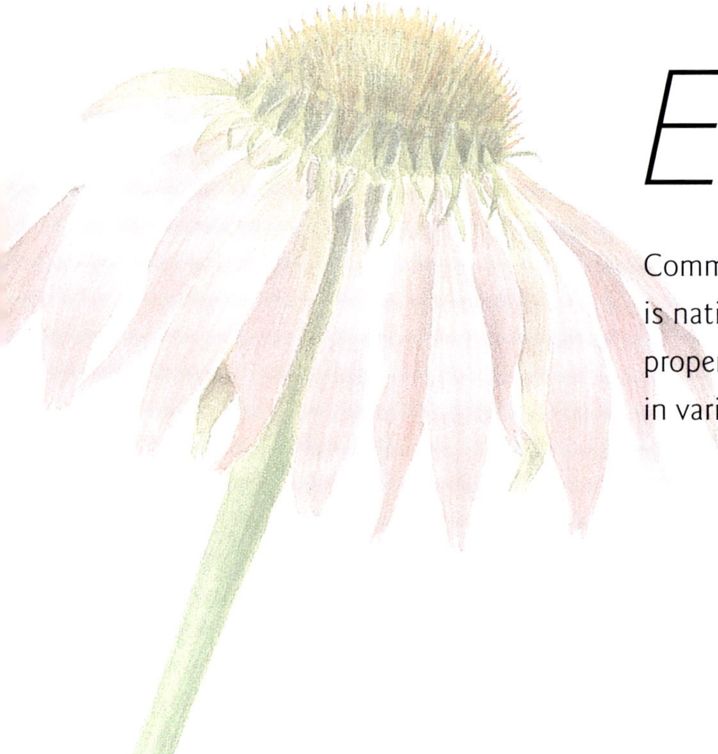

Echinacea

Commonly called the purple coneflower, *Echinacea purpurea* is native to North America and is known for its medicinal properties. It is a much-loved herbaceous plant and is available in various shades.

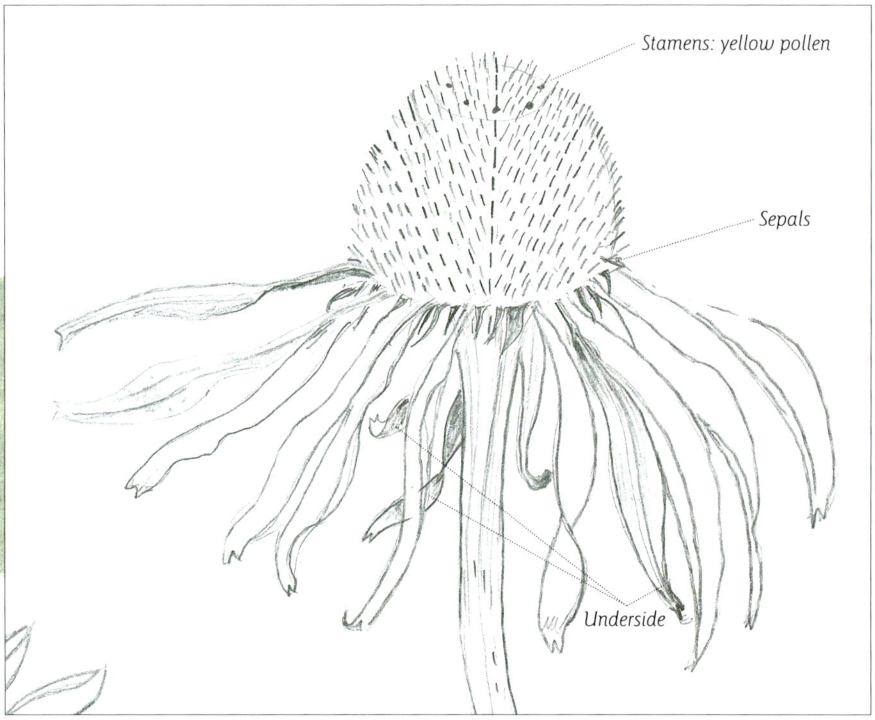

This section of the main flower shows the annotated undersides of the petals. Including these notes will help to avoid confusion when painting them.

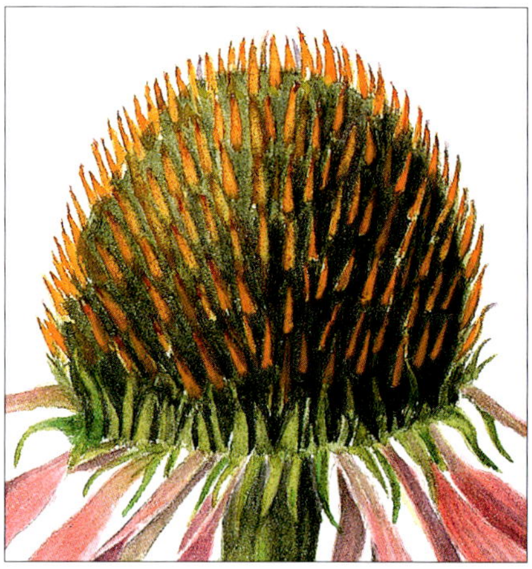

The small sepals were painted first as these were much lighter in colour, and the darker tones of the seed head were then painted behind them. Note the angles of the bracts on the seed head.

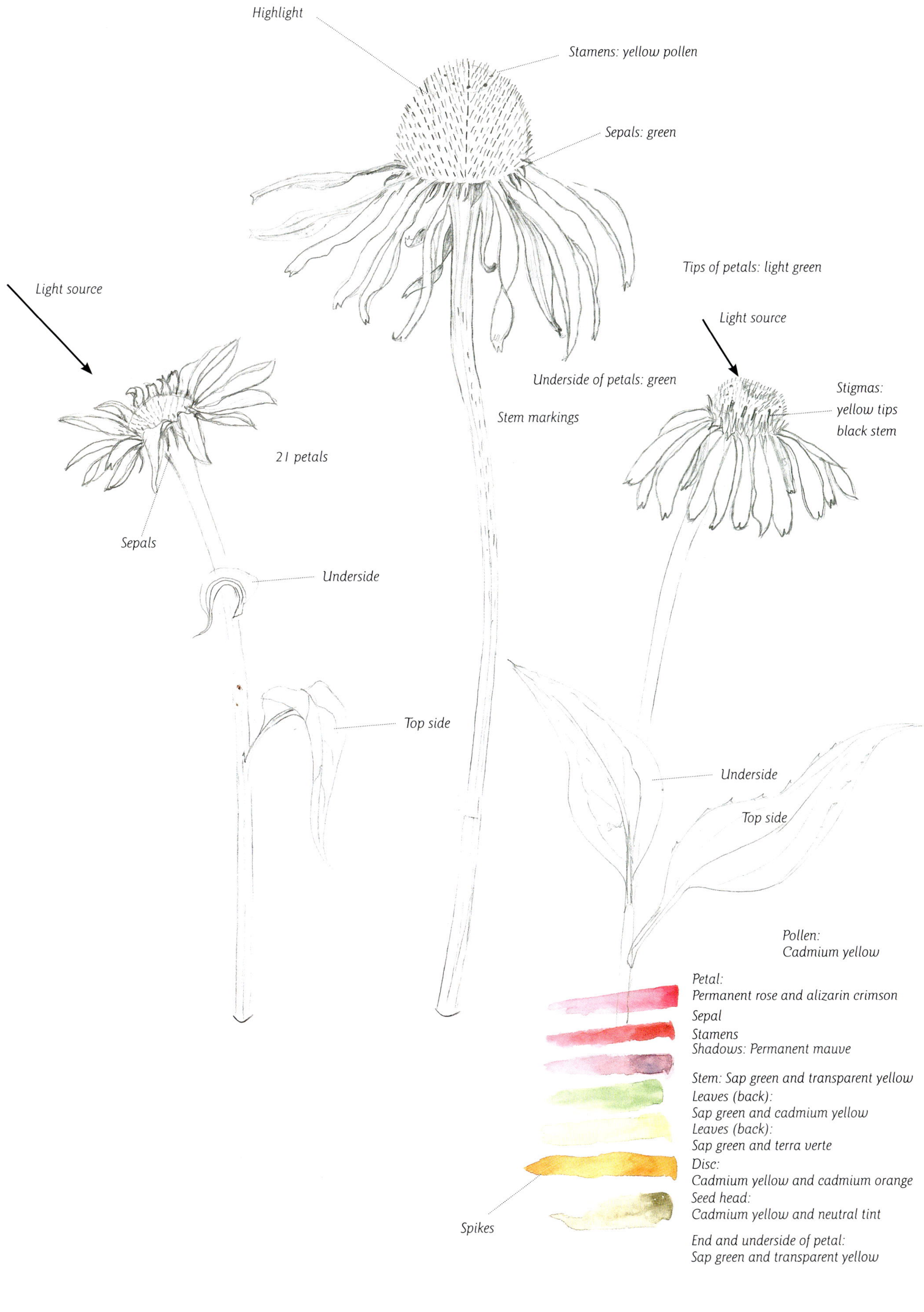
Highlight
Stamens: yellow pollen
Sepals: green
Tips of petals: light green
Light source
Light source
Underside of petals: green
Stigmas:
yellow tips
black stem
Stem markings
21 petals
Sepals
Underside
Top side
Underside
Top side
Pollen:
Cadmium yellow
Petal:
Permanent rose and alizarin crimson
Sepal
Stamens
Shadows: Permanent mauve
Stem: Sap green and transparent yellow
Leaves (back):
Sap green and cadmium yellow
Leaves (back):
Sap green and terra verte
Disc:
Cadmium yellow and cadmium orange
Seed head:
Cadmium yellow and neutral tint
End and underside of petal:
Sap green and transparent yellow
Spikes

Painting the *Echinacea*

Transfer the drawing to hot-pressed watercolour paper once you have your sketch and paints ready.

First wash

1 Use a size 3 brush to glaze all of the petals, seed head and stems with clean water and allow them to dry. Use a dilute mix of alizarin crimson and permanent rose to wash the top side of the petals, grading into the highlights and keeping the left-hand side of the flower petals a lighter tone. Repeat this on all of the flowerheads and leave them to dry.

2 Still using the size 3 brush, use a dilute mix of raw umber with a little neutral tint to paint in the seed heads, leaving a highlight on the top left of each.

3 Switch to a size 2 brush and a dilute mix of sap green and transparent yellow. Paint the underside of the petals and the small sepals, then swap to a size 3 to paint the stems with the same mix, grading from right to left.

4 Glaze the leaves with clean water and leave them to dry. Using a dilute mix of sap green and terra verte, paint in the tops of the leaves, grading into the highlights.

5 Use a dilute mix of sap green and cadmium yellow to wash the underside of the leaves, leaving the midribs free of paint.

6 With a size 1 brush and a dilute mix of cadmium yellow and cadmium orange, paint the centres of the two younger flowers (those to the left and right).

Tonal washes

1 Using the same size brushes and stronger mixes of the respective colours, repeat the above process on the different areas, grading the washes to achieve the necessary tone and build up the form. You will have to apply a number of washes in order to build up the required depth of colour.

2 Wash over the midrib with the leaf colour.

Crossovers

1 Use a size 1 brush and a dilute mix of alizarin crimson and permanent mauve to paint in the small areas where the petals overlap each other, in order to put the petals in their correct position.

2 Use the same size brush and a mix of neutral tint to paint in the small areas where the leaves overlapped the stems, grading the paint into the green of the stems.

Harmonisation

With a size 2 brush and a dilute mix of sap green and transparent yellow, apply a small wash to the lower parts of the petals. Paint a small wash of a dilute mix of permanent rose and alizarin crimson over the upper parts of the flower's leaves.

Details

1 Use a stronger mix of cadmium orange with a size 1 brush to paint the bracts on the cone of the central (oldest) flower, starting from the centre and working from left to right. Repeat this until the correct tone has been achieved, then add a little neutral tint to the mix for the bracts in the shadow area. Repeat the process on the other flowerheads.

2 Use a stronger mix of neutral tint and a size 0 brush to paint in the stamens and stigmas, then add the pollen using cadmium yellow. Still using the size 0 brush, use a dilute mix of neutral tint and raw umber to paint the speckled markings on the flower stems.

3 With a size 1 brush and sap green, paint in the tips of the petals, grading the colour into the pink of the petals. Use a 2mm (⅛in) flat brush to gently lift out the veins on the leaves.

Discretionary washes

I used a size 3 brush with a dilute mix of transparent yellow and sap green to wash over the top side of the leaves and the flower stems.

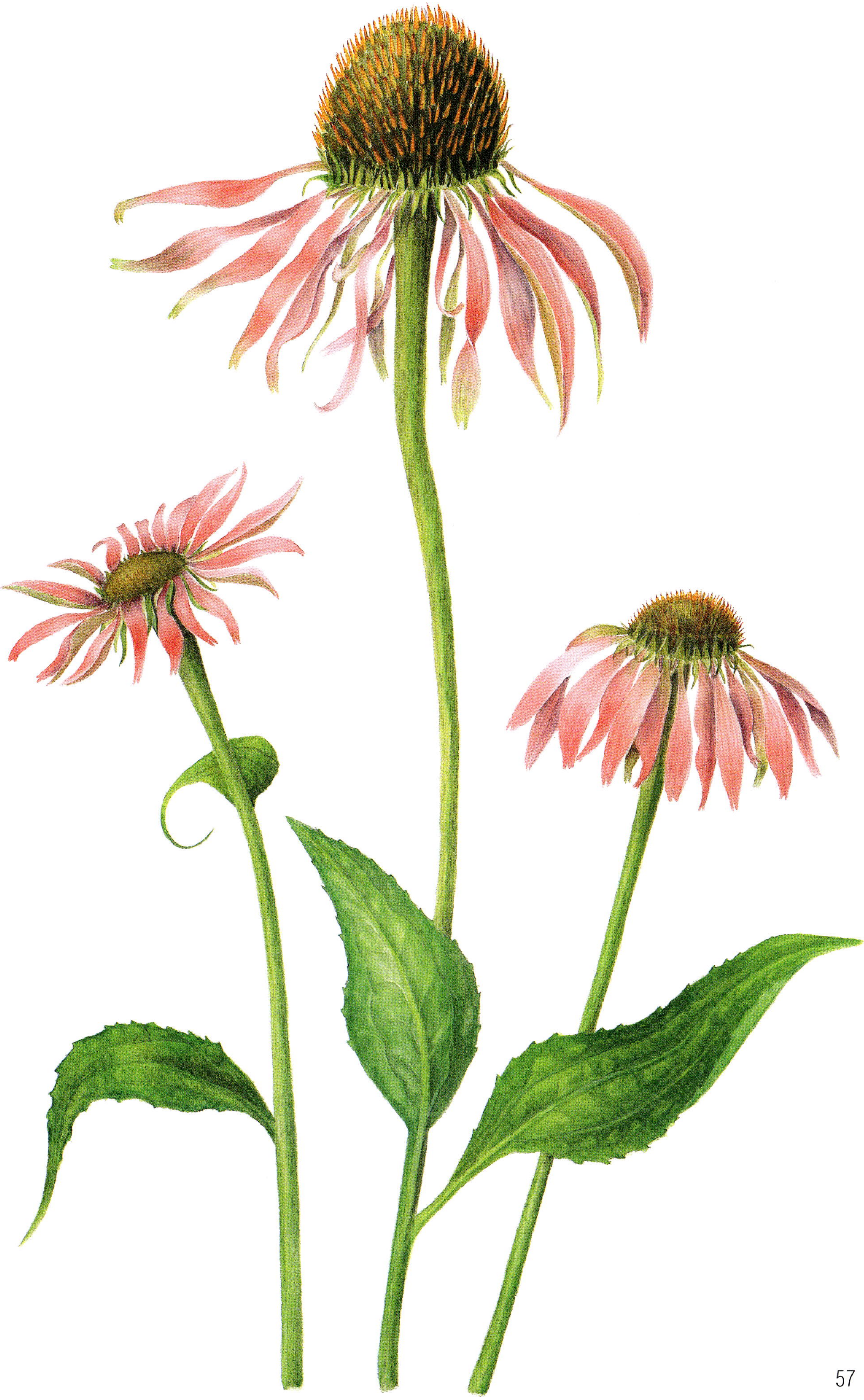

Fuchsia

Originally from Mexico, this flower was introduced to the gardens of England by Lee and Kennedy of Hammersmith in the 1780s. It is a delight to paint, as there are hundreds of colours. This variety is called 'Blacky', for obvious reasons.

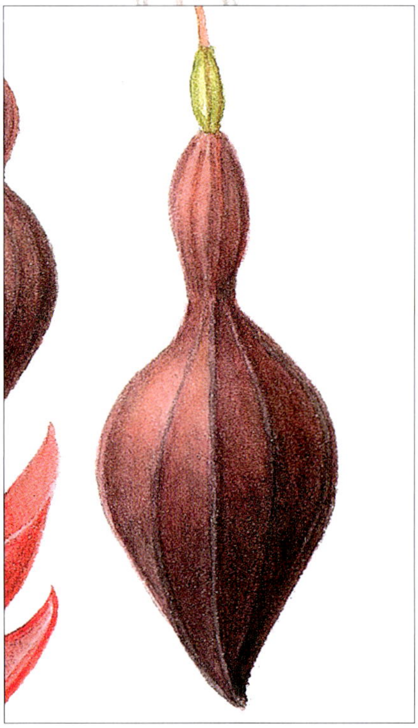

The bud was given several washes of the alizarin crimson and opera rose mix and allowed to dry. The raised sepal edges were then shadowed on the right-hand side to make them raised using the flower colour mix.

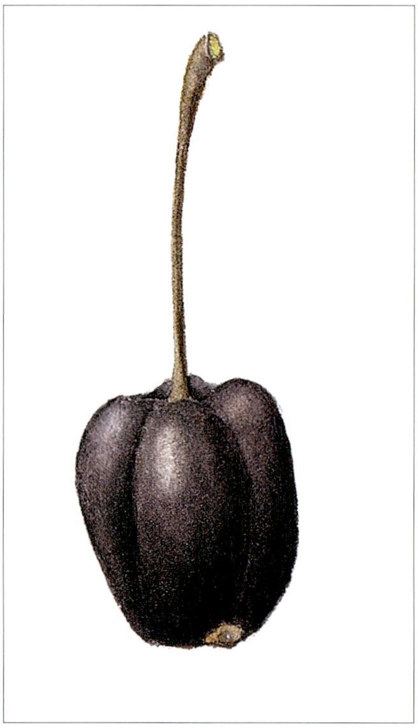

Shadowing was added in the ridges to create form and shape. Note the highlight on the top left – ensure that the light is falling from only one light source to avoid a confusing image.

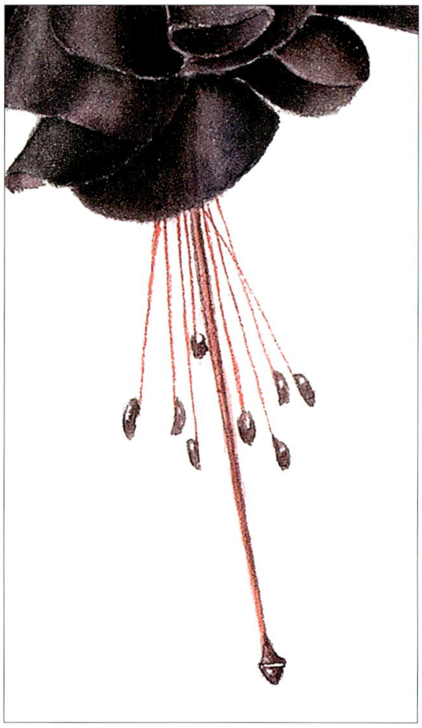

When painting in the stigmas and stamens, make sure that you leave a highlight. Although very small, they still have a shape.

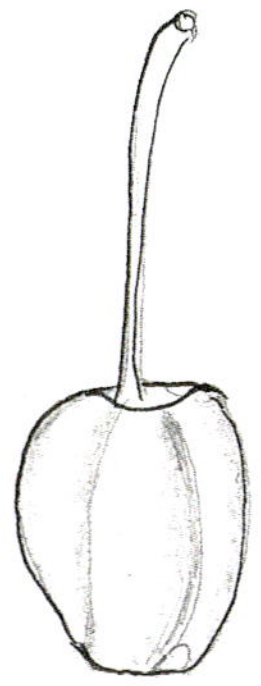

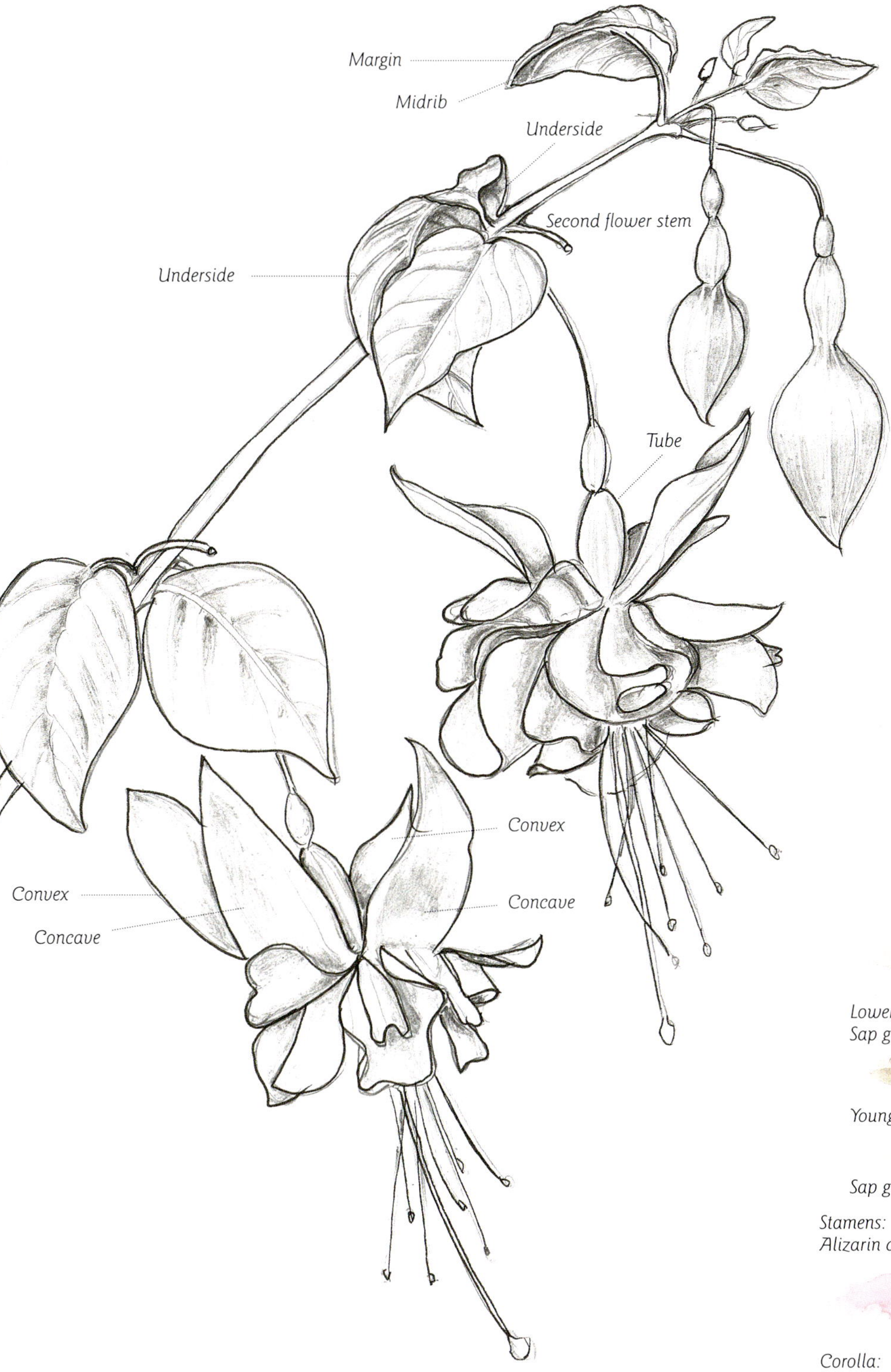

Fruit colour/seed pod:
Same as corolla plus
neutral tint

Buds:
Alizarin crimson
and opera rose

Fruit

Lower stem:
Raw umber and alizarin
crimson, same as stamens

Young stem upper

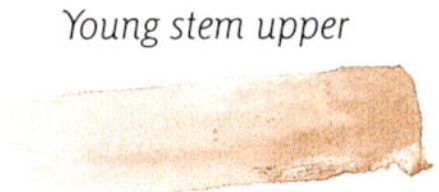

Lower, older leaves:
Sap green and alizarin crimson

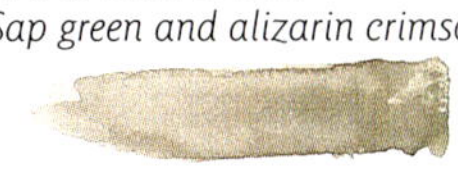

Young leaves:

Sap green and transparent yellow

Stamens:
Alizarin crimson and French ultramarine

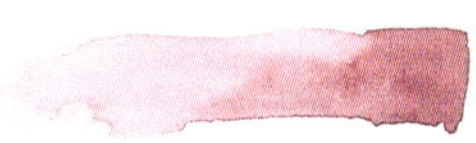

Corolla:
French ultramarine, alizarin crimson
Permanent magenta and cadmium yellow

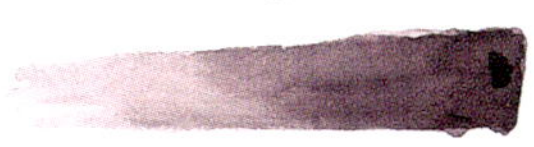

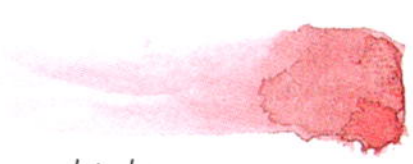

Petals and tube:
Alizarin crimson and opera rose

Ovaries:
Sap green and transparent yellow

Painting the *Fuchsia*

With your sketch to hand and your colours prepared, transfer the drawing to hot-pressed watercolour paper.

First wash

1 Use a size 2 brush to glaze all of the petals and sepals with clear water and leave them to dry.

2 Use the same brush to apply the first dilute wash of French ultramarine, alizarin crimson and permanent magenta with a touch of cadmium yellow to the corolla, leaving the highlight unpainted but grading into it. Allow to dry.

3 Paint the sepals and tube with a dilute mix of alizarin crimson and opera rose, again leaving the highlights unpainted but grading into them.

4 Glaze all of the leaves with clean water and a size 3 brush, then leave them to dry.

5 Using a dilute mix of sap green and alizarin crimson, paint in the first wash on the four larger leaves, working from the midrib to the left, leaving the highlights; then grade the paint to the right-hand side of the leaf.

6 With a size 2 brush and a dilute mix of sap green and transparent yellow, paint the two young leaves, leaving the midrib unpainted. Using the same brush and the same mix, paint the green stalks grading from right to left, then glaze the stem with clean water and leave to dry.

7 Still using the size 2 brush, use a dilute mix of raw umber and alizarin crimson paint the stem, grading it from right to left and add more alizarin crimson towards the upper part of the stem. Use the same mix of paint on the thin flower stems and the four flower buds, again grading into the highlights.

8 With the same mix as for the corolla, apply the first wash to the seed pod, grading each segment from right to left and leaving the highlights unpainted. Leave to dry.

Tonal washes

1 Using the size 2 round brush, start to build up the depth of colour on the corolla using a slightly stronger version of the same mix as before.

2 Carefully grade each petal to create form and tone, then use a slightly stronger sepal mix to paint the centres. When graded out to the lighter areas, this gives a concave look.

3 Paint the vertical lines on the tubes and the flower buds, then build up the depth of colour on the leaves, grading from each vein to create surface modelling.

4 Darken the stem to the required tone and build up the form on the seed pod to create a three-dimensional look.

Crossovers

1 Using a size 2 brush and a mix of alizarin crimson and neutral tint, paint in the small areas where the tubes overlap the sepals and where the sepals overlap the tubes to create the impression of distance.

2 Shade where the leaves overlap the stems.

Harmonisation

1 Using a size 2 brush, paint a dilute wash of alizarin crimson on the lower part of the two lower leaves.

2 Next apply a small wash, of a dilute mix of transparent yellow and sap green, to the upper petals of the flower sepals and to the flower and bud stalks.

Details

1 Use a slightly stronger mix of alizarin crimson and a size 1 brush to paint in the leaf veins and the small serrations on the leaves.

2 Use the same mix to paint in the styles and stigmas, then add more neutral tint to the mix to darken the stigma and stamens.

3 With a size 1 brush and a mix of raw umber and alizarin crimson, paint in the stem on the seed pod and the small circle at the top of the fitment.

Discretionary washes

Using a size 3 brush and a dilute mix of transparent yellow and sap green, I washed over all of the leaves keeping accurately to the edges, then left the portrait to dry.

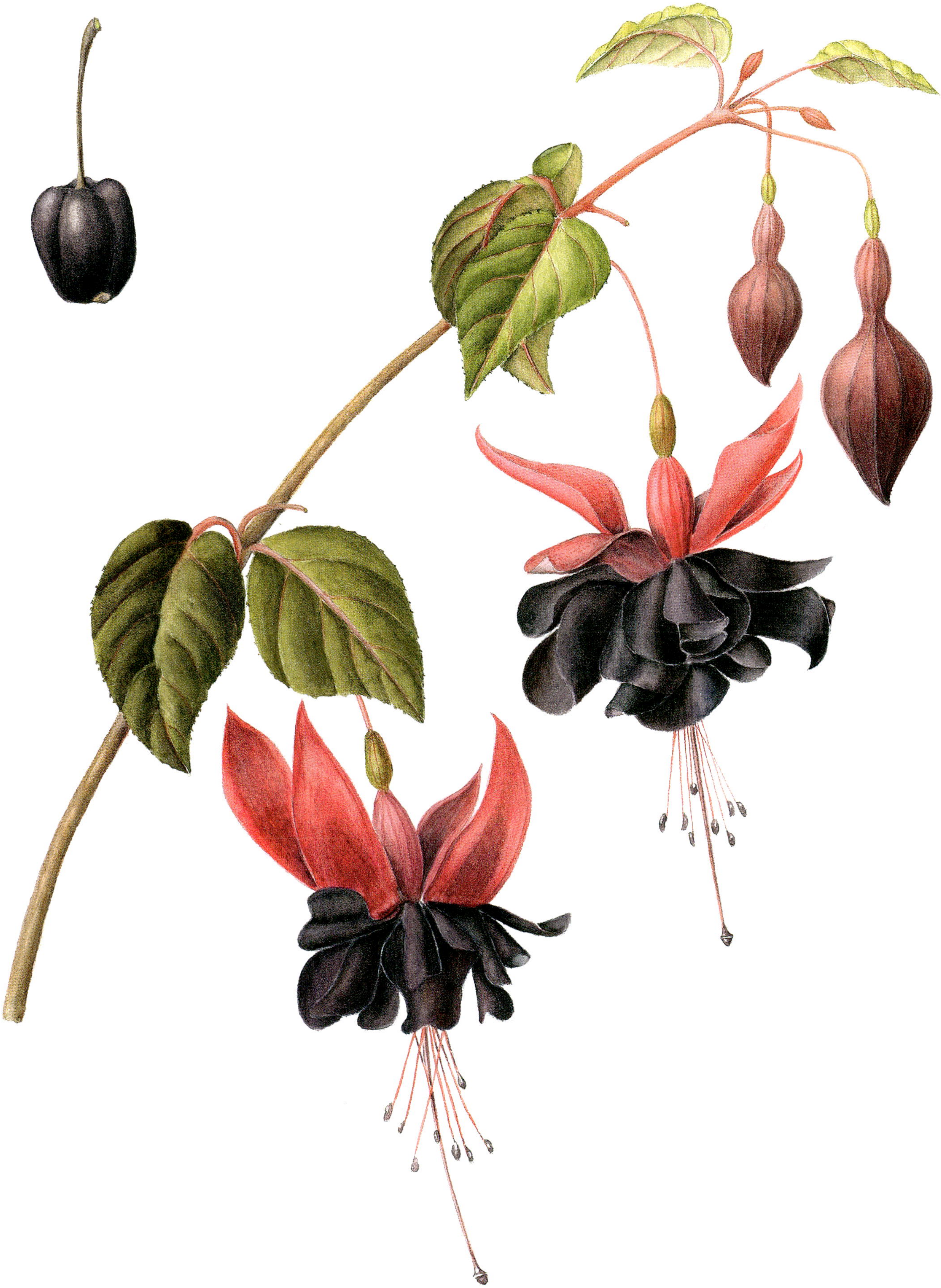

Galanthus

There are three main genera of snowdrops: the Turkish *elwesii*, the Russian *plicatus* and the *nivalis*, which is the most widespread and best known. The main difference between the three is the shape of the leaves, and the variety can be identified from the different markings on the inner petals.

This finished painting contains the three main genera. From left to right, they are *plicatus*, *nivalis* and *elwesii*.

Composition

Basic sketches were made of each of the varieties, and these were then rearranged for a more pleasing final composition.

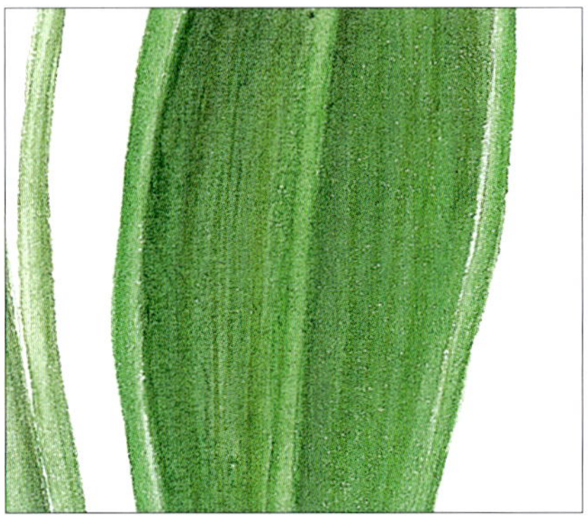

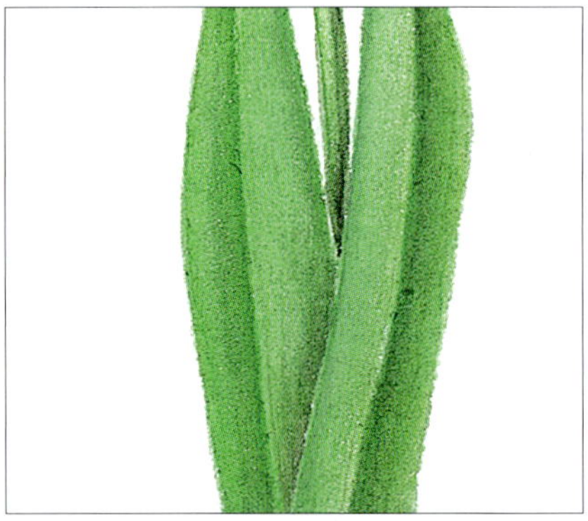

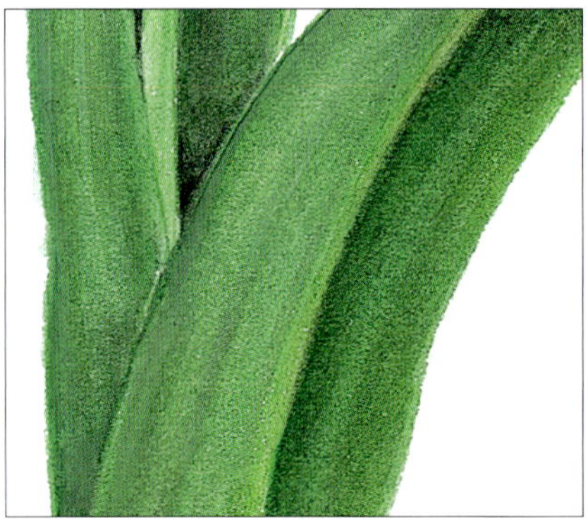

Snowdrop leaves on an individual plant do not vary much in hue, but different varieties have different hues. The plicatus *leaves (top) have more yellow in the mix than the other two, while the* elwesii *leaves (bottom) are much darker than the others and have comparatively more blue in the mix. Good observation is required to note the difference.*

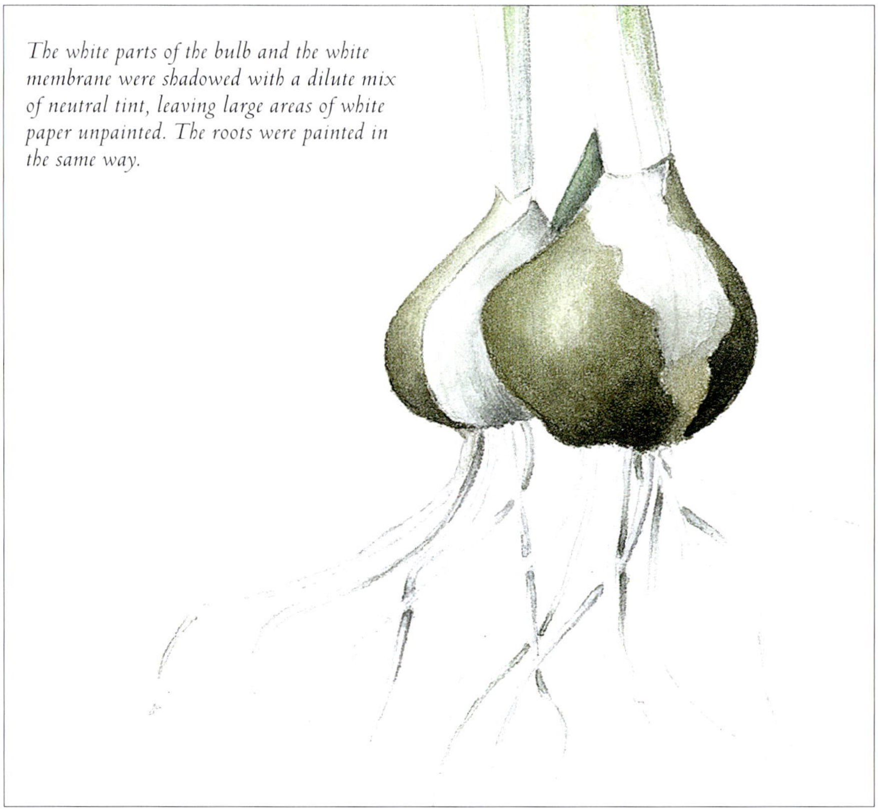

The white parts of the bulb and the white membrane were shadowed with a dilute mix of neutral tint, leaving large areas of white paper unpainted. The roots were painted in the same way.

Nivalis *(1) Centre*
Elwesii *(2) Right (on painting)*
Plicatus *(3) Left*

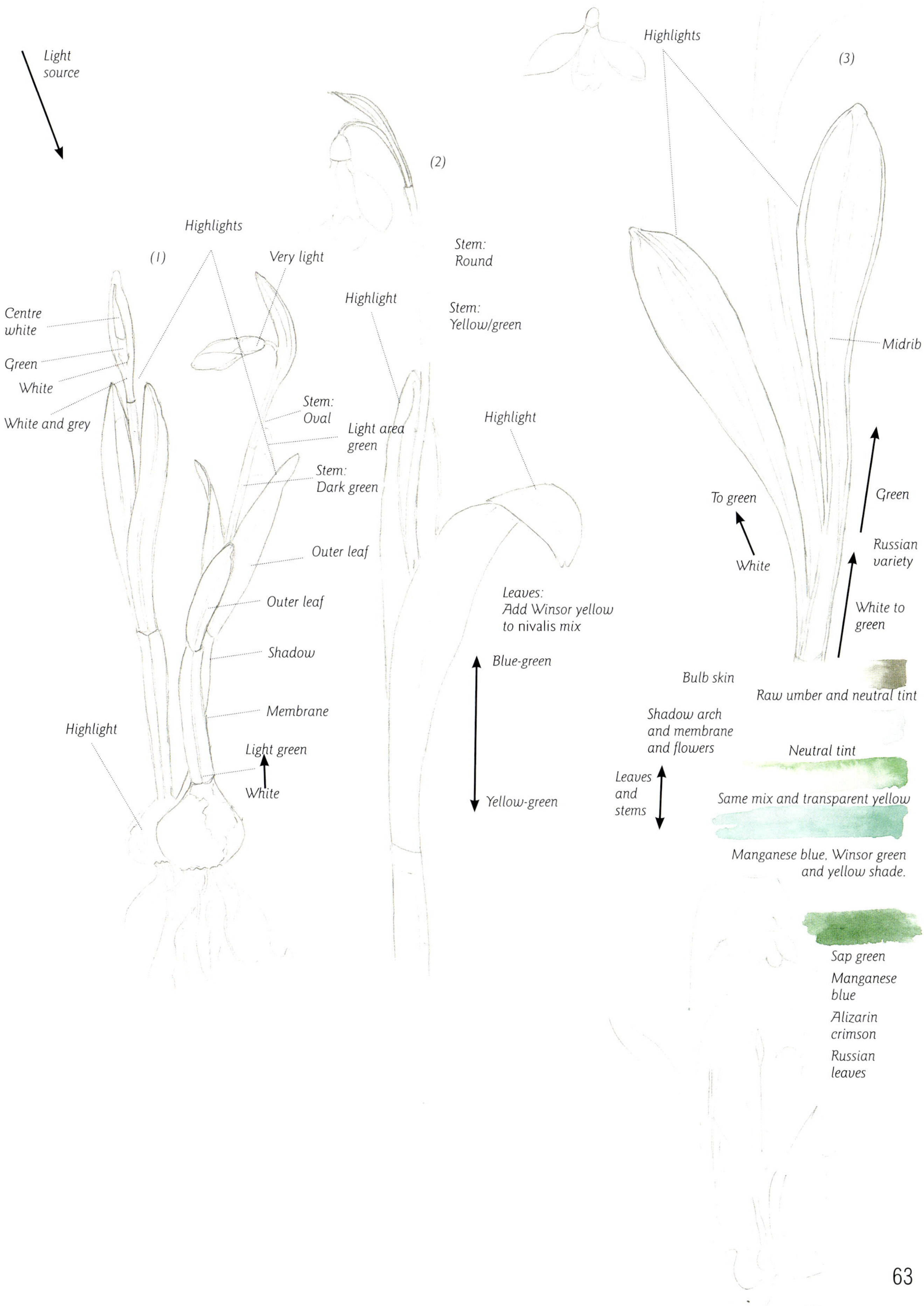

Painting the *Galanthus*

Transfer the drawing to your hot-pressed watercolour paper, prepare your wells of colour and place your sketch nearby for reference.

First wash

1 Glaze all of the leaves using a size 2 brush and clean water, then leave them to dry. Use a dilute mix of manganese blue and Winsor green (yellow shade) to paint the first wash on to the leaves of the *nivalis* and *elwesii*, grading into the highlights and leaving the lower membrane and midrib unpainted.

2 Use the same size brush with a mix of sap green, manganese blue and a little alizarin crimson to paint the leaves on the *plicatus* variety, leaving the lower membrane unpainted. Glaze the stems and flowerheads with clean water and leave them to dry.

3 Using a mix of manganese blue, Winsor green (yellow shade) and transparent yellow, paint the stems, leaving the highlights clean.

4 With a size 2 brush and a dilute mix of raw umber and neutral tint, apply a wash to the outer skin of the bulb, grading into the highlights.

5 Use a dilute mix of neutral tint and vertical strokes of the brush to paint the lower membranes on all of the three lower leaves, leaving the highlights unpainted. Using a size 1 brush and a dilute mix of neutral tint, paint in the shadows on the flower petals, grading from dark to the white areas.

Tonal washes

1 Develop the *nivalis* leaves with the stronger manganese blue and Winsor green (yellow shade) wells. Leave the midribs unpainted.

2 Again leaving the midribs unpainted, add Winsor yellow to the mix to paint the *elwesii* and *plicatus* leaves.

3 Replicate the previous steps, using the stronger wells to deepen the tone but ensure that you leave the highlights. Repeat until you achieve the correct tone.

Crossovers

1 Using a size 1 brush and neutral tint, shadow the areas where the leaves cross to separate and distance them from each other.

2 Use the same colour to add shadows to the roots where the roots cross, being careful to grade it into the white highlight areas.

3 Add shadows to the flower petals in the same way but be careful not to over-shadow them: you do not want grey flowers.

4 Repeat the crossover steps until you achieve the correct depth of tone.

Harmonisation

There is no harmonisation needed on this illustration.

Details

1 Use a size 0 brush with a mix of sap green and transparent yellow to paint in the green area of the bud on the *nivalis* and also the ovary on all of the flowers, leaving a highlight on each one.

2 With the same mix and brush, paint in the patterning on the inner petals. Next, use a dilute mix of neutral tint to paint the vertical lines on the membrane of the lower leaves and the curved lines on the bulbs.

3 Add further detail to the roots and the lines on the petals with the same mix.

Discretionary washes

I used a size 3 brush and a dilute mix of transparent yellow to apply a wash to the leaves on the *elwesii* and *plicatus* and a dilute mix of manganese blue to wash over the petals on the *nivalis*.

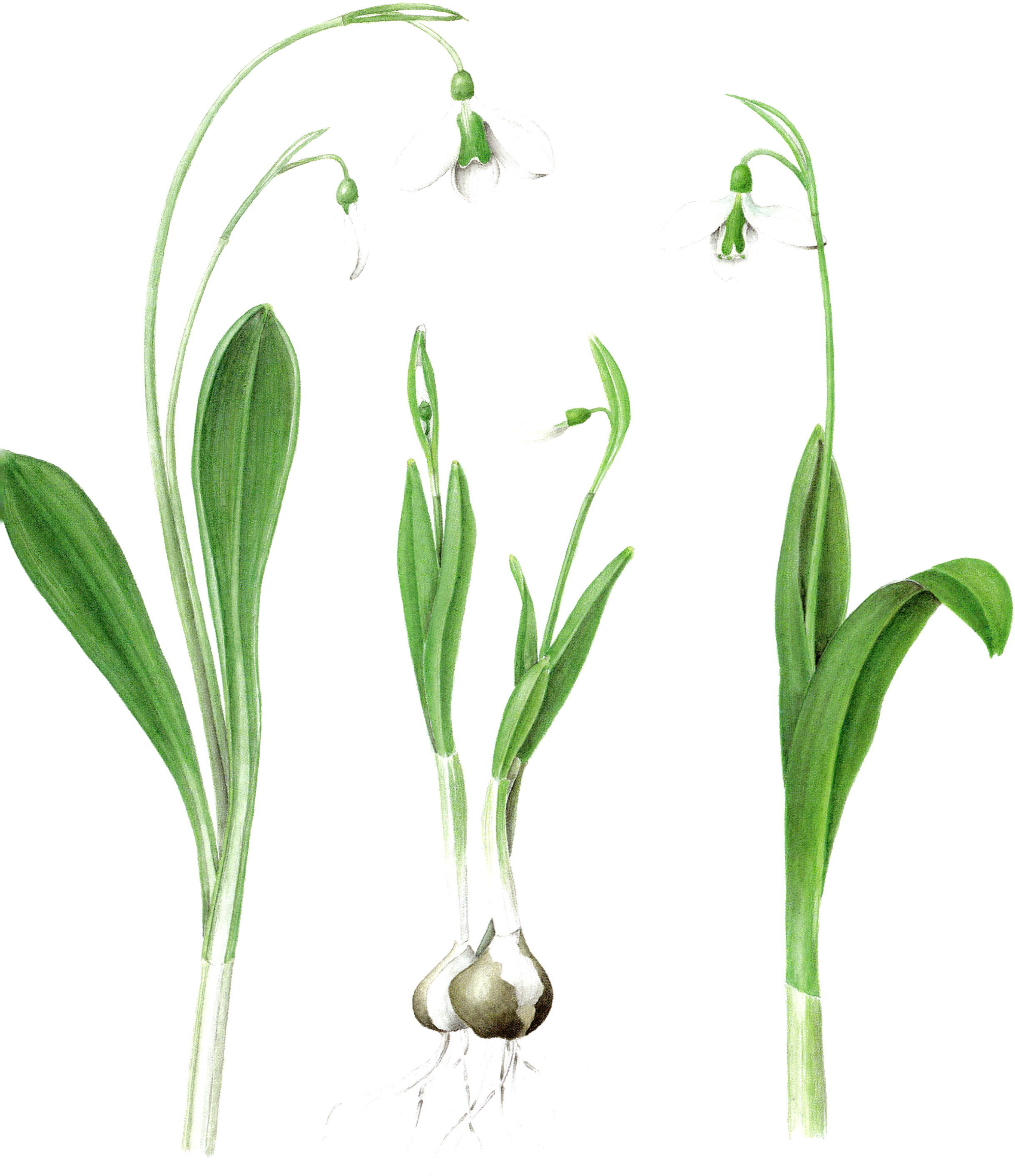

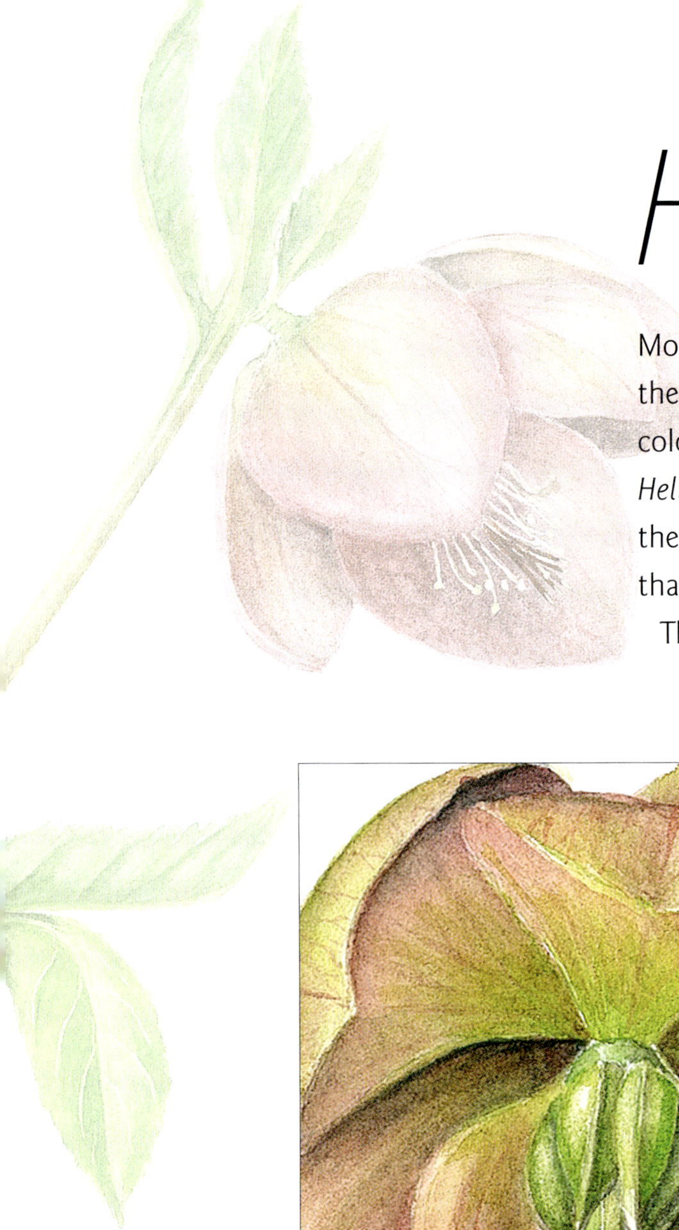

Helleborus

Modern varieties of hellebores are commonly hybridised, and their petals range from almost black to light pink, with various coloured speckles on their petals. Traditional hellebores, like the *Helleborus orientalis* shown here, and *Helleborus niger*, from which these modern hybrids derive, more commonly have white petals that fade to pink.

They are prized by gardeners because they flower in winter.

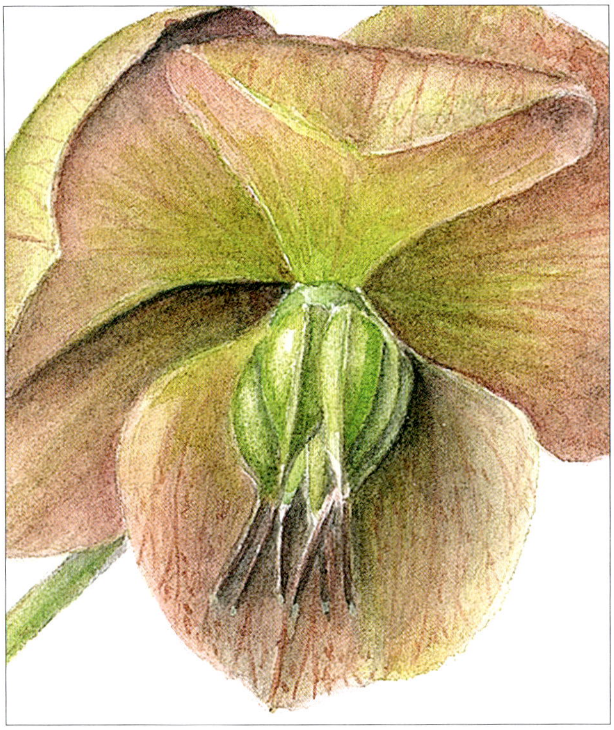

This older flower has started to turn to seed. This detail shows the early green seed pods, which later turn dark brown before releasing their seeds.

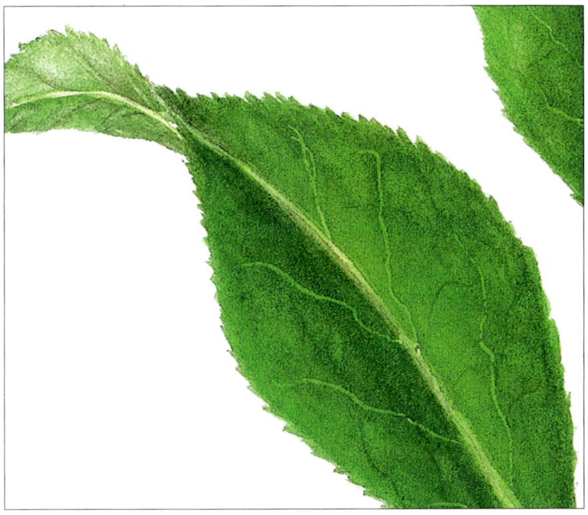

This detail shows both the top and underside of the leaf. Note the curved, serrated shape plus the difference in colour and the angles of the serrations as the leaf curls. Note also that the midrib does not continue from the top of the leaf to the underside. A gap is left to allow for the twist.

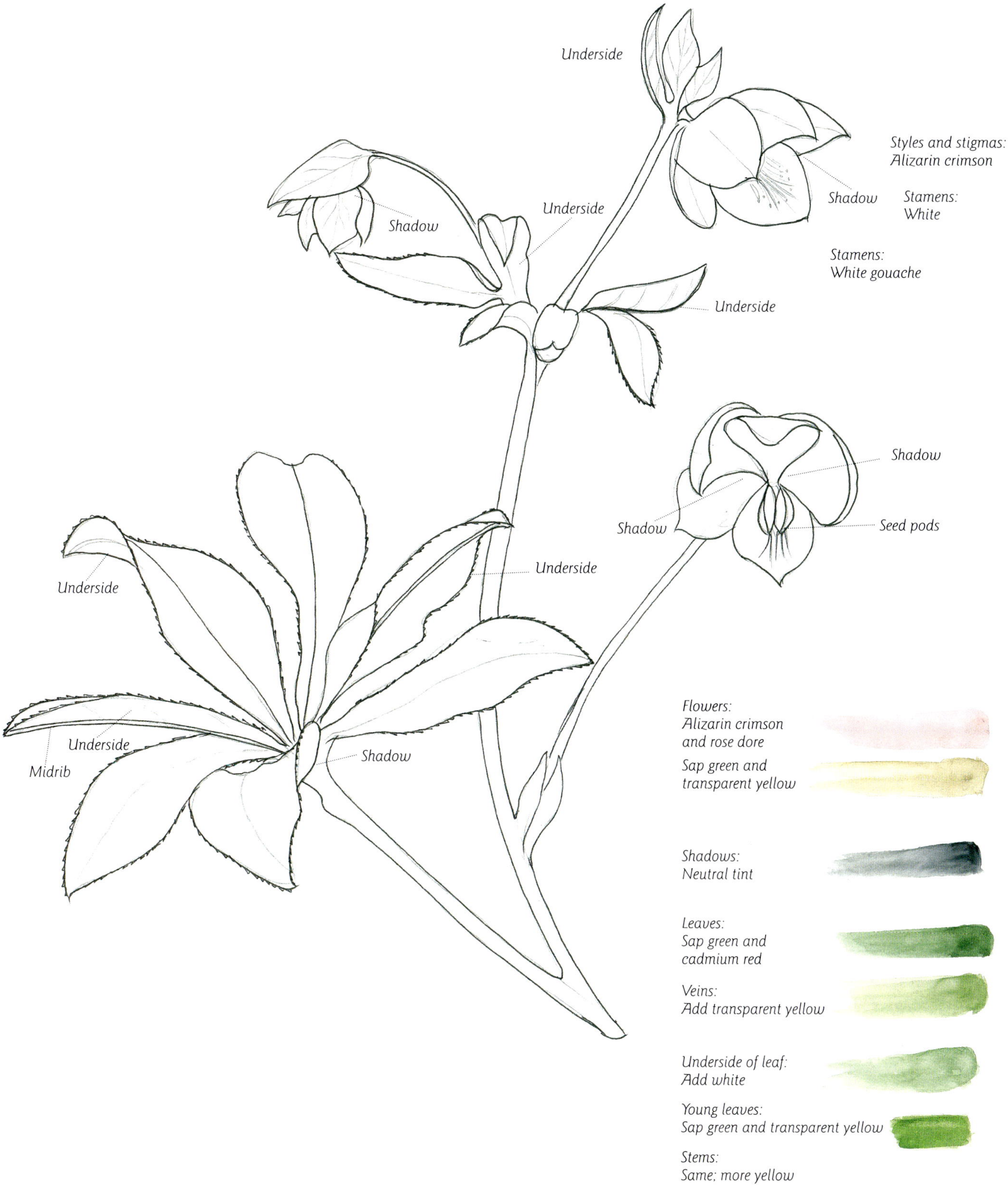
Underside
Styles and stigmas:
Alizarin crimson
Shadow
Underside
Shadow
Stamens:
White
Stamens:
White gouache
Underside
Shadow
Shadow
Seed pods
Underside
Underside
Underside
Midrib
Shadow
Flowers:
Alizarin crimson
and rose dore
Sap green and
transparent yellow
Shadows:
Neutral tint
Leaves:
Sap green and
cadmium red
Veins:
Add transparent yellow
Underside of leaf:
Add white
Young leaves:
Sap green and transparent yellow
Stems:
Same; more yellow

Painting the *Helleborus*

With your sketch to hand and your colours prepared, transfer the drawing to hot-pressed watercolour paper.

First wash

1 Use a size 3 brush to glaze all of the flower components and leave them to dry. With a dilute mix of sap green and transparent yellow, apply the first wash to the petals, seed pods and bud, grading the paint into the highlights.

2 Once dry, use the same size brush with a dilute mix of alizarin crimson and rose dore to paint the shadow areas, grading into the highlights and blending the paint with the previous layer.

3 Glaze all of the leaves and stems with clean water and allow them to dry. Use a size 5 brush with a dilute mix of sap green and cadmium red to apply the first wash to the main older leaf, leaving the midrib unpainted and grading outwards from the midrib to suggest form on the leaves.

4 Swap to the size 2 brush and use a dilute mix of sap green and transparent yellow to apply the first wash to the top side of the young leaves. Add more transparent yellow to the mix and paint the first wash to all of the stems, grading from the right to left, leaving the centres of the stems much lighter to give a three-dimensional look.

5 Still using the size 2 brush, use a dilute mix of sap green and cadmium red, with a little titanium white added, to paint the undersides of all of the leaves, leaving the midribs unpainted.

Tonal washes

1 Using the same size brushes as for the first wash, build up the form, keeping the shadow areas darker and keeping the highlights a lighter tone. Refer to the first wash instructions for the correct colours for each section, but use the stronger wells.

2 Paint the midribs on the leaves with a dilute mix of sap green and transparent yellow. Allow to dry, then repeat the washes until the tones are correct.

3 Use a 2mm (⅛in) flat brush and a little water to lift out the small subsidiary veins on the leaves.

Crossovers

1 With a size 2 brush and a dilute mix of neutral tint, paint in the small areas where the leaves overlap each over, where the leaves overlap the stems, and where the petals overlap each other. This creates distance between them and places them in the correct position.

2 Repeat the small washes until the tones are correct.

Harmonisation

1 Using a size 2 brush and a dilute mix of sap green and transparent yellow, apply a small wash to the tops of the flower petals under the leaves.

2 Use the same brush with a mix of alizarin crimson and rose dore to paint a small wash to the upper parts of the stems and on the tips of the right-hand side of both the old and new leaves.

Details

1 Use a size 0000 brush and a little white gouache to paint in the stamens on the top open flower.

2 Still using the same brush, paint in the stigmas on the flowers with a mix of alizarin crimson and a little neutral tint.

3 With the same mix, add small shadows on the right-hand sides of the veins on the underside of the leaves (to make them look convex) and on the flower petals' veins.

4 Repeat until the tones are correct.

Discretionary washes

Using a size 5 brush and a dilute mix of transparent yellow, I washed over all of the leaves and stems and allowed them to dry. I used the same mix to wash the tops of the petals and seed pods.

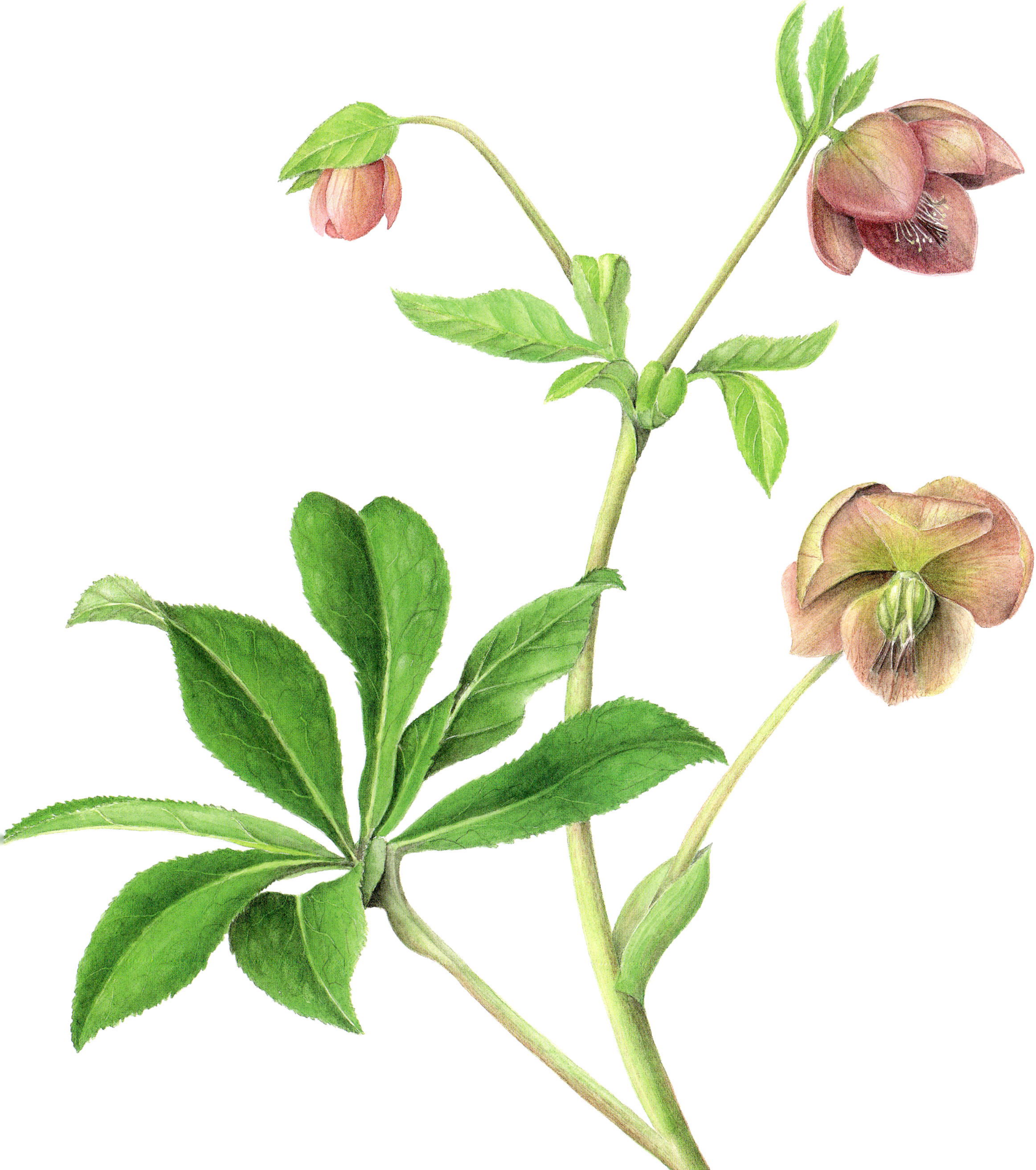

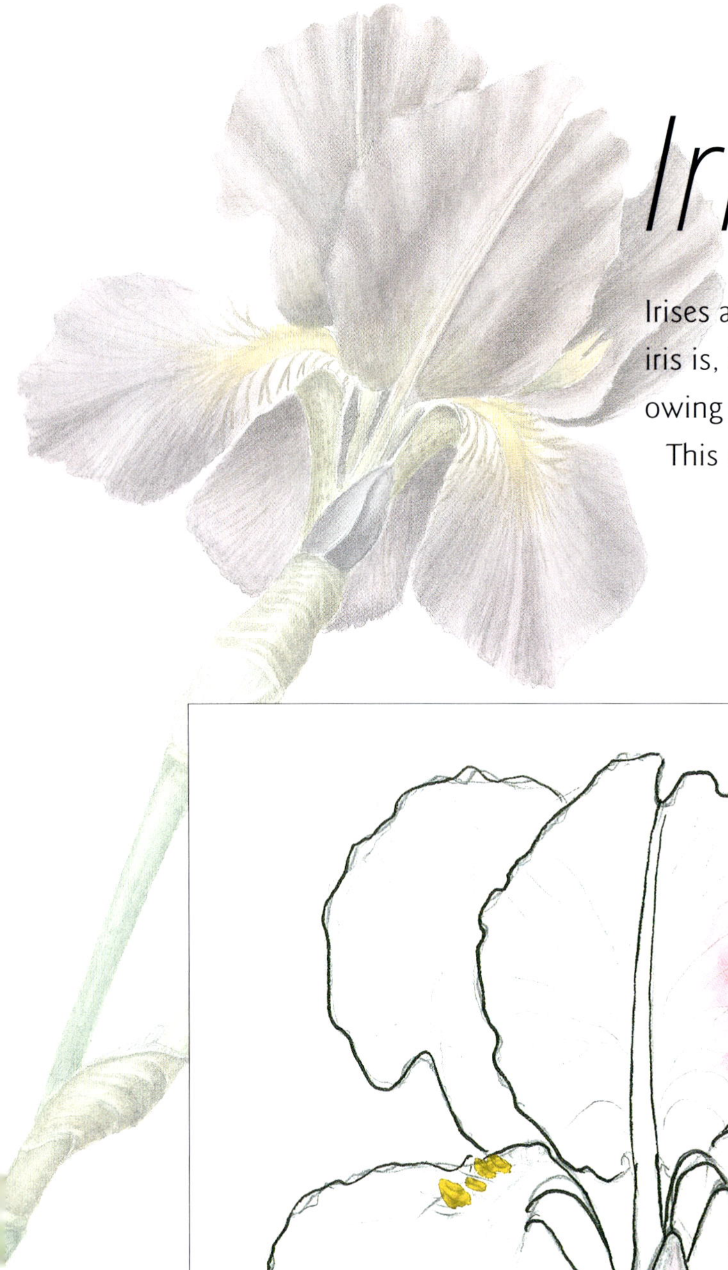

Iris

Irises are rhizomatous plants and originate from Turkey. The bearded iris is, to me, a very exotic flower and it is an excellent one to paint owing to the large variety of colours in which it appears.

This particular cultivar is *Iris germanica* 'Caliente'.

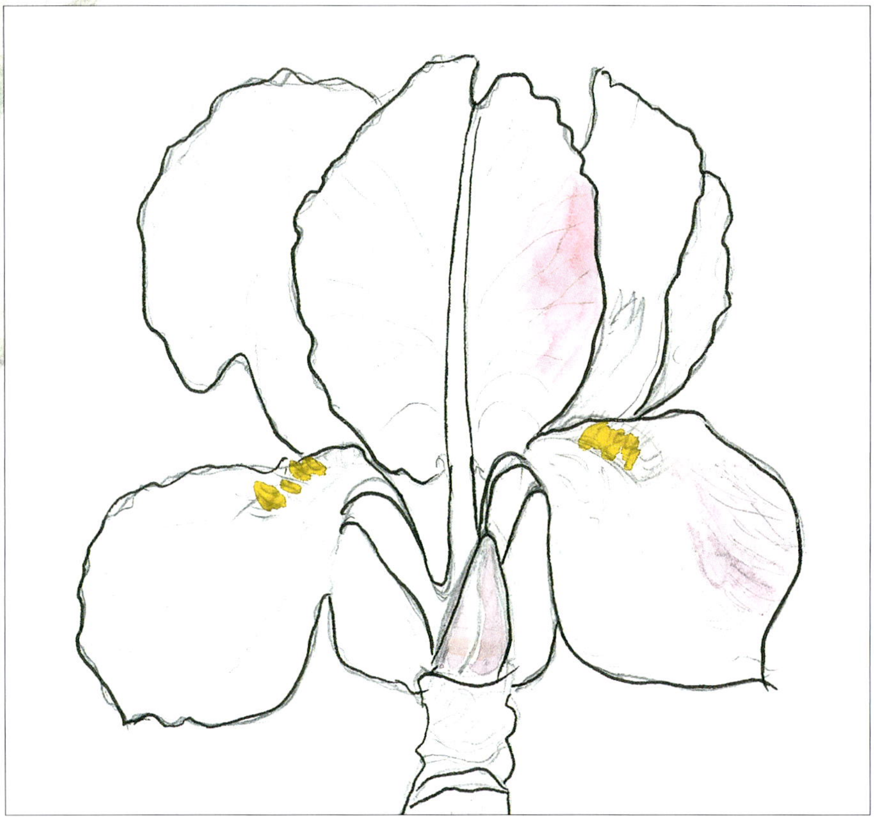

All irises have three standards (the upper, vertical petals) and three falls (the lower petals). The two types of petal are different in shape and colour. The falls of Iris germanica *have stigmas and stamens attatched to them and have more venation and texture than the standards.*

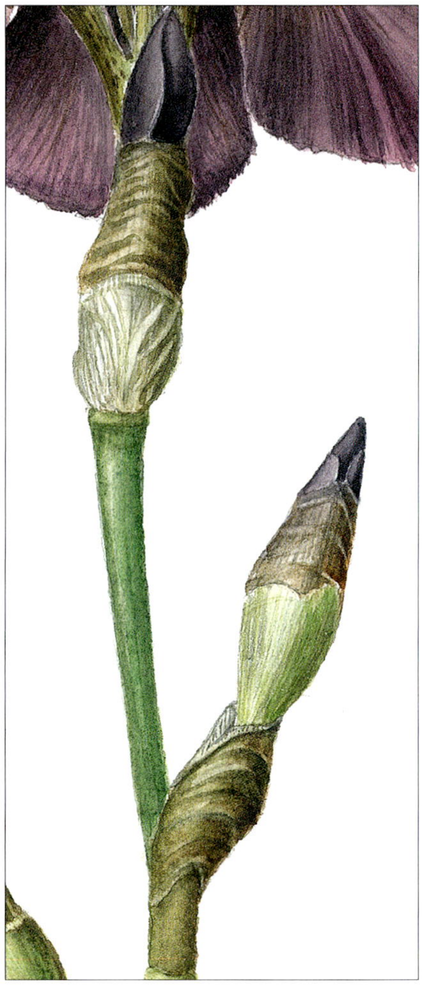

The vertical and horizontal lines of the membrane on the buds must be given subtle highlights to give the crinkled look.

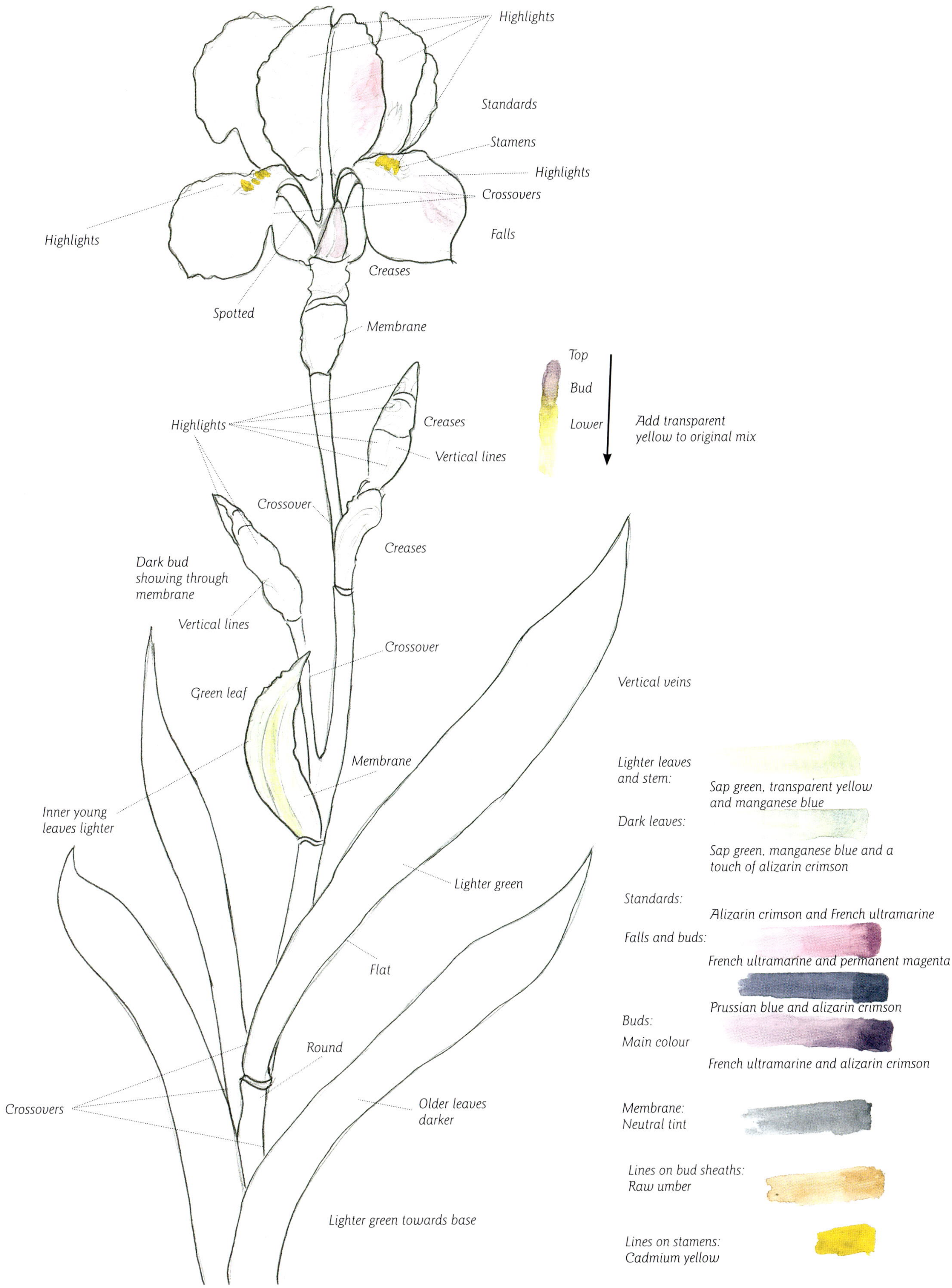
Highlights
Standards
Stamens
Highlights
Crossovers
Falls
Highlights
Creases
Spotted
Membrane
Top
Bud
Lower
Add transparent yellow to original mix
Highlights
Creases
Vertical lines
Crossover
Creases
Dark bud showing through membrane
Vertical lines
Crossover
Green leaf
Vertical veins
Membrane
Inner young leaves lighter
Lighter leaves and stem:
Sap green, transparent yellow and manganese blue
Dark leaves:
Sap green, manganese blue and a touch of alizarin crimson
Lighter green
Standards:
Alizarin crimson and French ultramarine
Falls and buds:
French ultramarine and permanent magenta
Flat
Prussian blue and alizarin crimson
Buds:
Main colour
French ultramarine and alizarin crimson
Round
Crossovers
Older leaves darker
Membrane:
Neutral tint
Lines on bud sheaths:
Raw umber
Lighter green towards base
Lines on stamens:
Cadmium yellow

Painting the *Iris*

With your sketch to hand and your colours prepared, transfer the drawing to hot-pressed watercolour paper.

First wash

1 Using a size 5 brush and clean water, glaze all of the petals, stems and buds and allow them to dry. Then, using a dilute mix of alizarin crimson and French ultramarine, start to paint in the three standards (the upright petals), leaving the midrib of the petals unpainted. Allow these to dry completely.

2 Using the same size brush and a dilute mix of French ultramarine and permanent magenta, apply the first wash to the three falls (the other petals), grading into the highlight areas. Use the same mix to paint the first wash on the three buds, grading into the highlights.

3 With a size 3 brush and a dilute mix of sap green, manganese blue and a little transparent yellow, apply the first wash to all of the stems. Grade the paint from right to left, leaving the centres lighter to suggest the form.

4 Use a size 5 brush to glaze all of the leaves with clean water and allow them to dry. Using the same brush and the same green mix, apply the first wash to the upper two leaves (these are the younger leaves), working in long vertical strokes to create the veins in the leaves.

5 Using the same brush, and a dilute mix of sap green, manganese blue and a little alizarin crimson, apply the first wash to the lower two leaves using the same method.

6 With a size 3 brush and a dilute mix of sap green and transparent yellow, paint the centre part of the opening leaf. To the same mix, add a little manganese blue and paint the outer parts of the young leaf.

7 Using a size 2 brush and a dilute mix of sap green and transparent yellow, paint the underside of the two falls, applying the same mix to the midrib on the standards.

Tonal washes

1 Referring to the first wash steps for the brushes and colours to use, but with the slightly stronger wells, replicate the work done above until the correct depth of tone has been achieved, creating form. This can take as many as twelve layers of washes; be sure to let each dry before applying the next.

Crossovers

1 Using a size 2 brush and a dilute mix of neutral tint, apply small washes where the falls and standards overlap, ensuring the effect is darker in the shadow areas.

2 Apply the shadows where the leaves overlap, again using dilute neutral tint. Repeat this process until the correct tone has been achieved to give each component distance and detach them from each other.

Harmonisation

1 With a size 3 brush and a dilute mix of alizarin crimson and French ultramarine, apply a small wash at the tops of the leaves and a little at the top half of the main flower stems. Be careful not to apply too much of the mix as you do not want to change the character of the leaves.

Details

1 Using a size 1 brush and a dilute mix of neutral tint, start to paint the membrane on all of the buds, ensuring that you retain the form of the buds by using fine lines and keeping the right-hand sides darker.

2 Add the creases (folds) just below the main dark buds using French ultramarine and permanent magenta, and adding transparent yellow to the mix for the lower parts of the buds.

3 When dry, use the same brush and a slightly stronger mix of raw umber to paint in more vertical and horizontal lines to the buds; then add more neutral tint to the mix and paint in the spotted areas under the two fans.

4 Use the same mix to paint in the many thin lines on all of the petals. When this has dried, use a size 0 brush and a slightly stronger mix of cadmium yellow to paint in the stamens and stigma.

Discretionary washes

With a size 5 brush and a dilute mix of transparent yellow and manganese blue, I washed over all of the leaves and stems. Using the same size brush with a dilute mix of alizarin crimson and French ultramarine, I washed over all of the standards and falls to harmonise the whole portrait.

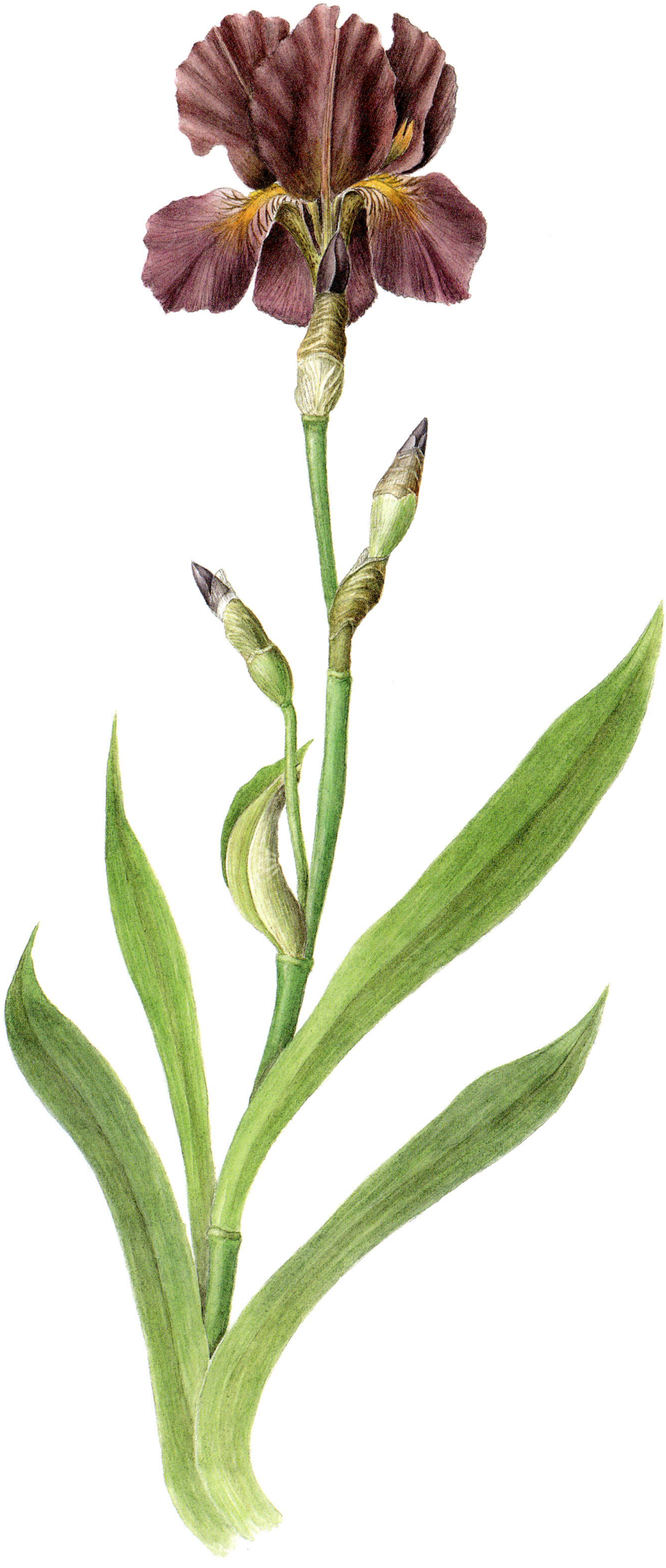

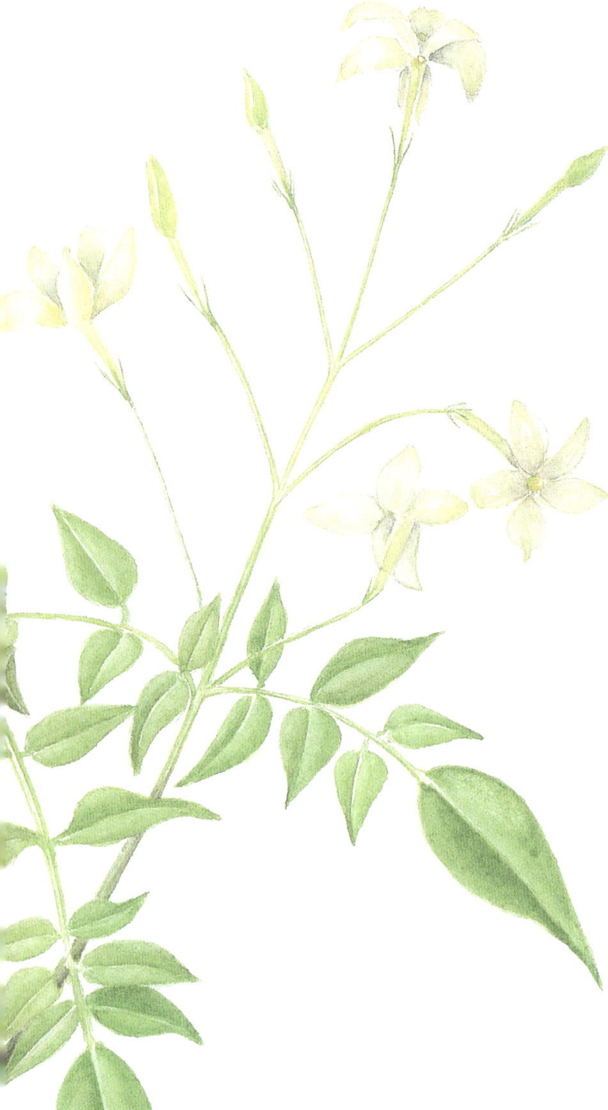

Jasminum

This variety of jasmine flower (*Jasminum officinale*) rejoices in the name 'Clotted Cream', and is extremely fragrant. It is a hardy climber, deciduous and evergreen. The flowers are small and prolific.

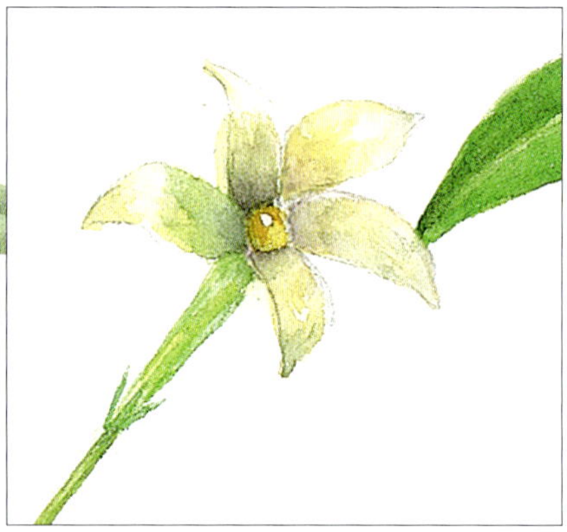

The cream colour of the jasmine flowers has to be shadowed with a little neutral tint to create form and depth.

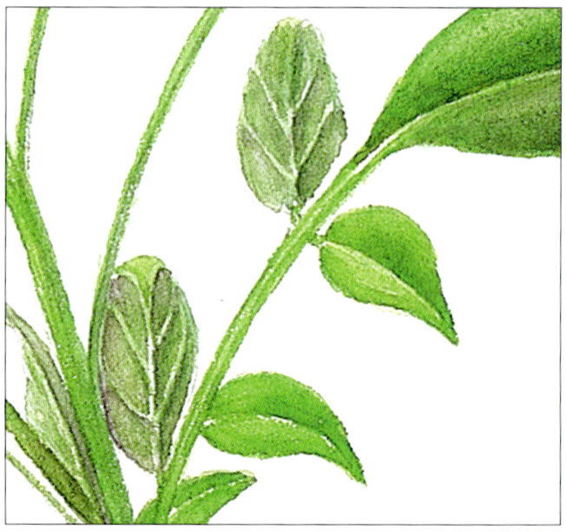

The underside of the small leaves are different shades of green and have raised veins. The illusion of dimensionality is achieved by putting a shadow on the side of the vein further from the light source.

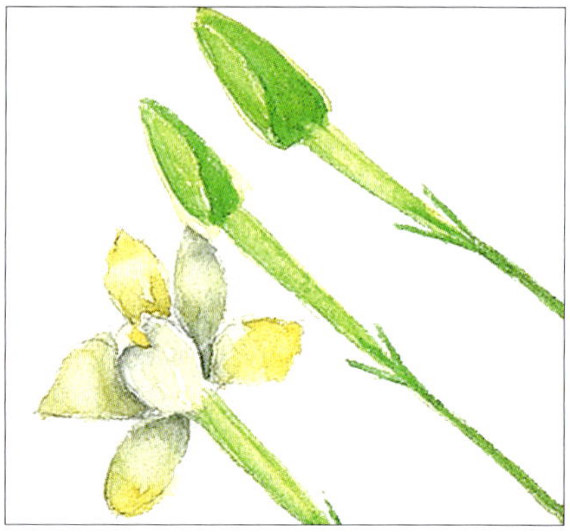

The small buds must be given the same amount of care and accuracy as the larger components.

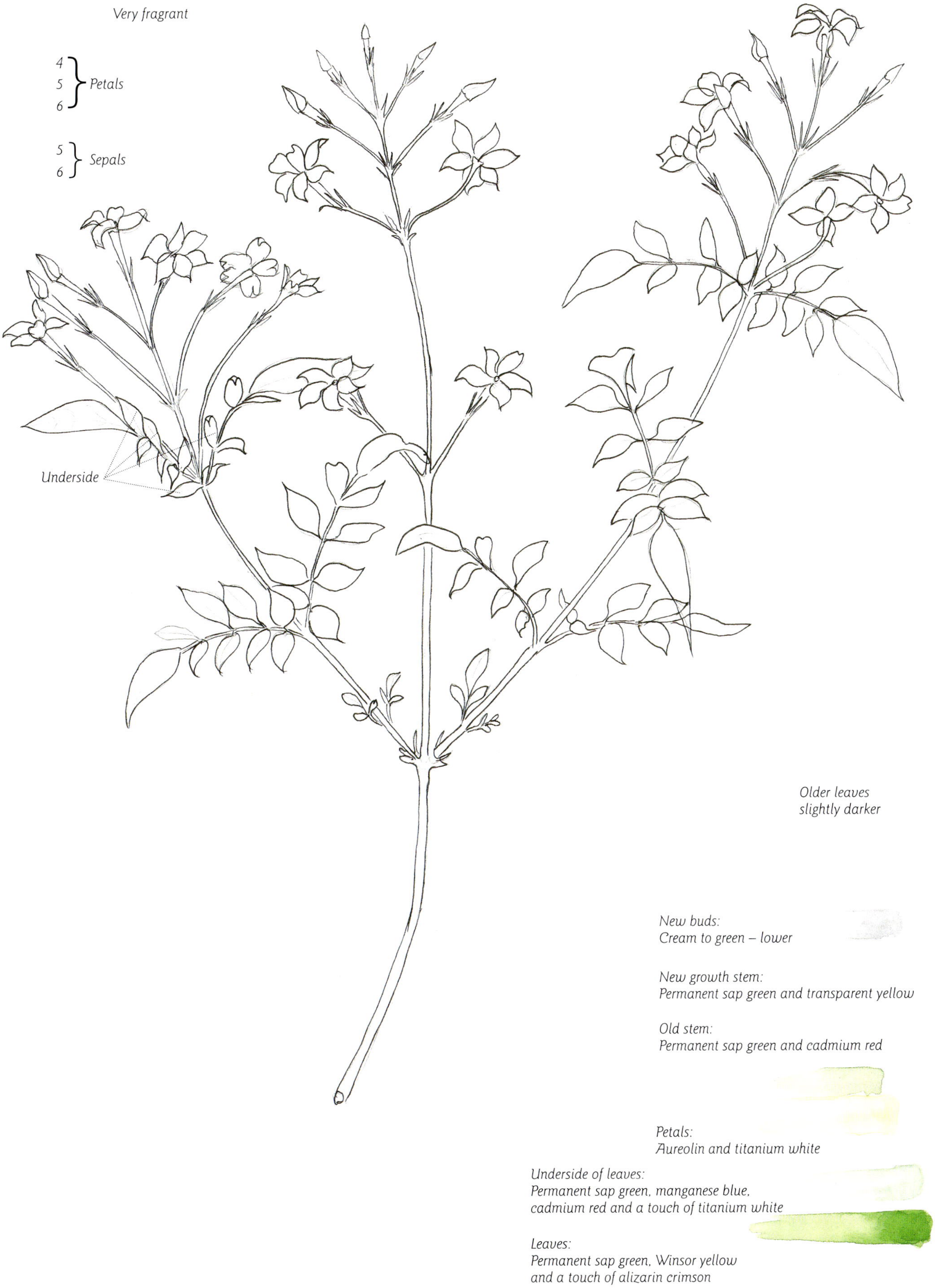
Very fragrant
4
5
6
Petals
5
6
Sepals
Underside
Older leaves slightly darker
New buds:
Cream to green – lower
New growth stem:
Permanent sap green and transparent yellow
Old stem:
Permanent sap green and cadmium red
Petals:
Aureolin and titanium white
Underside of leaves:
Permanent sap green, manganese blue, cadmium red and a touch of titanium white
Leaves:
Permanent sap green, Winsor yellow and a touch of alizarin crimson

Painting the *Jasminum*

Transfer the drawing to hot-pressed watercolour paper, prepare your colours and have your sketch close at hand for easy reference.

First wash

1 Using a size 2 brush, glaze over all of the leaves with clean water and leave them to dry.

2 With the same size brush and a dilute mix of sap green, Winsor yellow and a little alizarin crimson, paint the leaves, accurately grading into the highlights, leaving the midribs unpainted.

3 Once dry, use the same size brush to glaze the stems, flowerheads and buds, then leave them to dry.

4 With a dilute mix of sap green and cadmium red, paint the older main stems; then use a dilute mix of sap green and transparent yellow to paint the new growth of the stems and the fine flower stems, grading the paint into the highlights to create form.

5 Using a size 1 brush and a dilute mix of neutral tint, paint the shadows on each petal, making them darker in the throat of each flower and leaving as much white paper as possible.

6 With a size 1 brush and a mix of sap green, manganese blue, a little cadmium red and a little white gouache, paint the underside of the leaves, leaving the veins unpainted.

Tonal washes

1 Using the same size brushes and a stronger mix of the leaf colour, build up the form of each leaf making the leaves on the right-hand stems darker.

2 Add more Winsor yellow to the mix and build up the leaves on the left-hand side in the same way.

3 Continue to build up the tone of the stems and flowers using a slightly stronger mix of the colours in the first wash instructions (above).

4 When the form of the petals on all the flowerheads has been achieved, use a dilute mix of aureolin and a little white gouache to paint over all the petals and give them a cream look.

5 With a dilute mix of sap green and transparent yellow, paint the buds grading into the highlights, then paint the small tubes under the buds with the cream mix.

Crossovers

1 With a size 2 brush and a dilute mix of neutral tint, paint the small areas at the point where the leaves overlap the stems and the flowerheads overlap the leaves.

2 Do the same where the leaves overlap each other. Sometimes, a stronger mix may be needed to give distance to each component.

Harmonisation

1 Using a size 1 brush and a dilute mix of sap green and transparent yellow, paint a small wash on to the flower petals closest to the leaves or buds.

Details

1 With a size 0 brush and a mix of cadmium yellow, paint in the small stigmas, leaving a small highlight in the centre and repeating until they are the correct dark tone.

2 Using the same size brush and a mix of sap green and transparent yellow, paint in the small sepals at the base of the flower tubes.

Discretionary washes

Using a dilute mix of transparent yellow, I washed over all of the leaves, being careful to keep the edges neat and crisp.

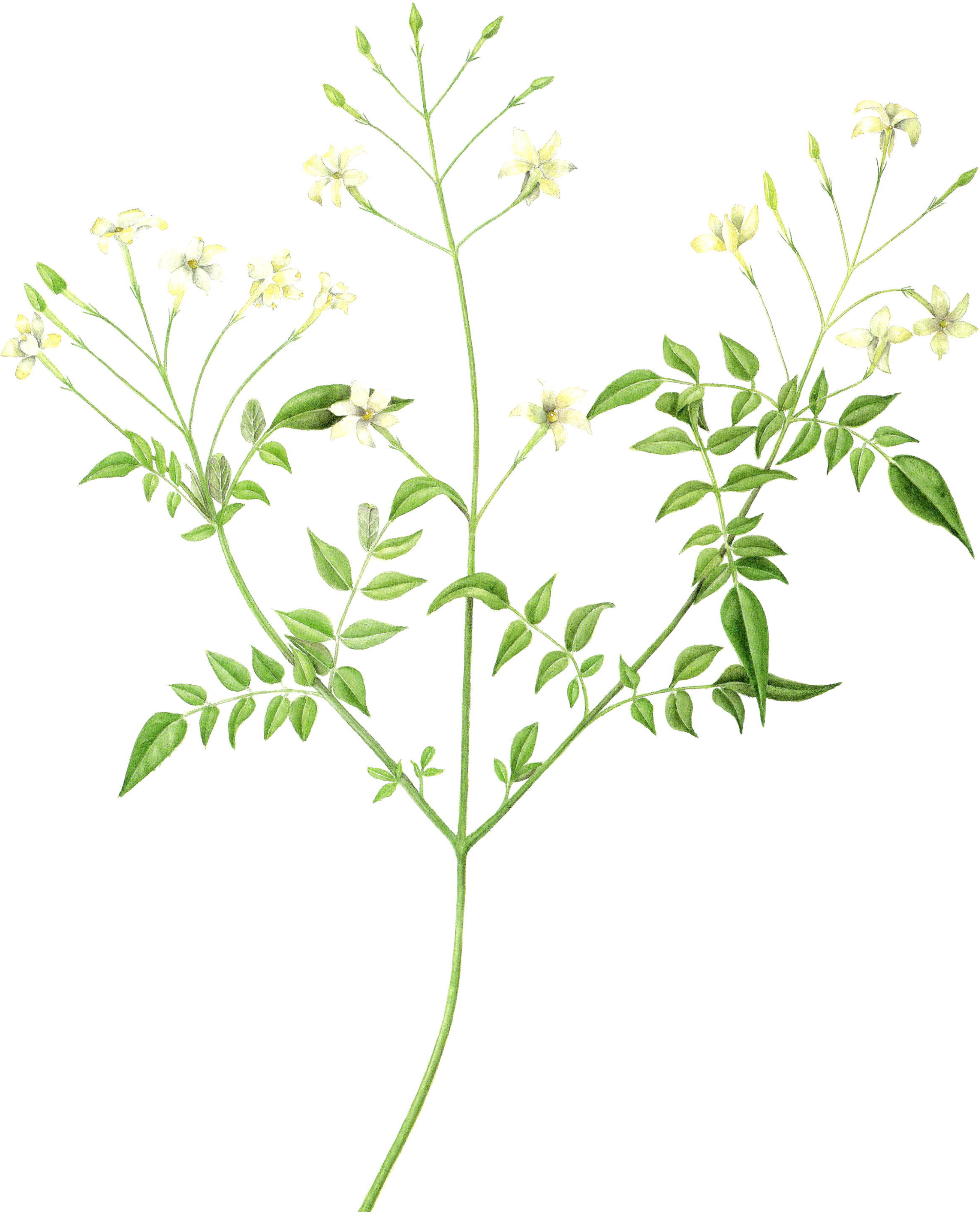

Kniphofia

Commonly called red hot pokers, an alternative name for the striking *Kniphofia uvaria* is 'Torch lily'. They originate from South Africa and first reached Europe in 1707.

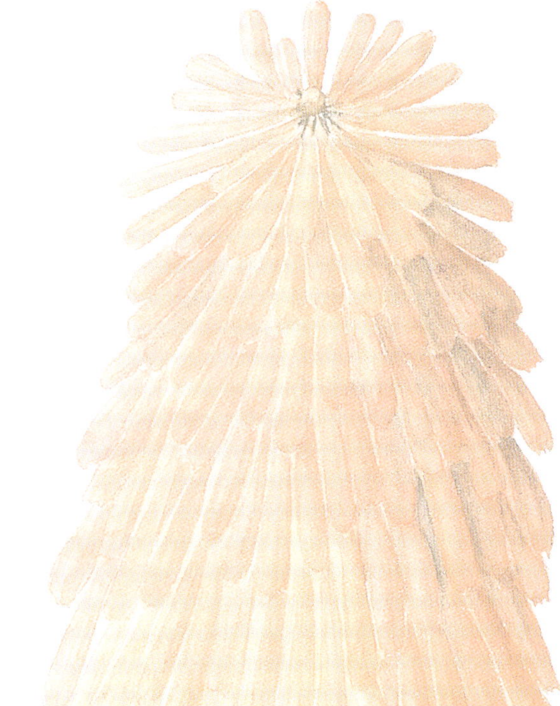

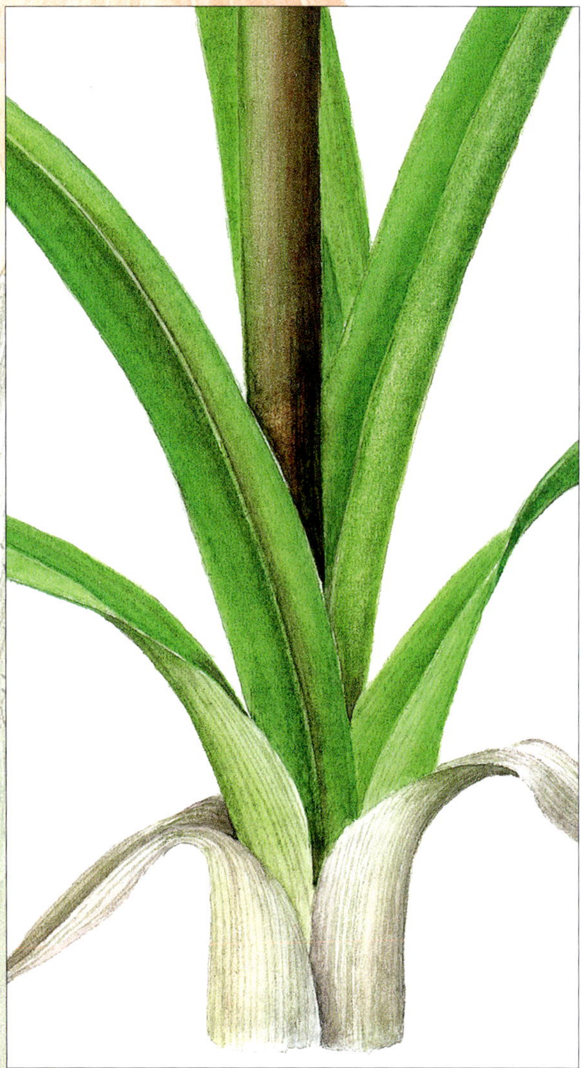

The leaves of Kniphofia *are strap leaves, all feeding into the basal stem. Care must be taken to paint in the overlaps so the leaves appear in the correct positions.*

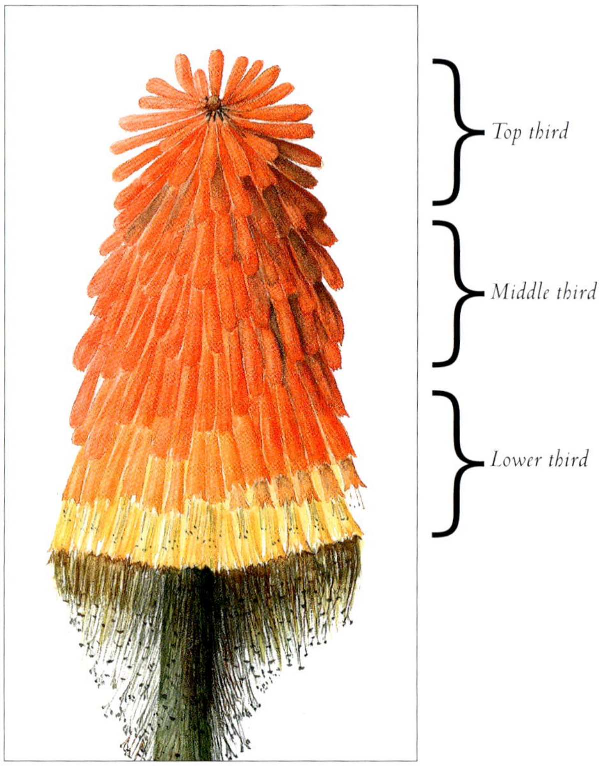

The flowerhead has to be graded in both tone and colour. Start with a mix of lemon yellow and cadmium red for the top third, and add more yellow for the middle third. The lowest petals are fully open and show the stamens.

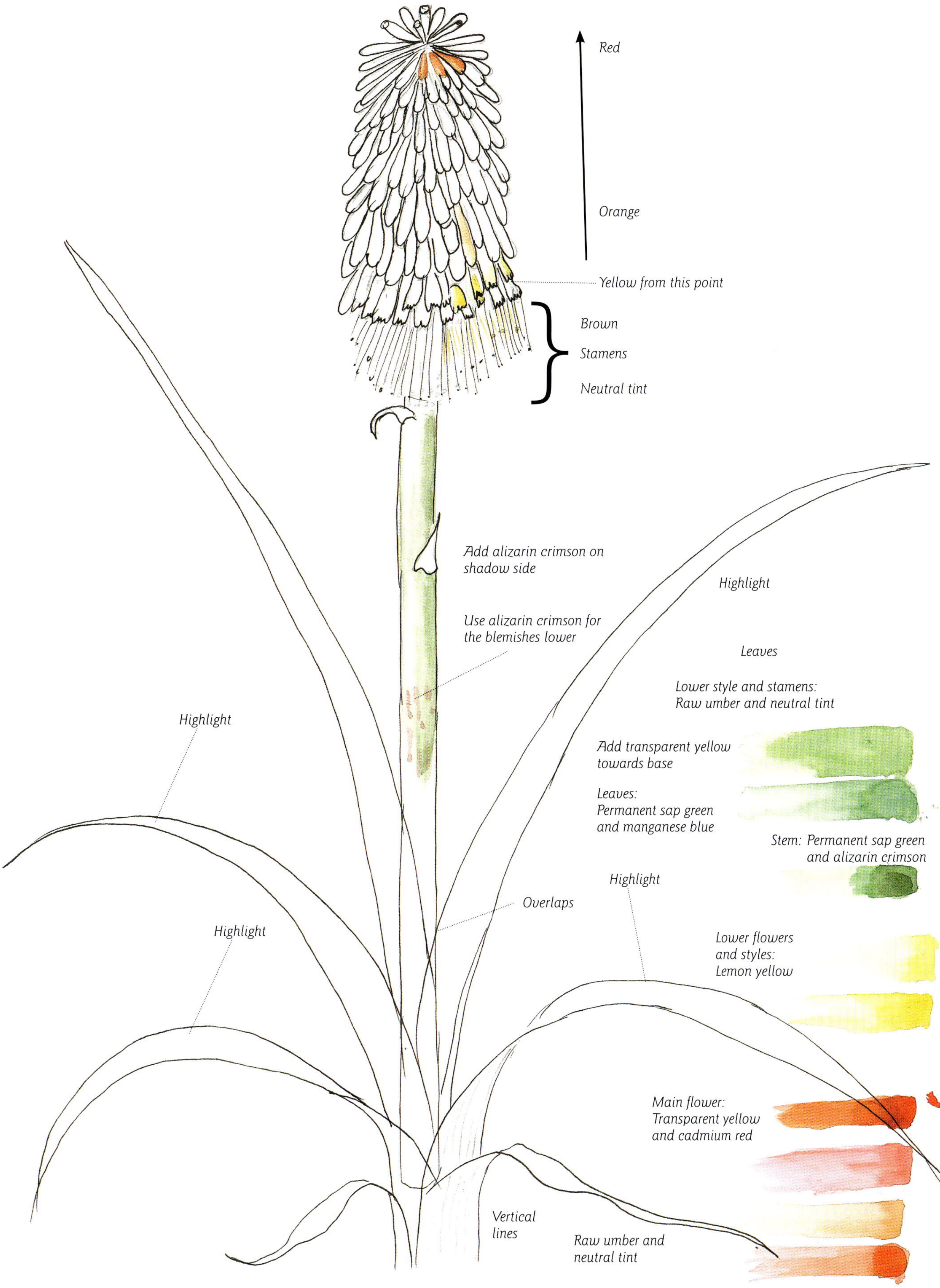
Red
Orange
Yellow from this point
Brown
Stamens
Neutral tint
Add alizarin crimson on shadow side
Highlight
Use alizarin crimson for the blemishes lower
Leaves
Lower style and stamens: Raw umber and neutral tint
Highlight
Add transparent yellow towards base
Leaves: Permanent sap green and manganese blue
Stem: Permanent sap green and alizarin crimson
Highlight
Overlaps
Highlight
Lower flowers and styles: Lemon yellow
Main flower: Transparent yellow and cadmium red
Vertical lines
Raw umber and neutral tint

Painting the *Kniphofia*

With your finished sketch to hand and your colours prepared, transfer the drawing to hot-pressed watercolour paper.

First wash

1 Use a size 3 brush to glaze all of the petals and stem with clear water, then leave them to dry.

2 Using a dilute mix of cadmium red and transparent yellow, paint in the top third of the petals, painting each tube individually and grading them from right to left.

3 Add more transparent yellow to the mix to make a light orange for the middle third of the petals and paint them in the same way.

4 Paint the bottom third of the flowerhead using pure lemon yellow.

5 With the same size brush and a dilute mix of sap green and alizarin crimson, paint the stem grading from right to left.

6 Change to a size 5 brush and glaze all of the leaves with clean water. Once dry, use a mix of sap green and manganese blue with a little transparent yellow to paint the leaves, grading into the highlights. Add more transparent yellow towards the base of the leaves and leave them to dry.

Tonal washes

1 With a size 3 brush and the slightly stronger wells, build up the form and tonal values on each petal, keeping the upper left area of the flowerhead lighter in tone and adding more yellow towards the base of the flowerhead. Refer to the first wash instructions above for the colours to use on the flowerhead.

2 Referring to the first wash instructions for the leaf and stem colours, build up the tone on the leaves and stem in the same way, leaving the highlights as white paper but grading into them. Add shadow to the two older, dying leaves at the base with a mix of raw umber and neutral tint.

Crossovers

1 Using a size 2 brush and a dilute mix of neutral tint, paint in the small shadow on the right-hand side of each flower petal and underneath each petal in order to put them in their correct position.

2 Use the same mix to paint in the small areas where the leaves cross, using a darker tone on the one in the background and lighter tones towards the front.

3 Repeat the washes until the correct depth of colour has been achieved, putting the leaves in their correct position.

Harmonisation

1 Use a dilute mix of cadmium red and transparent yellow with a size 3 brush to paint a small wash over the upper part of the two larger leaves.

2 Use a small wash of sap green and magnanese blue on the lower part of the flowerhead.

Harmonisation

As the flowerhead is much higher than the leaves, only a small amount of colour is transmitted from the flower to the leaf and vice versa.

Details

1 Use a 00 brush and a mix of raw umber to paint in the styles and stamens at the base of the flower, adding neutral tint for the lower ones.

2 Add alizarin crimson to the mix for the older sepals and for the blemishes on the stem.

3 Paint the vertical lines on the underside of the leaves with the same mix.

Discretionary washes

With a size 5 brush and a dilute mix of transparent yellow, I applied a wash over all of the leaves and stem and left the portrait to dry.

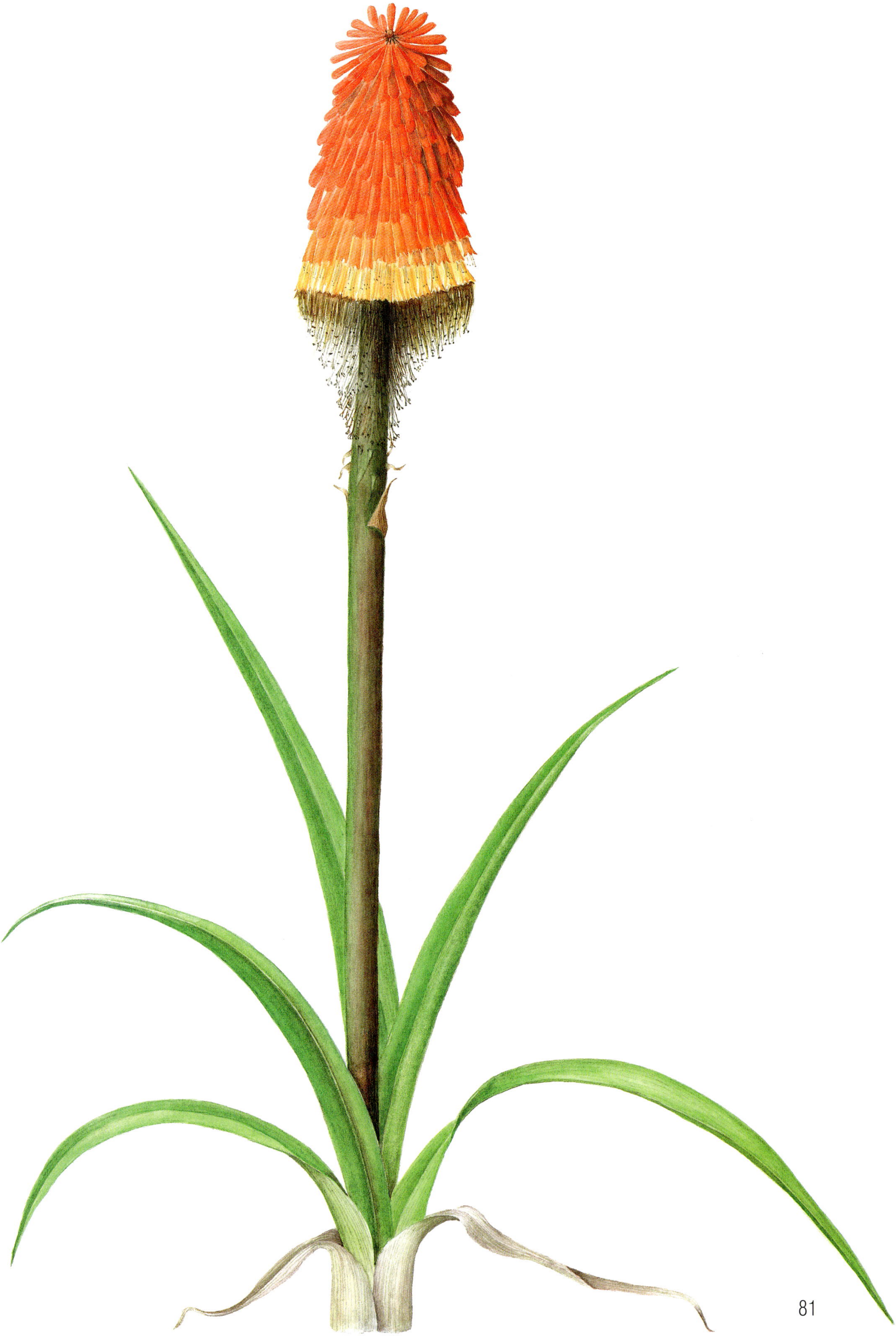

Lathyrus

This perennial flower (*Lathyrus latifolius*) is very vigorous and hardy, qualities at odds with its rather delicate common name of sweetpea! It is native to the Mediterranean region from Sicily to Crete, and first appeared in Britain in 1699, where it quickly became popular.

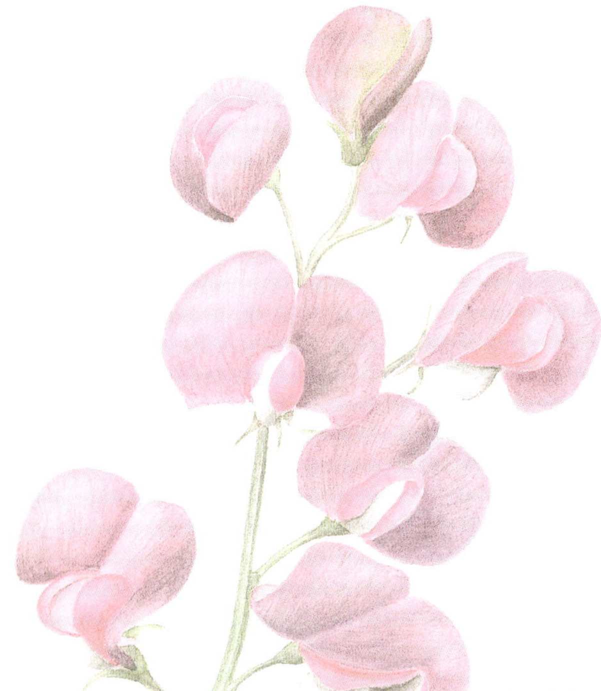

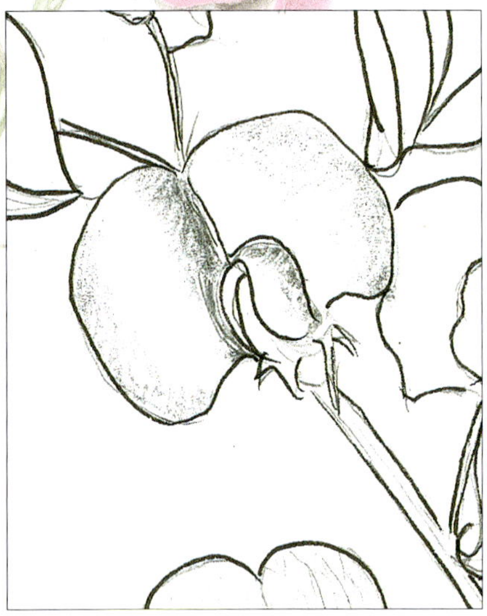

Working out the shadows on our sketch in pencil will help give you confidence when you come to suggesting the form with paint.

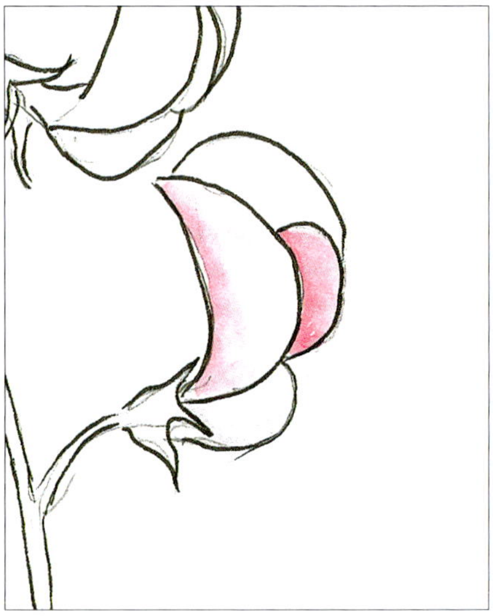

Adding a delicate wash of colour to show the form of the petals in the sketch will help your final piece; much in the same way as planning the tonal values (see left).

Note the different colours and venation of the leaves. The underside is painted blue-green and the veins emphasised while the topside of the leaves are a warmer yellow-green and the veins are left unshadowed.

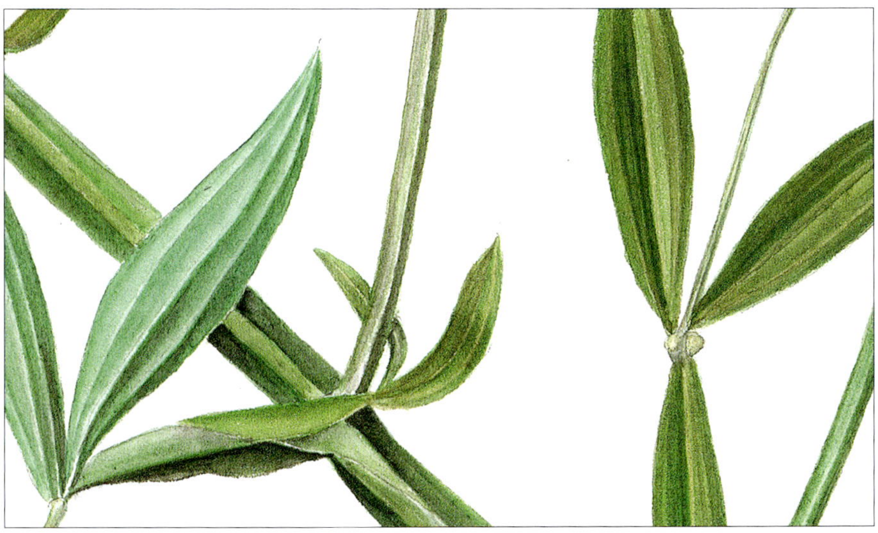

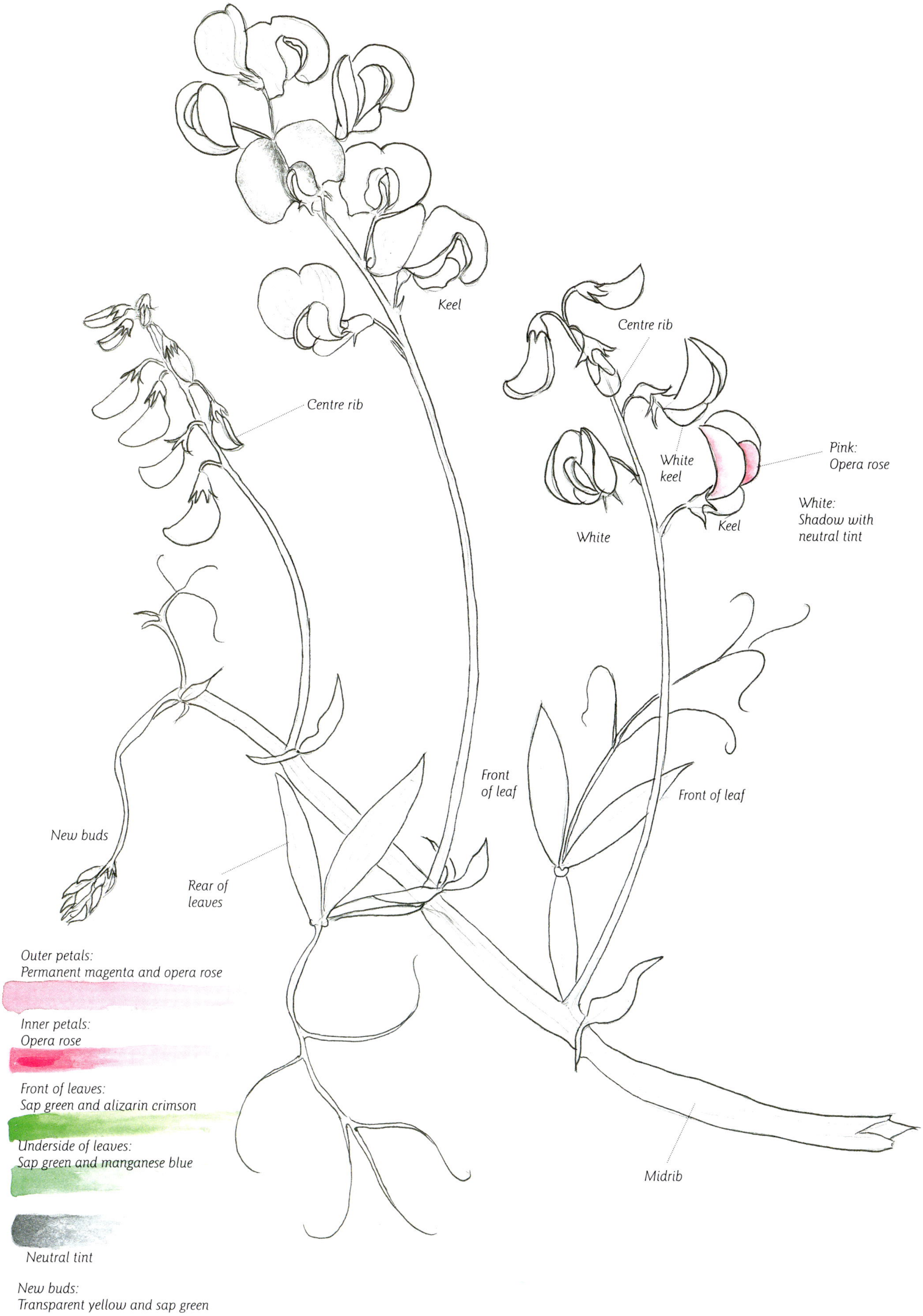
Keel
Centre rib
Centre rib
White keel
Pink:
Opera rose
White
Keel
White:
Shadow with neutral tint
Front of leaf
Front of leaf
New buds
Rear of leaves
Midrib
Outer petals:
Permanent magenta and opera rose
Inner petals:
Opera rose
Front of leaves:
Sap green and alizarin crimson
Underside of leaves:
Sap green and manganese blue
Neutral tint
New buds:
Transparent yellow and sap green

Painting the *Lathyrus*

After drawing the *Lathyrus* in your sketchbook and preparing your colours, transfer the drawing to hot-pressed watercolour paper.

First wash

1 Using a size 3 brush, glaze all of the flowers and buds with clean water and leave them to dry.

2 With a dilute mix of permanent magenta and opera rose, begin to paint the petals, starting in the darker areas and grading out to the highlights. Repeat this process on all of the petals and leave them to dry.

3 Using the same brush and a dilute mix of opera rose, paint in the corollas, grading into the highlight to create form and depth.

4 Once dry, use a dilute mix of neutral tint to create shadows and develop form on the lower parts of the flowers.

5 Use a size 2 brush with a dilute mix of transparent yellow to paint in the buds. Grade the colour from right to left and into the highlights. Before this is completely dry, add a little opera rose towards the base of the buds.

6 Using a size 1 brush, start to paint in the sepals on all of the flowers and buds with a dilute mix of sap green and a little alizarin crimson. When dry, use a size 3 brush to glaze all of the stems and leaves with clean water and then leave them to dry.

7 Use a dilute mix of sap green and alizarin crimson to paint the flower stems. As the flower stems are square in section, make the right-hand side darker, with no gradation. Give the small flower stems a graded form as these are round in section.

8 Still using the size 1 brush, paint the front side of the leaves with a dilute mix of sap green and alizarin crimson, grading the paint out from the midrib to give a ribbed effect. Using the same size brush and a mix of sap green and manganese blue, paint in the backs of the leaves with the same method.

9 Using the sap green and alizarin crimson mix, paint in the main stem, painting outwards from the shadow side to the highlights.

Tonal washes

1 Following the order given in the steps above, and substituting the stronger wells in place of the dilute mixes, build up the form of the components of the plant until the correct depth of colour has been achieved.

Crossovers

1 With a size 2 brush and a dilute mix of neutral tint, paint in the small areas where the petals overlap each other.

2 Use the same mix and brush to paint in the areas where the stems overlap the leaves and tendrils.

3 Repeats these steps, overlaying the colour where necessary, until the parts appear the correct distance from each another.

Harmonisation

1 Use a size 1 brush to paint a small wash of sap green and transparent yellow on the petal areas closest to the sepals, where the reflection from the green affects the pink petal.

2 Using the same size brush with a dilute mix of opera rose, paint a small wash on to the stems of the flowers.

Details

1 Using a size 0 brush with a mix of sap green and alizarin crimson, paint the tendrils and the sepals on the cluster of buds. Sharpen up all of the sepal points with the same brush and mix.

2 With permanent magenta and opera rose, paint the very small buds on the cluster, grading the colour to suggest the form.

Discretionary washes

Using a size 3 brush and a dilute mix of manganese blue, I washed over the main stem and slightly into the flower stems. I also used this wash on the backs of the leaves. With the same size brush and a dilute mix of sap green I washed over the flower stems and fronts of the leaves.

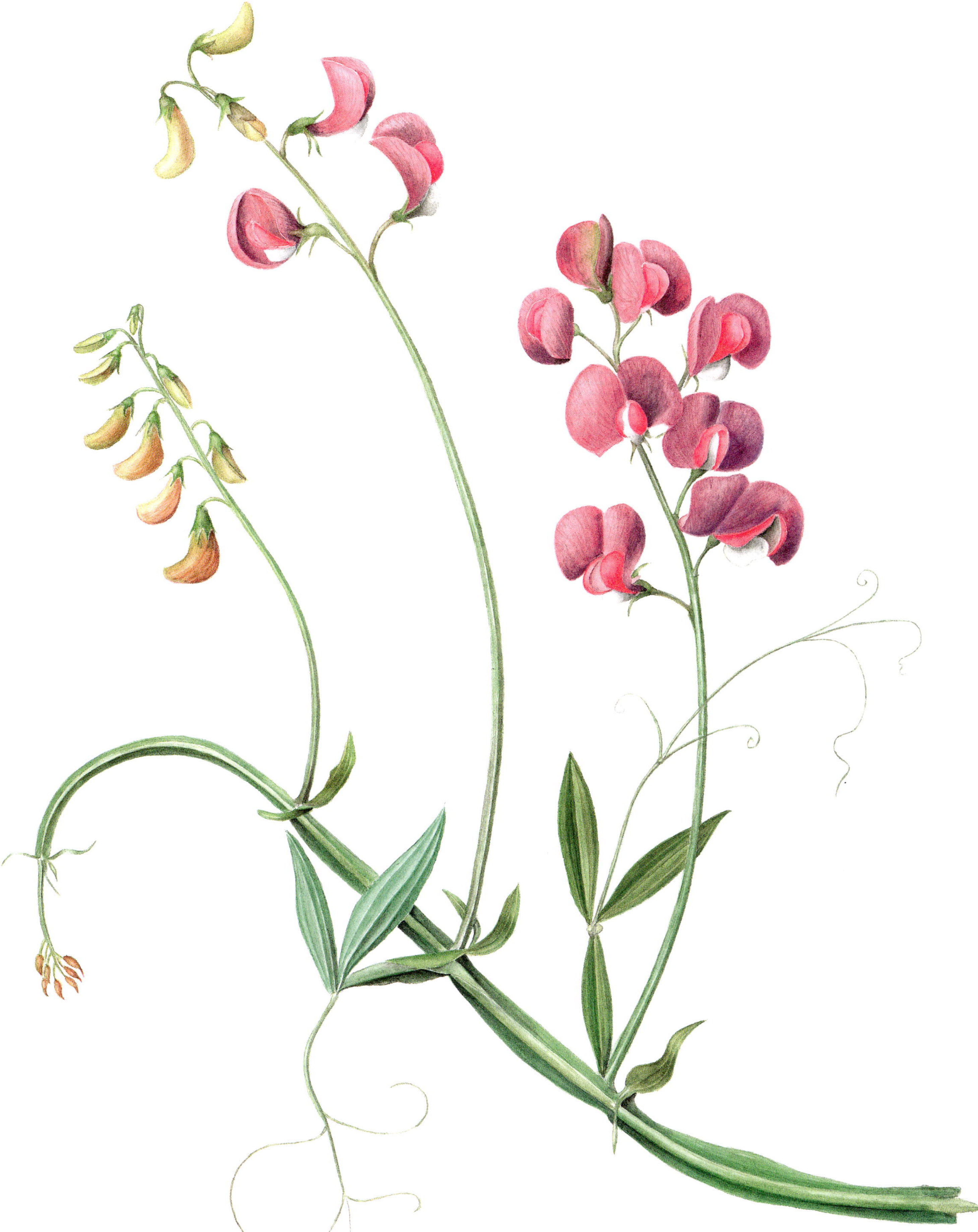

Magnolia

In spring, these flowers start with a furry brown sheath, then burst into a spectacular array of pink or white flowers. After the petals have fallen, you can see the stigmas and stamens standing proud. The leaves appear after the flowers have finished.

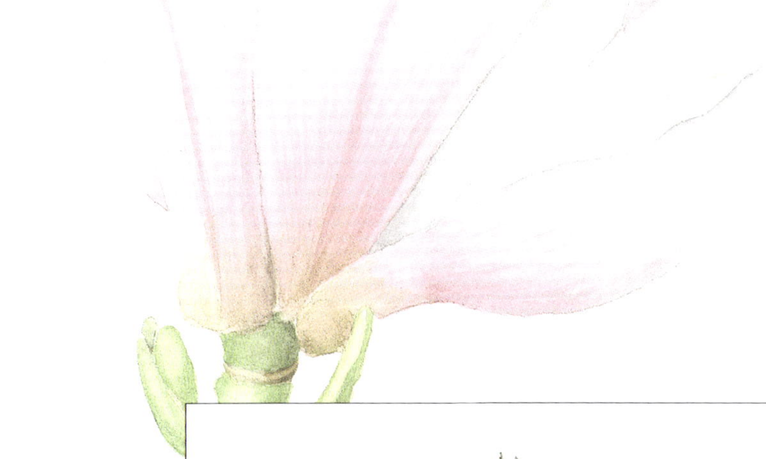

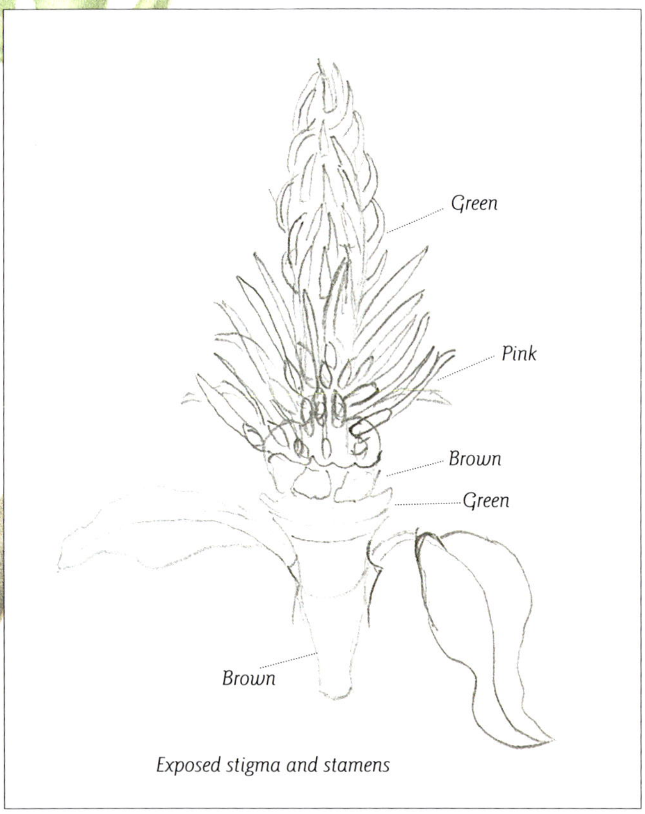

Exposed stigma and stamens

The initial pencil drawing was used to note the various colours of the stigmas, stamens and sepals. Complex areas like this benefit from additional notes before you start to paint.

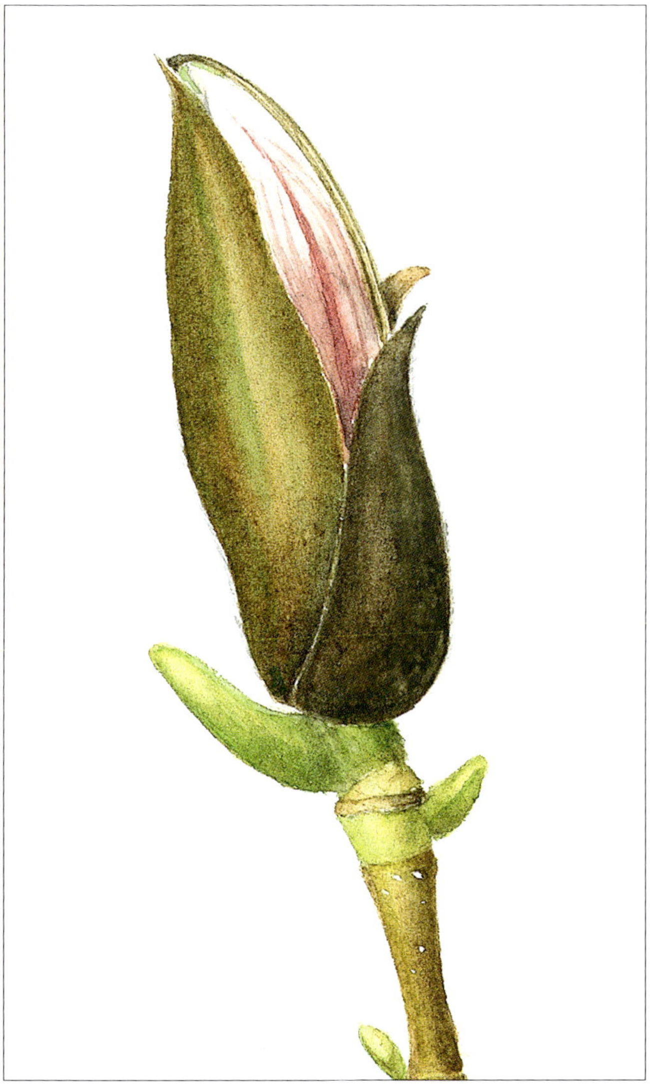

The bud casings of the flowers have a furry texture to them. You will have to work slightly wet-in-wet to achieve this, but note that it is a careful balance: if your paper is too wet the effect will be lost.

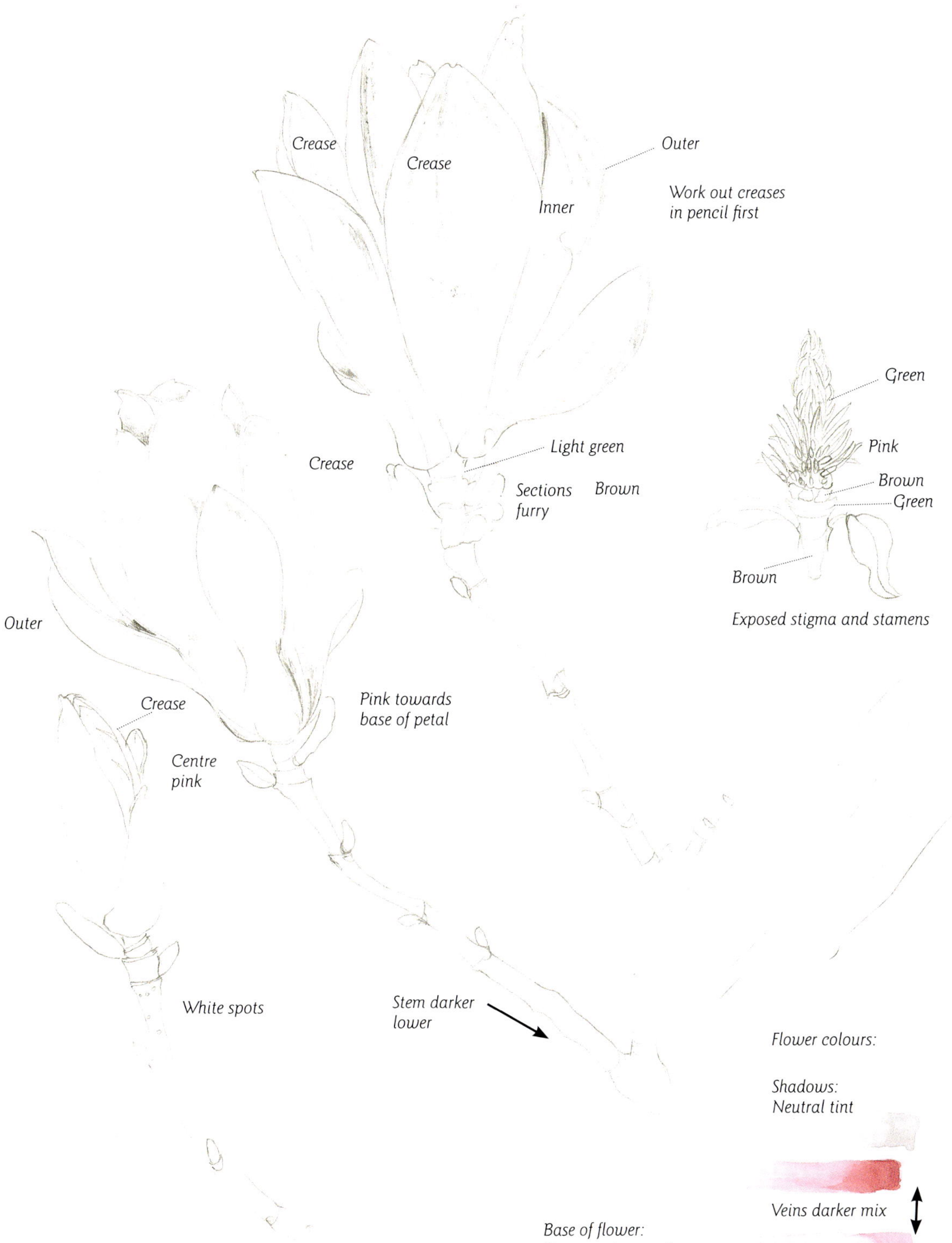

Flower colours:

Shadows:
Neutral tint

Veins darker mix

Base of flower:
Permanent magenta and alizarin crimson

Bud colours:

Outer sepal:
Raw umber and Payne's gray

Inner bud:
Yellow ochre and raw umber

Main stem:
Raw umber and Payne's gray

New buds:
Sap green, transparent yellow and cadmium red

Painting the *Magnolia*

With your sketch to hand and your colours prepared, transfer the drawing to hot-pressed watercolour paper.

First wash

1 Use a size 5 brush and clean water to glaze all of the petals, then leave them to dry.

2 Using a dilute mix of neutral tint, paint in the shadows on the right-hand side of the petals, grading out into the white paper. Take care to distinguish between the inner and outer petals.

3 Once the paint is dry, change to a size 3 brush and glaze all of the stems including the new bud stems with clean water. Use a dilute mix of raw umber and Payne's gray to paint the stems leaving the new buds unpainted.

4 With a size 2 brush, paint the segments below the petals and at the top of the stem with a dilute mix of sap green, transparent yellow and a little cadmium red. Grade the paint into the highlights, then use the same dilute mix to paint in the new buds.

5 Change to a size 1 brush and glaze the exposed stigma and stamens, then leave them to dry. Using the same brush with a dilute mix of transparent yellow and sap green, paint in the young leaves, making sure to leave the highlights unpainted.

6 Using a size 3 brush, glaze the sepals of the new bud and allow them to dry. With the same size brush and a mix of raw umber and Payne's gray, paint the right-hand sepal, grading the colour into the highlights.

7 Once the right-hand sepal is dry, use the same brush with a mix of raw umber and yellow ochre to paint the outer sepal, again grading into the highlights. Leave to dry.

Tonal washes

1 Repeat the first wash steps with the same size brushes and the stronger wells of the colours noted above to build up the depth of colour.

2 With a wet-into-wet technique, paint the outer petals of the flower with a size 3 brush and a dilute mix of permanent magenta and alizarin crimson. Allow the mix to bleed into the white paper but ensure the highlights are kept clean.

3 Once dry, use the same mix and brush to paint the pink petal of the bud.

Crossovers

1 With a size 2 brush and neutral tint, paint in the small areas where the flower petals cross, applying a darker wash at the base of the petals and to the petals in the shadow area.

Harmonisation

1 There is very little harmonisation on the main magnolia illustration as no leaves are included. However colour reflected from the flowers to stems and vice versa is needed. Use a size 2 brush to apply a small mix of the flower colour to the upper stems and the stem mix to the lower petals.

Details

1 With a size 0 brush and a mix of raw umber and neutral tint, add the small rings at the stem joints and the segments below the flower petals.

2 Using the same size brush and neutral tint, paint in the small detail on the flower bud and the finer details on the stigma, stamens and the veins on the small leaves.

3 Still using the size 0 brush, add the small white spots on the stem with a little white gouache.

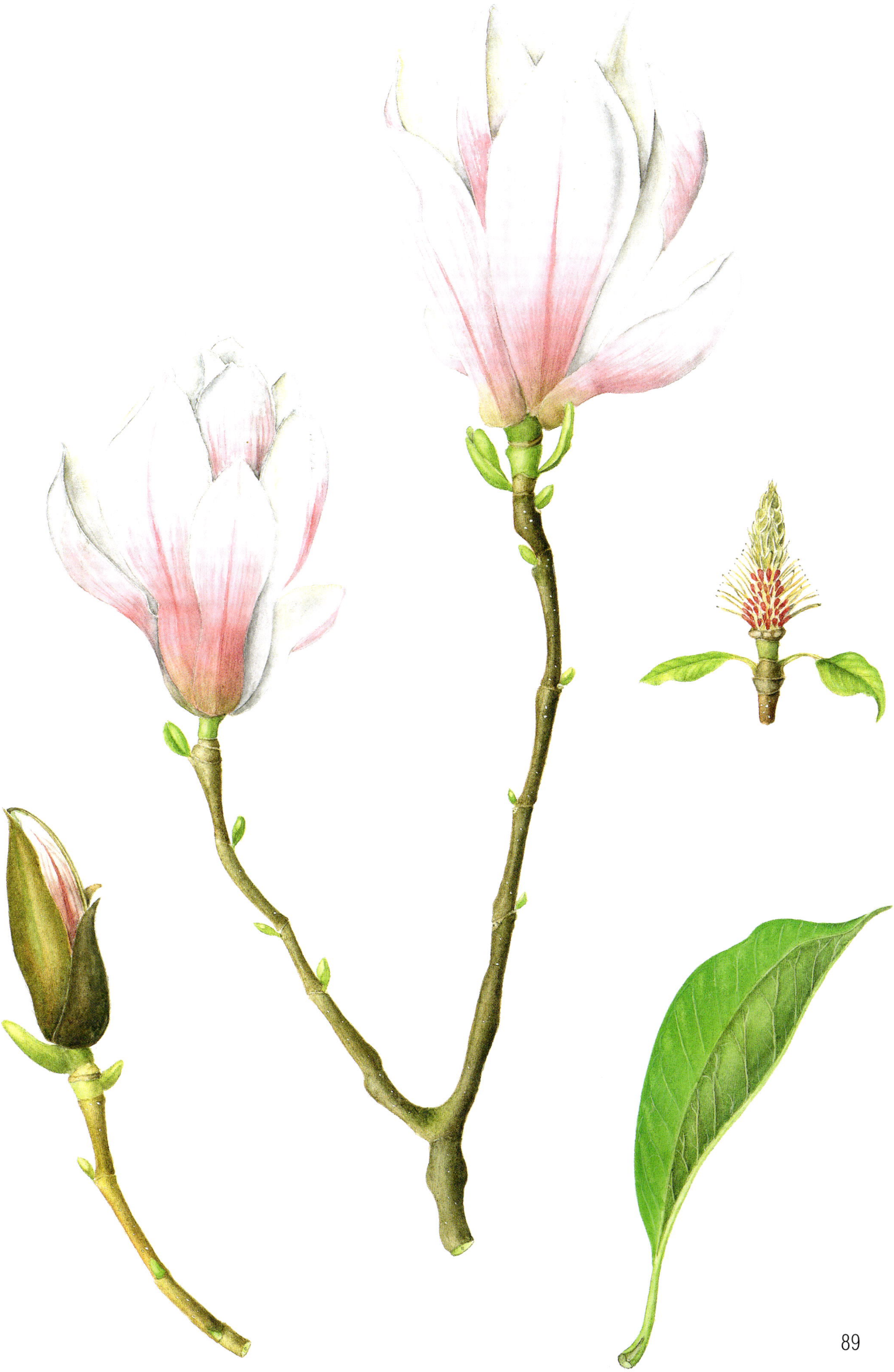

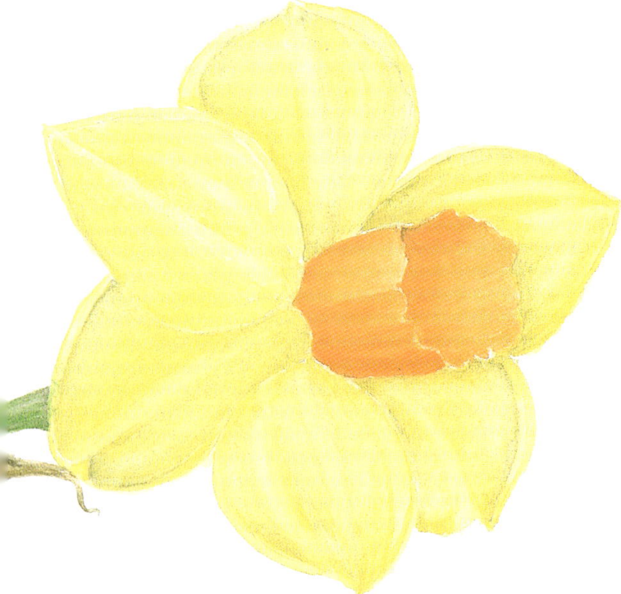

Narcissus

Narcissus is a perennially popular spring flower, with varieties ranging in colour from white to yellow to orange. Over 25,000 varieties have been identified since the 1870s. The variety shown here is 'Pipe Major'.

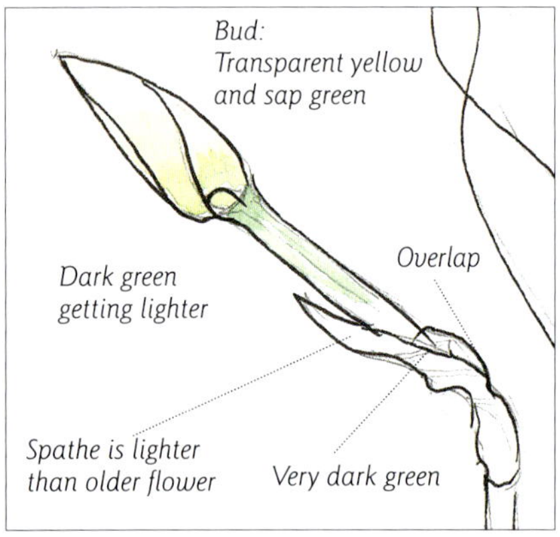

A few notes and test washes in the planning stage are beneficial, as they can act as a useful reference later on. Here, the colours are noted before the real painting begins.

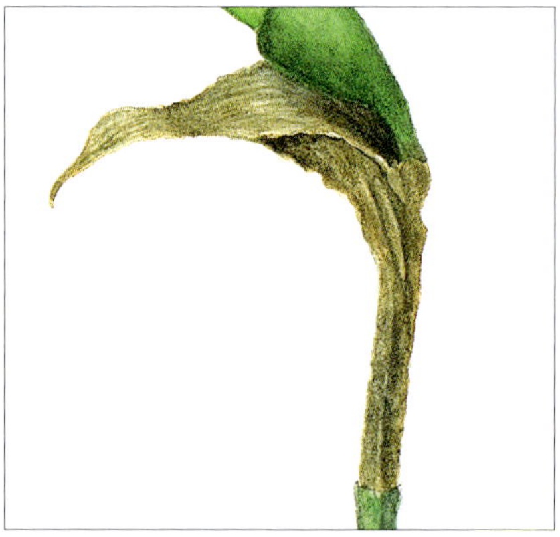

This detail show the spathe, a type of modified leaf which protects the bud before it flowers. Once the flower blossoms, the spathe starts to die, so a crinkled effect is required. Wavy lines leaving highlights will give this effect.

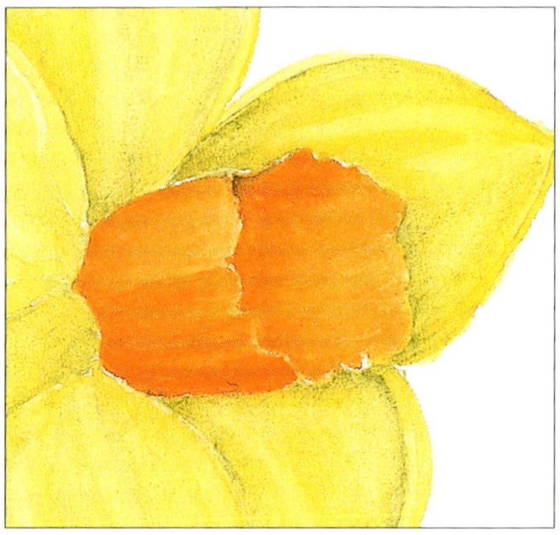

A slightly stronger mix of cadmium orange is used to darken the inside of the throat of the trumpet. This must be graded towards the outer edge otherwise the depth will be lost.

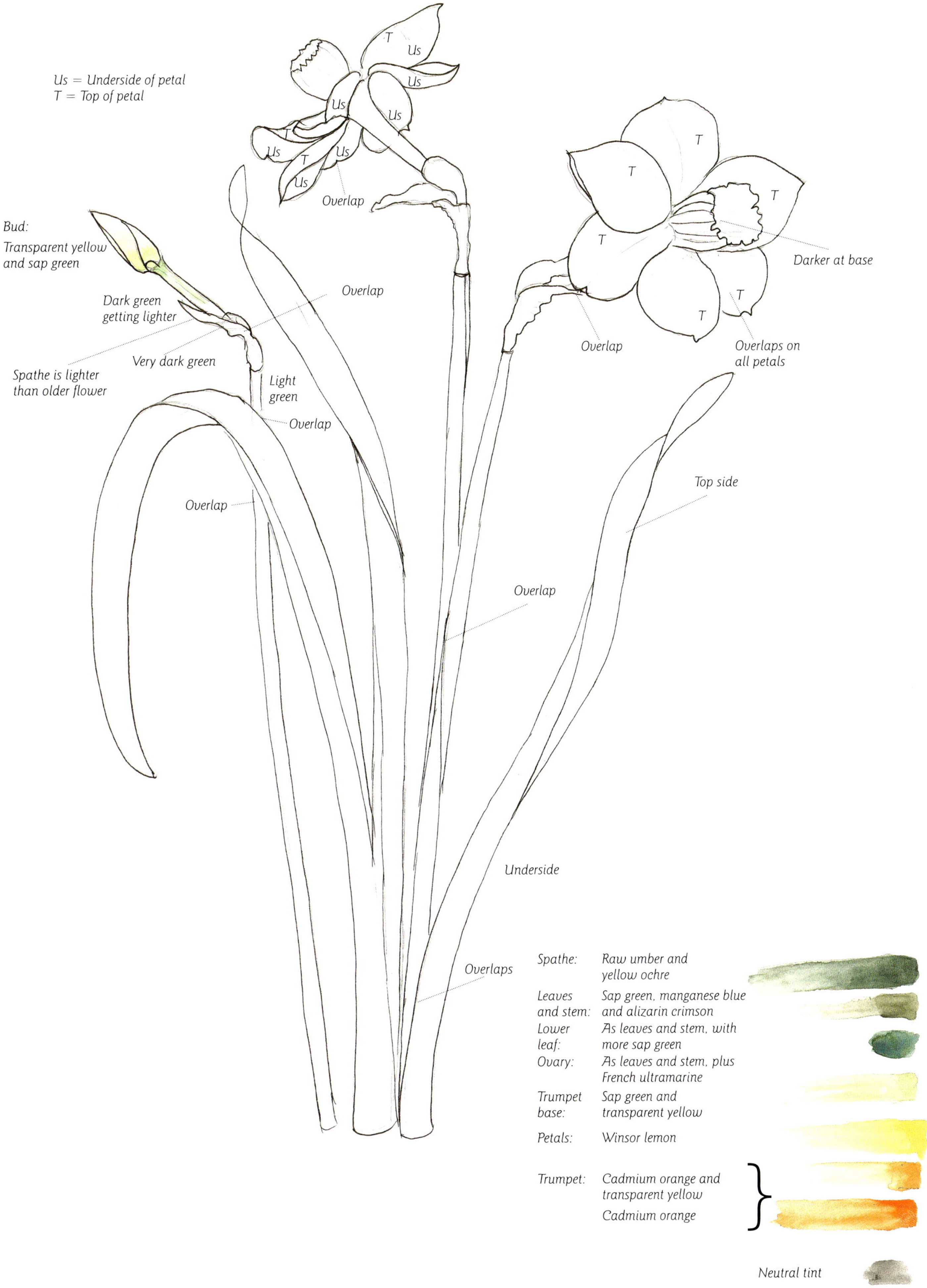
Us = Underside of petal
T = Top of petal
T
Us
Us
Us
Us
Us
T
Us
Us
Overlap
T
T
T
T
T
T
T
Darker at base
Bud:
Transparent yellow and sap green
Dark green getting lighter
Overlap
Spathe is lighter than older flower
Very dark green
Light green
Overlap
Overlap
Overlaps on all petals
Overlap
Top side
Overlap
Underside
Overlaps
Spathe: Raw umber and yellow ochre
Leaves and stem: Sap green, manganese blue and alizarin crimson
Lower leaf: As leaves and stem, with more sap green
Ovary: As leaves and stem, plus French ultramarine
Trumpet base: Sap green and transparent yellow
Petals: Winsor lemon
Trumpet: Cadmium orange and transparent yellow
Cadmium orange
Neutral tint

Painting the *Narcissus*

With your sketch to hand and your colours prepared, transfer the drawing to hot-pressed watercolour paper.

First wash

1 Use a size 3 brush to glaze all of the petals and leaves with clean water. Once dry, use a dilute wash of Winsor lemon to paint the top side of each petal, grading into the highlights.

2 Paint the underside of the petals, grading into the highlights and leave them to dry. Using the same size brush with a dilute mix of permanent sap green, manganese blue and a little alizarin crimson, paint the leaves. Add a little more sap green towards the base of the leaves.

3 Use a size 2 brush to glaze the spathe, ovary and base of the flower trumpet with clean water. Add a little French ultramarine to the leaf mix (see step 2) and paint the ovaries, grading into the highlights.

4 Paint the lower trumpet tubes of the flowers and bud with a mix of sap green and transparent yellow, adding more green at the top under the petals.

5 Use a dilute mix of raw umber and yellow ochre to paint in the three spathes, leaving highlights on the top left.

6 Glaze the two trumpets and use a dilute mix of cadmium orange and transparent yellow to paint them, painting in the guide lines and grading out to give the ribbed effect.

7 Glaze the flower bud and leave it to dry. Paint the bud with a dilute mix of transparent yellow and sap green, grading into the highlights and adding more sap green towards the base of the bud.

8 Glaze the flower stems with clean water using a size 3 brush and leave them to dry. With the leaf mix, paint the stems grading from dark on the right to light on the left.

First wash

When painting the petals, remember to work non-adjacent petals so the mix does not run between wet areas. Once dry, return and fill in the remaining petals.

Tonal washes

1 Repeat the first wash steps using the stronger wells of the same colours above. Add a little neutral tint in the shadow areas on the left-hand flower. When painting the leaves, use long strokes to give them a striped look.

Crossovers

1 With a size 1 brush and a dilute mix of neutral tint, paint in the small areas at the base of the petals on both flowers to put them into position.

2 Use the same mix to shade where the leaves cross the stems and where the spathes cross the ovaries.

3 Still using the size 1 brush, add a little neutral tint to the cadmium orange mix and darken the throats of the flower trumpets.

4 Repeat the steps above until each component appears the correct distance from the others.

Harmonisation

1 Use a size 3 brush and a dilute mix of transparent yellow to wash over the tops of the two straight leaves and over the bend on the curved leaf.

2 Add a little sap green to the dilute mix and wash the lower parts of the petals closest to the leaves.

Details

1 With a dilute mix of raw umber and neutral tint and a size 0 brush, paint the crease lines on the three spathes and the horizontal lines at the base of the spathes.

Discretionary washes

The lines on the leaves looked a little heavy, so I washed over them with a dilute mix of the same leaf colour.

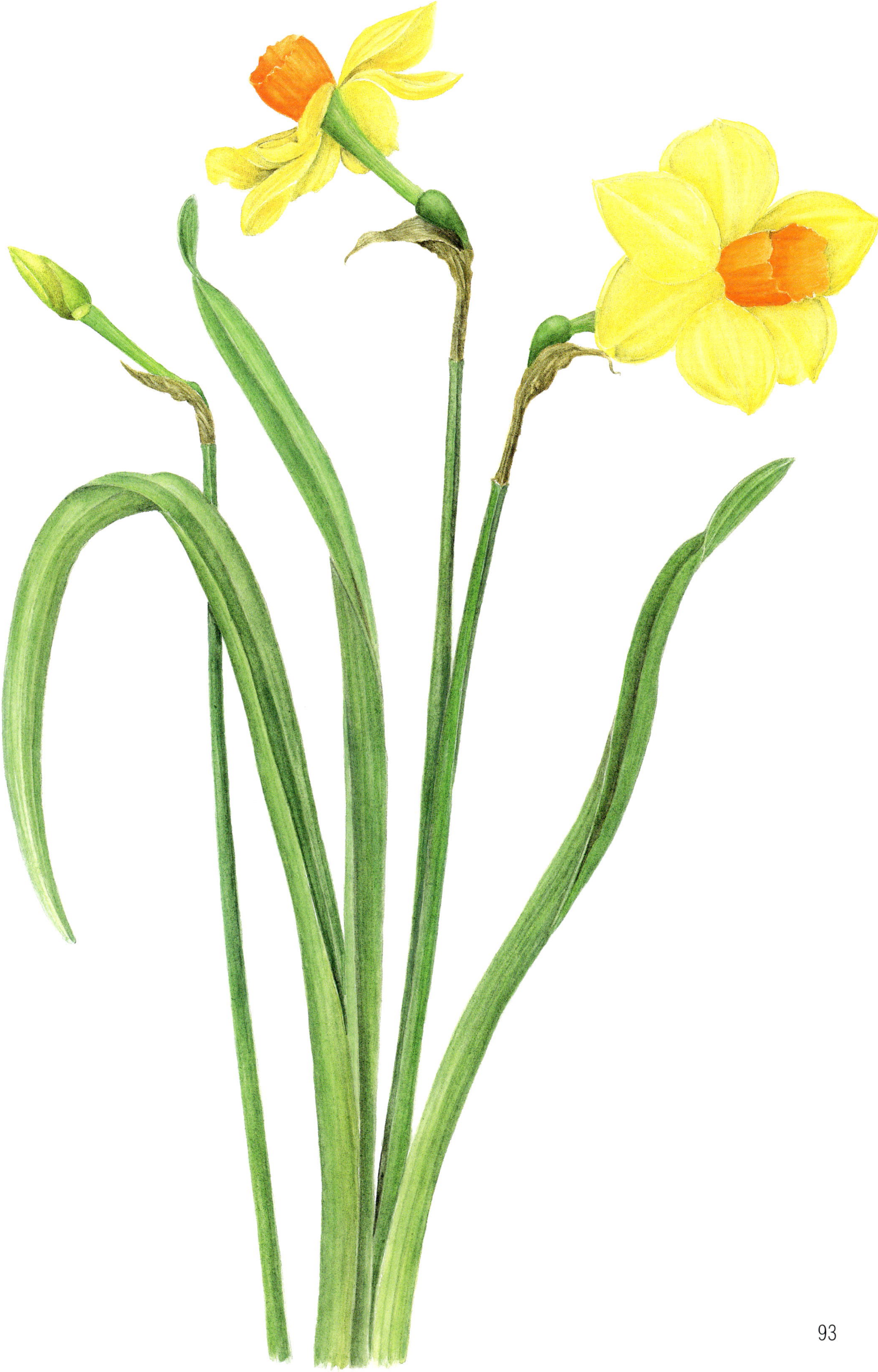

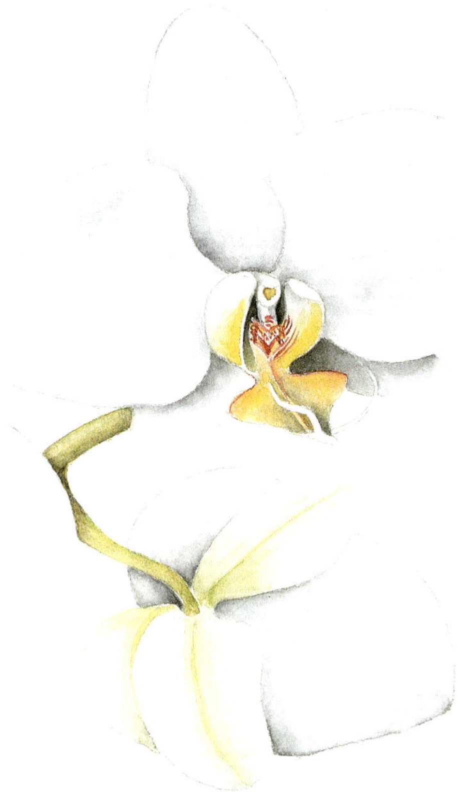

Orchid

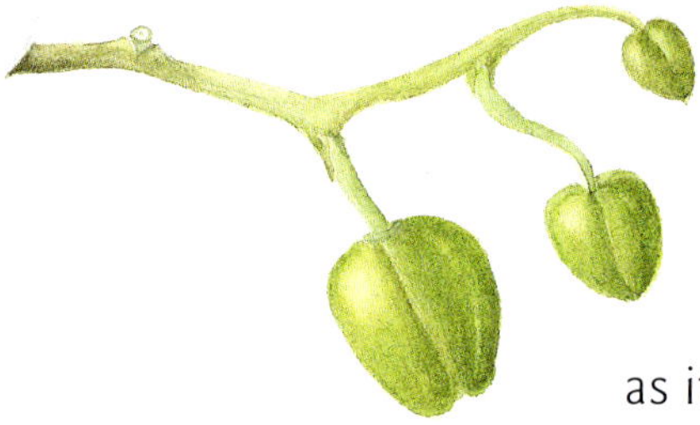

This flower is *Orchid phalaenopsis*, one of the most common varieties of this much-loved houseplant, and it is a real favourite with botanical artists as it presents a great challenge.

One of the great advantages of painting orchids is that you have plenty of time, as the flowers can last for months.

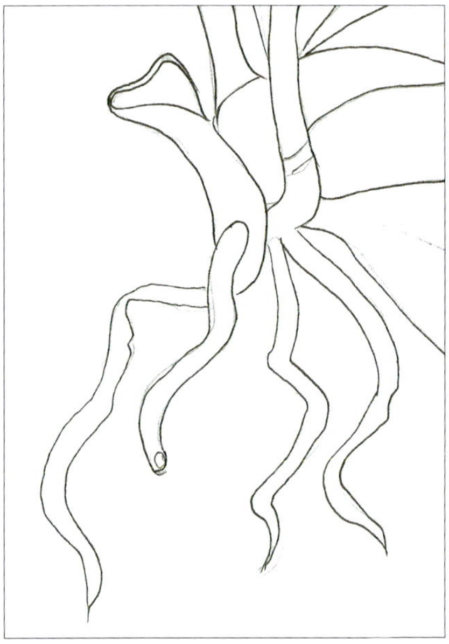

The root systems on plants should be given the same amount of thought and observation as the rest of the plant. That said, having too many roots can overcrowd your painting, so choose your specimen with this in mind.

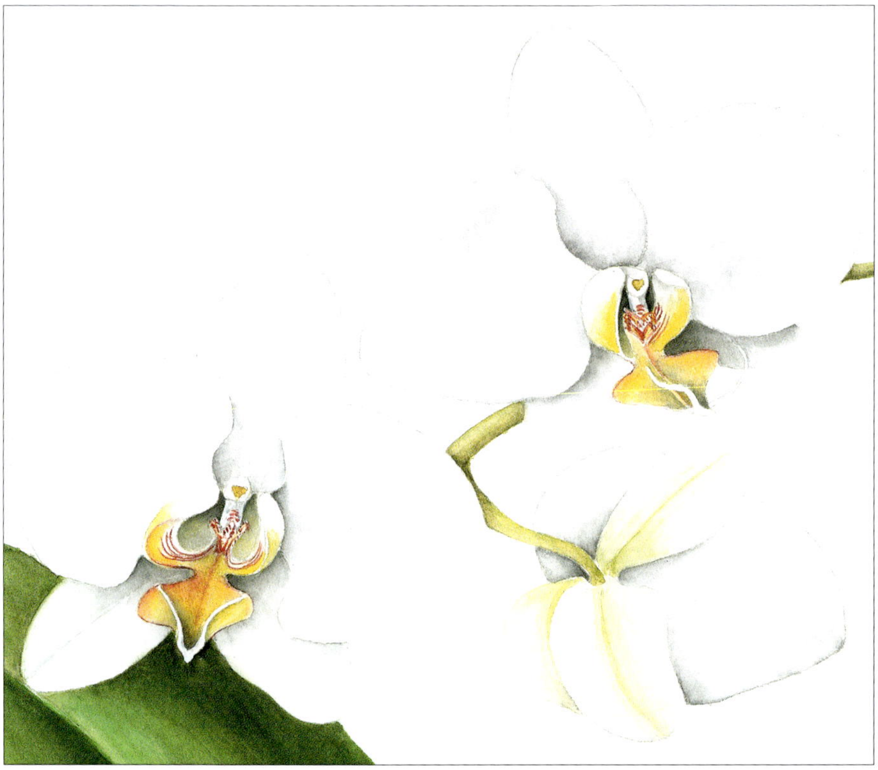

Painting white flowers is a balance between adding shadows in the dark areas and leaving as much white paper as possible. If too much shadow colour is used you will finish up with a grey flower. In this detail, note how dark the shadows are in the centre of the flowers: this is essential to achieve the correct depth and distance.

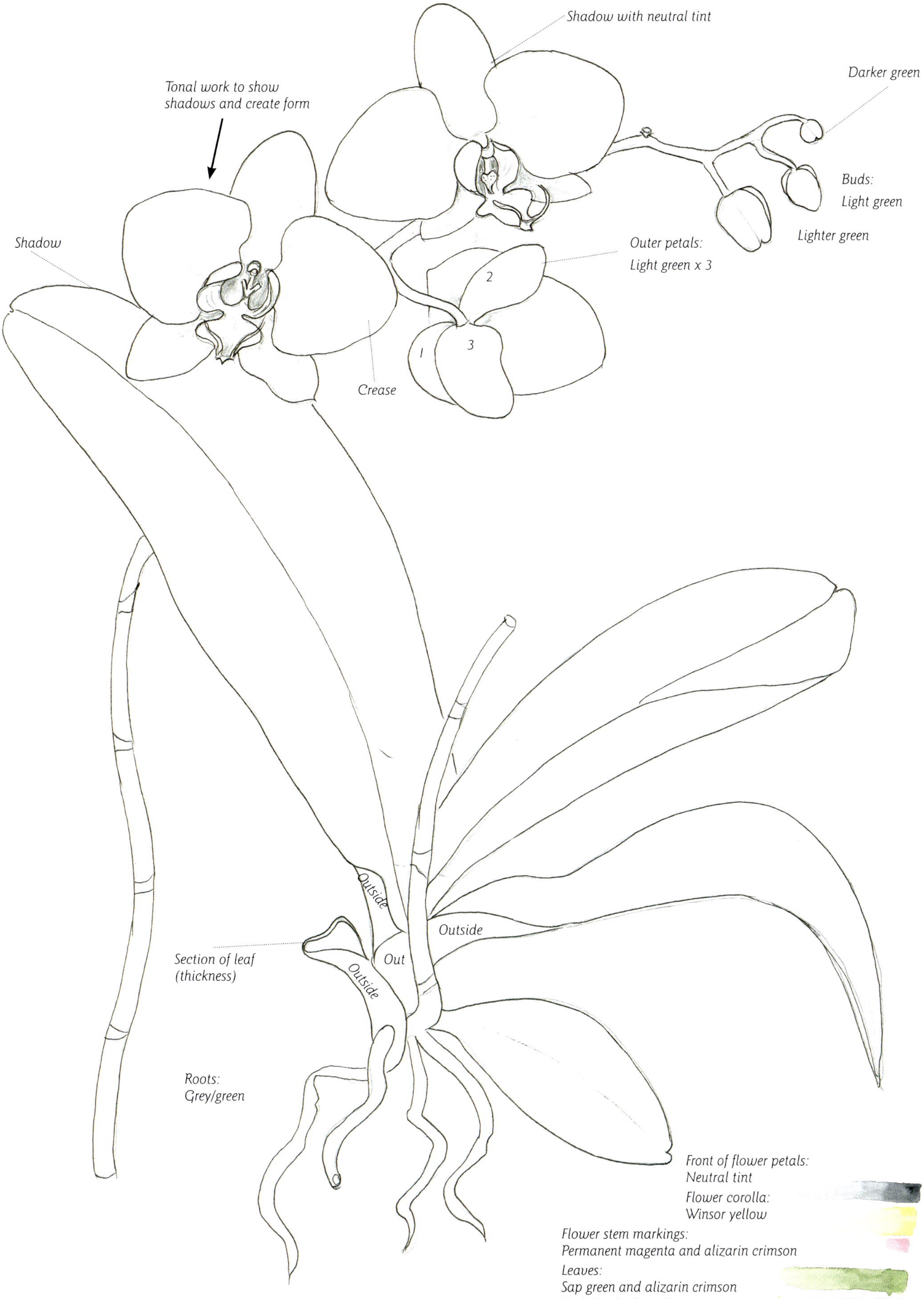

Front of flower petals:
Neutral tint
Flower corolla:
Winsor yellow
Flower stem markings:
Permanent magenta and alizarin crimson
Leaves:
Sap green and alizarin crimson
Buds/back of petals:
Sap green and transparent yellow
Roots:
Neutral tint and sap green

Painting the *Orchid*

With your sketch to hand and your colours prepared, transfer the drawing to hot-pressed watercolour paper.

First wash

1 Using a size 2 brush, glaze all of the petals with clean water and allow to dry. Next, use a dilute mix of neutral tint to wash the three rear petals at the point where the two front ones overlap. Grade the colour out to the white of the paper to form a shadow. Repeat this on the second flower.

2 Glaze the back of the flower and the buds with clean water and allow them to dry. Still using the size 2 brush, apply a dilute mix of neutral tint to the back of the third flower where the petals meet the stem.

3 Return to the two open flowers and wash neutral tint under the centre rib of each petal to form a crease in the petals. Allow to dry thoroughly.

4 Use a size 5 brush to glaze all of the leaves with clean water and then leave them to dry. With a dilute mix of permanent sap green and alizarin crimson, paint the first wash grading into the highlights. Make sure not to paint in the lower outer parts of the leaves.

5 Using a size 3 brush, glaze the flower stems with clean water and allow to dry. Then, with a dilute mix of sap green, transparent yellow and a little alizarin crimson, apply the first wash to all of the stems, grading the paint from right to left and leaving the centre of the stems lighter to give form.

6 Repeat the process on the lower parts of the crown with a dilute wash of Winsor yellow and a size 2 brush. Apply additional washes until the correct tone is achieved.

7 Using a size 2 brush and a dilute mix of sap green and transparent yellow, apply a first wash to the buds grading into the highlights.

Tonal washes

1 Use the same size brushes and colour mixes to repeat the first wash steps above, building up the form and shadow areas. Leave each wash to dry and repeat until the tones are dark enough to suggest that the image is three-dimensional.

2 Paint the backs of the leaves with a size 3 brush and a dilute mix of transparent yellow and sap green.

3 Glaze the roots using the size 3 brush and clean water, then allow them to dry. Paint the roots with a mix of neutral tint and sap green, grading into the highlights.

Crossovers

1 With a dilute mix of neutral tint and a size 1 brush, paint the small areas at the base of the petals where they overlap and where the petals overlap the stems.

2 Use the same brush and mix to paint in the areas where the leaves overlap each other.

3 Repeat these steps until the components are correctly distanced from each other and put in their correct place.

4 Apply a small amount of the same mix to the right-hand side of the stem nodes to make them stand out.

Harmonisation

1 Use a size 3 brush and a dilute mix of transparent yellow to paint a small wash on to the lower flower petals and the centres of the back of the three petals on the lower flower.

Details

1 Using a size 000 brush and a mix of alizarin crimson and permanent mauve, paint the inner markings on the corollas of both flowers.

2 Use the same colour to paint the thin outline to the labium.

3 Add a little neutral tint to the mix to darken the tone in the shadow areas.

Discretionary washes

I used a size 6 brush and a dilute mix of manganese blue to apply a wash over all the leaves.

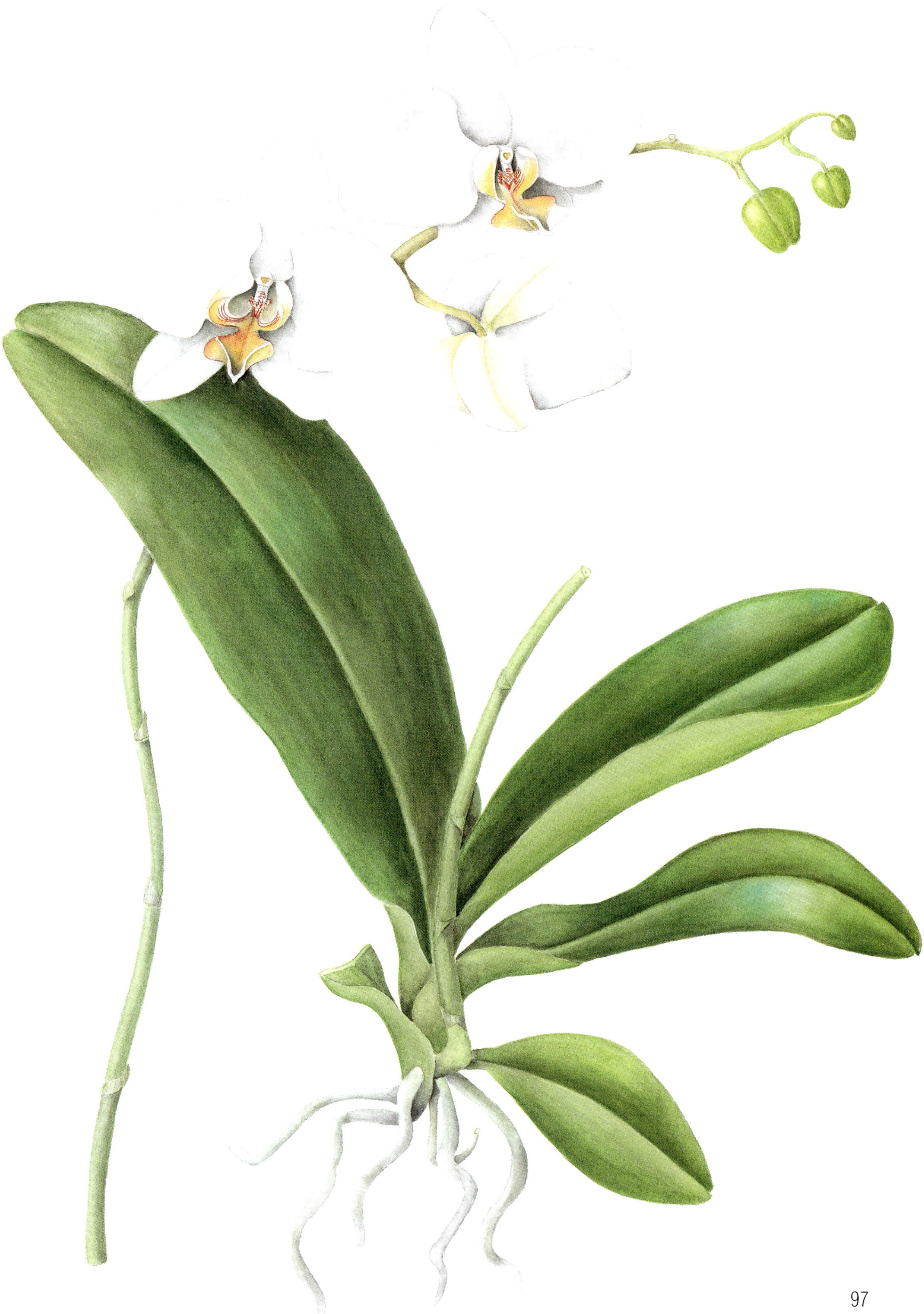

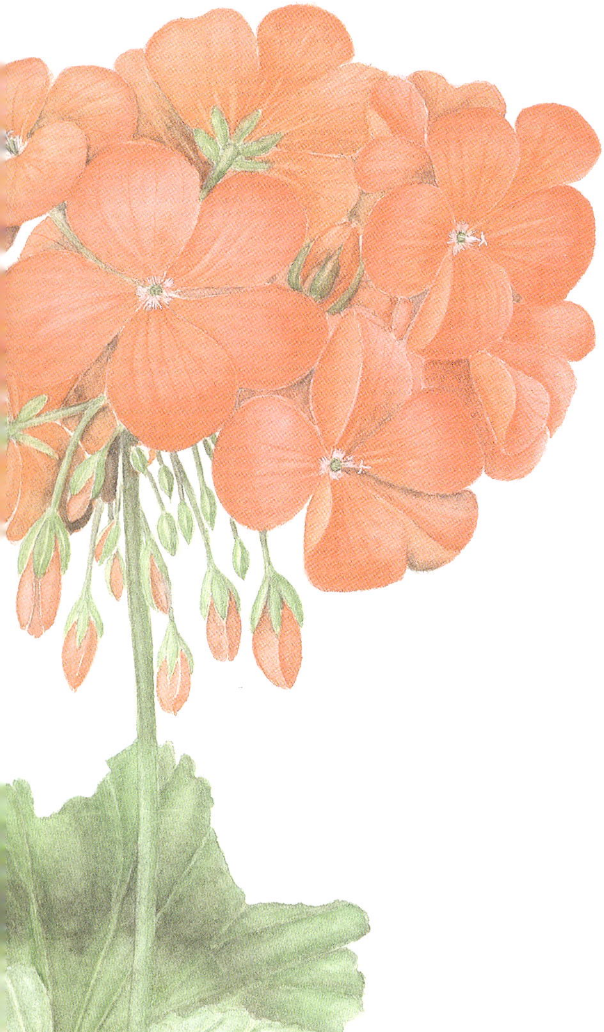

Pelargonium

Geraniums have been popular with European growers since 1701 and have never really gone out of fashion. Doubtless some of their popularity stems from their great variety of vibrant colours: reds, whites and pinks are eye-catching and striking. This variety is *Pelargonium zonale* 'Ricard Orange'.

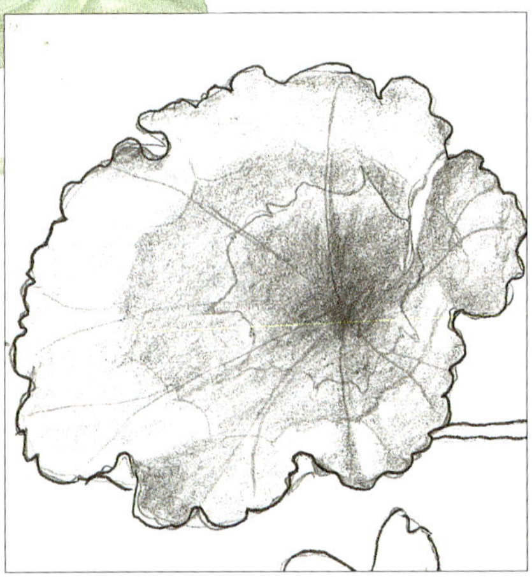

Tonal work in pencil is beneficial to accentuate the sometimes complex form of a component such as this geranium leaf.

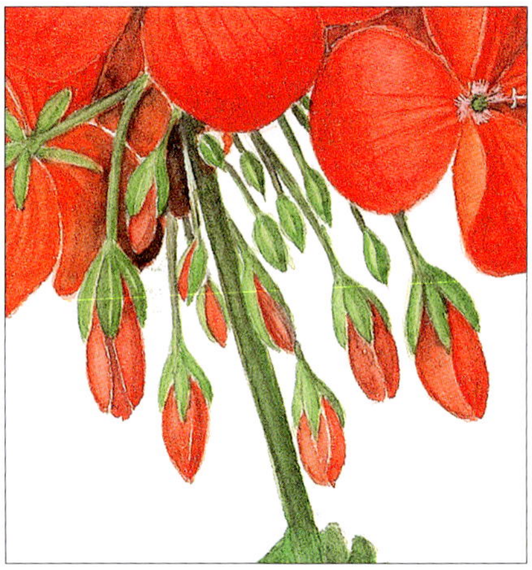

Although small, the new flower buds have a distinct shape. To suggest this, leave a highlight aiming towards the light source.

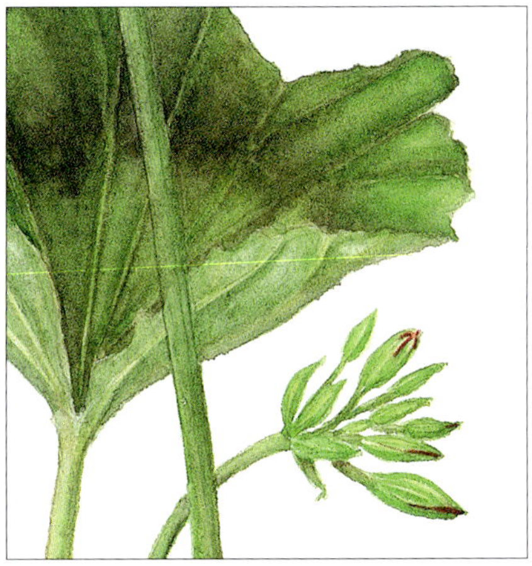

A small overlap was required for the main flower stem in front of the smaller one. The dark tones of the leaf form the shadow for the main stem.

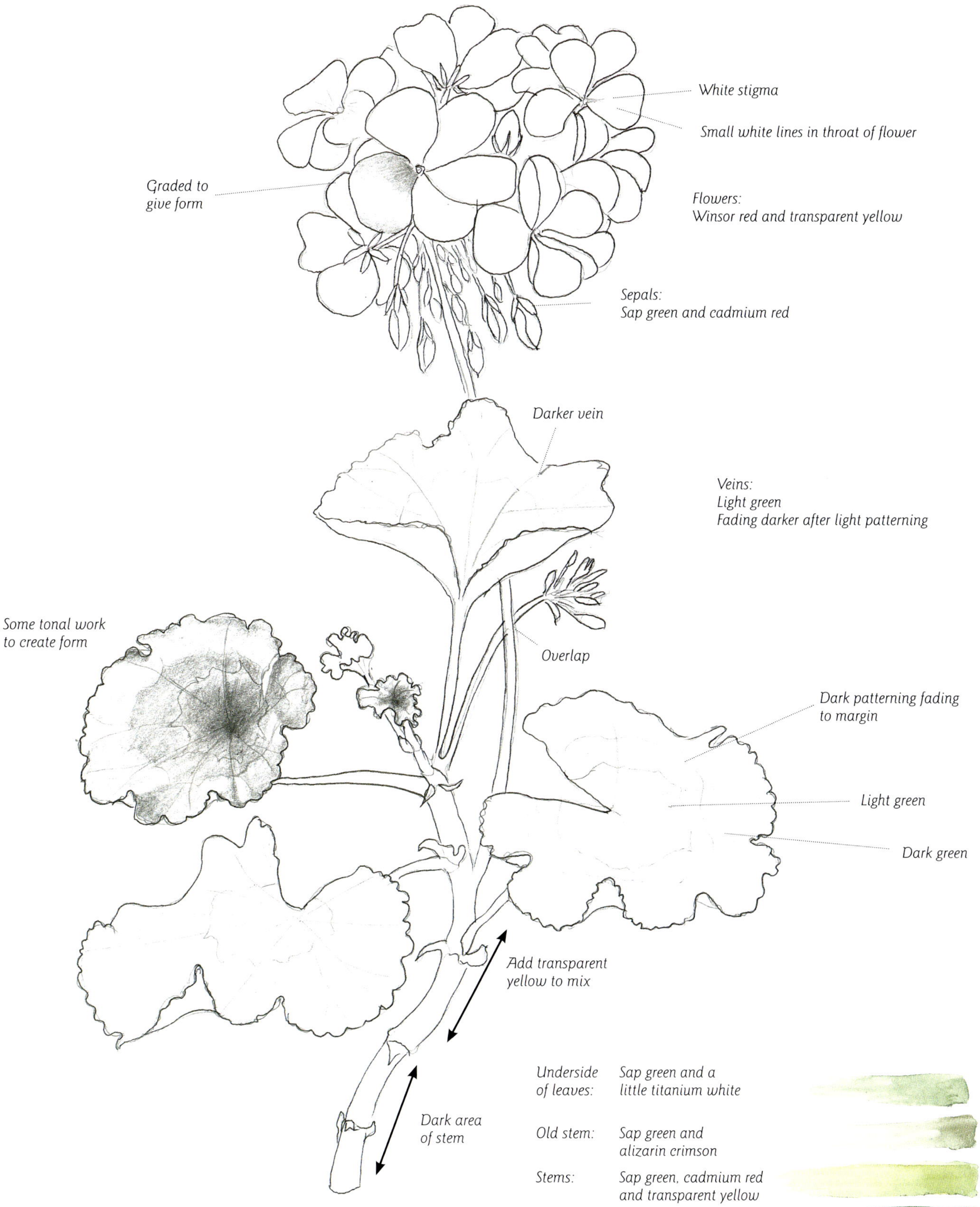

Underside of leaves:	Sap green and a little titanium white
Old stem:	Sap green and alizarin crimson
Stems:	Sap green, cadmium red and transparent yellow
Dark parts of leaf:	Sap green, Payne's gray and cadmium red
Light areas of leaf:	Sap green and cadmium red
Flower:	Winsor red
	Winsor red and transparent yellow
Shadows:	Neutral tint

Painting the *Pelargonium*

With your sketch to hand and your colours prepared, transfer the drawing to hot-pressed watercolour paper.

First wash

1 Using a size 3 brush and clean water, glaze all of the petals individually and leave to dry. Using a dilute mix of Winsor red and a little transparent yellow, paint every alternate petal. Start each at the throat of the flower, grade the colour out towards the highlights on the bends of the petals and strengthen the colour towards the outer margin of the flowers.

2 Once dry, repeat this process on all of the remaining petals. Using the same brush, glaze all of the leaves and stems with clean water and leave the painting to dry.

3 Apply a dilute mix of sap green and cadmium red to the undulating leaf, grading into the highlights and leaving the veins unpainted.

4 Still using the size 3 brush and a dilute mix of sap green and alizarin crimson, paint the older lower part of the stem, grading from right to left and leaving the leaf nodes unpainted.

5 With a dilute mix of sap green, cadmium red and transparent yellow, paint the small stems of the flower buds and sepals, the young leaves and the main flower stem. Grade from right to left for each stem.

Tonal washes

1 Using a size 3 brush and a dilute mix of sap green, Payne's gray and a little cadmium red, paint the darker areas of the leaves and blend the paint into the lighter green, keeping the form as before.

2 Using a size 2 brush and a stronger mix of Winsor red, build up the form on the flower petals and buds.

3 Continue to build up the leaves with the mix in step 1 until the depth of colour has been reached. On the last two or three washes paint over the leaf veins to achieve a subtle colour.

Crossovers

1 Using a size 2 brush and a mix of neutral tint, darken the small areas where the leaves overlap the stems, the stems overlap the leaves and the bud stems cross each other, in order to put them in the correct position.

Harmonisation

1 Using a size 3 brush and a dilute mix of Winsor red and transparent yellow, apply a small wash to the leaf closest to the flowerhead.

2 Still using the size 3 brush, add a small wash of sap green and transparent yellow to the lower flower petals and buds.

Details

1 Using a size 0000 brush and a little white gouache, paint in the stigmas and stamens of the open flower.

2 Switching to a size 1 brush and a mix of sap green with a little white gouache, paint the undersides of the leaves, leaving the veins unpainted.

3 With a mix of sap green and transparent yellow, paint in the small leaves at the nodes, grading the paint to keep the form.

Discretionary washes

Using a size 5 brush and a dilute mix of transparent yellow and sap green, I washed over all of the leaves and stems. Using a size 1 brush and transparent yellow, I then washed over the individual petals on the left of the portrait.

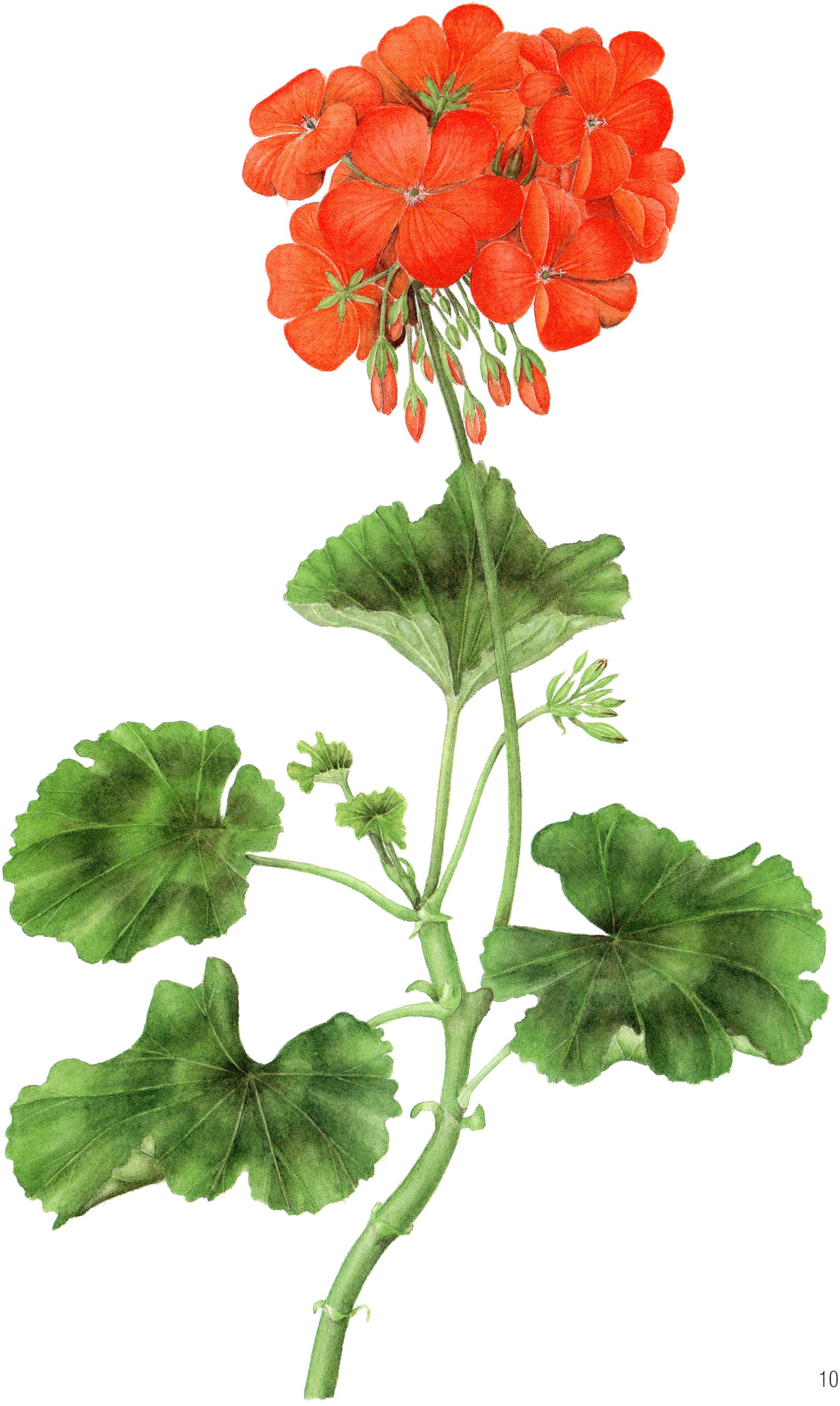

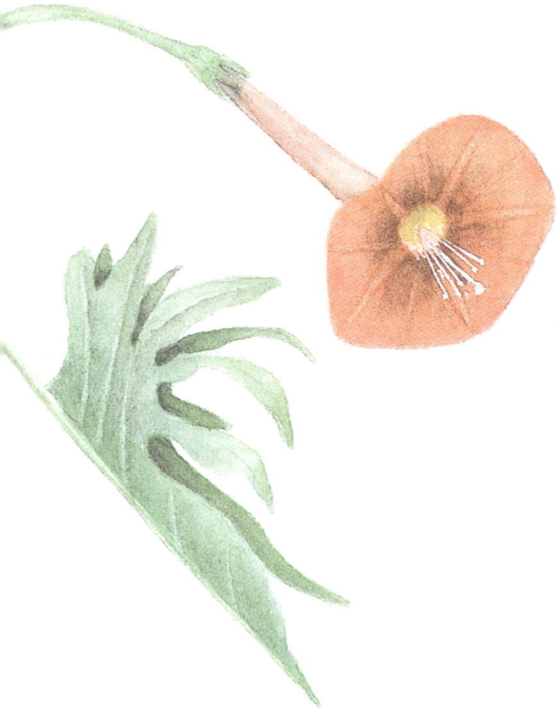

Quamoclit

This annual climber, *Quamoclit coccinea*, with its delicate trumpet-shaped flowers, is from the *Ipomoea* genus of the Convolvulaceae family that originates from Mexico. Convolvulaceae is a large family that encompasses shrubs, vines and herbs as well as vines such as the bindweeds and this particular flower.

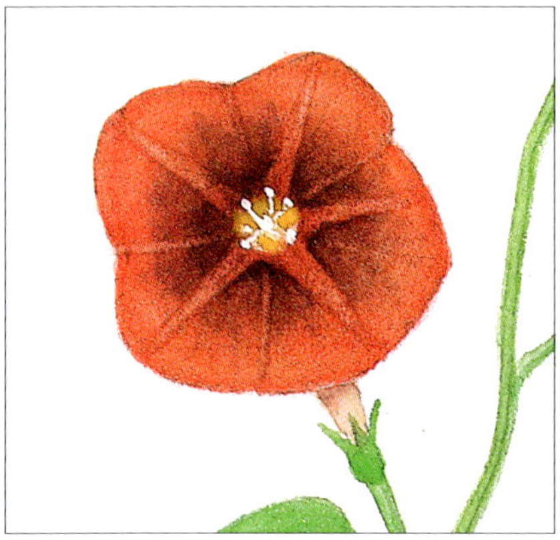

The small flowers of Quamoclit coccinea *have star-like patterns on their petals which are lighter in colour. This effect can be achieved by lifting out with a small flat brush.*

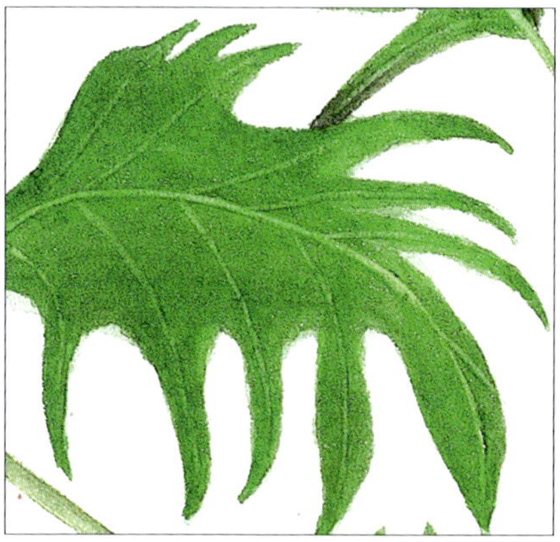

The veins on the topside of the leaves are a very pale green. Again these were lifted out with a small flat brush.

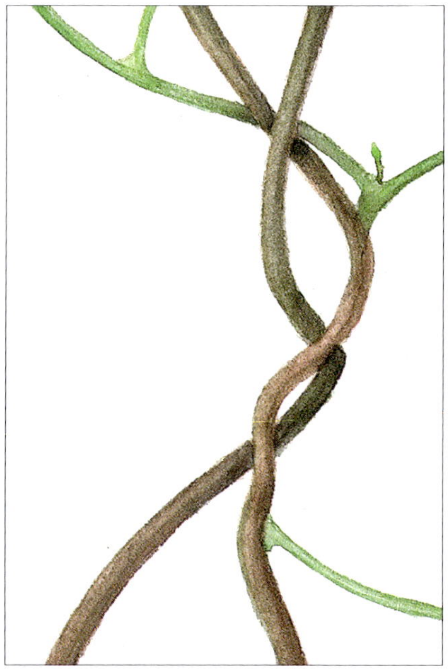

The twisting stems have many crossovers and each one should be shadowed with neutral tint.

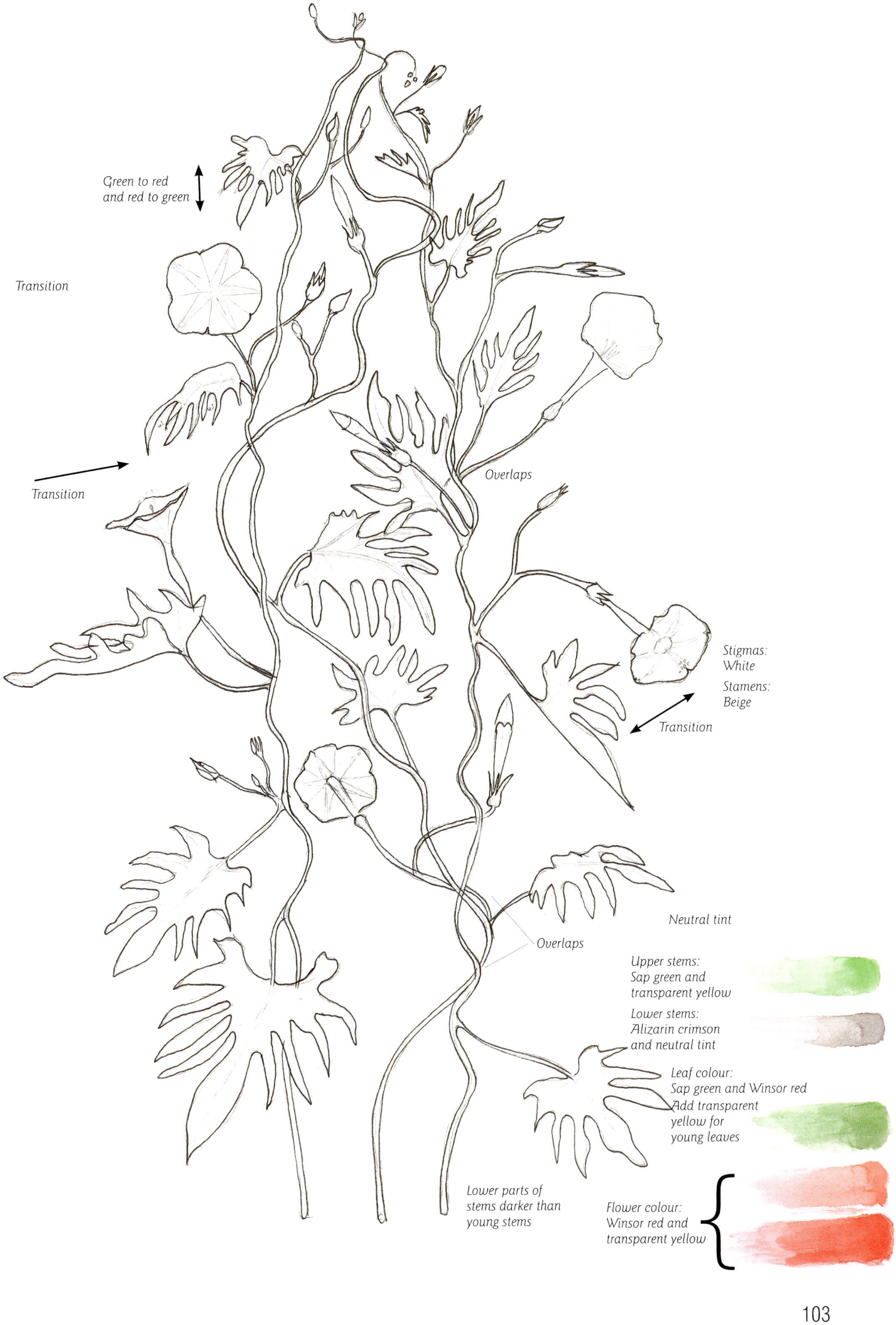

Green to red
and red to green
Transition
Transition
Overlaps
Stigmas:
White
Stamens:
Beige
Transition
Neutral tint
Overlaps
Upper stems:
Sap green and
transparent yellow
Lower stems:
Alizarin crimson
and neutral tint
Leaf colour:
Sap green and Winsor red
Add transparent
yellow for
young leaves
Lower parts of
stems darker than
young stems
Flower colour:
Winsor red and
transparent yellow

Painting the *Quamoclit*

With your sketch to hand and your colours prepared, transfer the drawing to hot-pressed watercolour paper.

First wash

1 Use a size 2 brush to glaze the flowers. Once dry, give the flowers a wash using a dilute mix of Winsor red and transparent yellow, grading from the centre outwards to give depth.

2 Change to a size 3 brush and give a wash of sap green and Winsor red to the top sides of all of the leaves except the small young leaves. Give these a wash of the same mix with transparent yellow added.

3 Returning to the size 2 brush, give the stems a dilute wash of alizarin crimson and neutral tint, changing the colour to a mix of sap green and transparent yellow towards the top of the stems.

4 Give the backs of the two flowers a very dilute wash of Winsor red.

Tonal washes

1 Using the same brush sizes and colours as in the first wash instructions, but with the slightly thicker wells, repeat the steps above. Grade into the highlights. Leave to dry thoroughly.

Crossovers

1 The light is coming from the top left, so use a size 2 brush and neutral tint to shadow each stem at the point where it crosses another on the right-hand side. Repeat this process until the stems in the foreground look separate and detached from the ones behind.

Harmonisation

1 Use a size 2 brush with a dilute mix of Winsor red and transparent yellow to wash the leaf closest to the flowers.

2 With diluted sap green and transparent yellow, wash the flower petals closest to the leaves.

Details

1 Use a size 1 brush with a dilute wash of sap green and transparent yellow to give the small buds a first wash, making sure to leave a highlight. When all these have been completed, leave them to dry.

2 With a wash of Winsor red, paint in the buds, leaving the highlight.

3 Still using the size 1 brush and Winsor red, add the detail to the back and front of the flowers.

4 With a 2mm (⅛in) flat brush and clean water, lift out the veins on the leaves.

5 Use a 0000 brush with a little white gouache to paint in the stamens and stigma.

Discretionary washes

I used a size 3 brush and a dilute mix of transparent yellow to wash every leaf just once and then left the painting to dry.

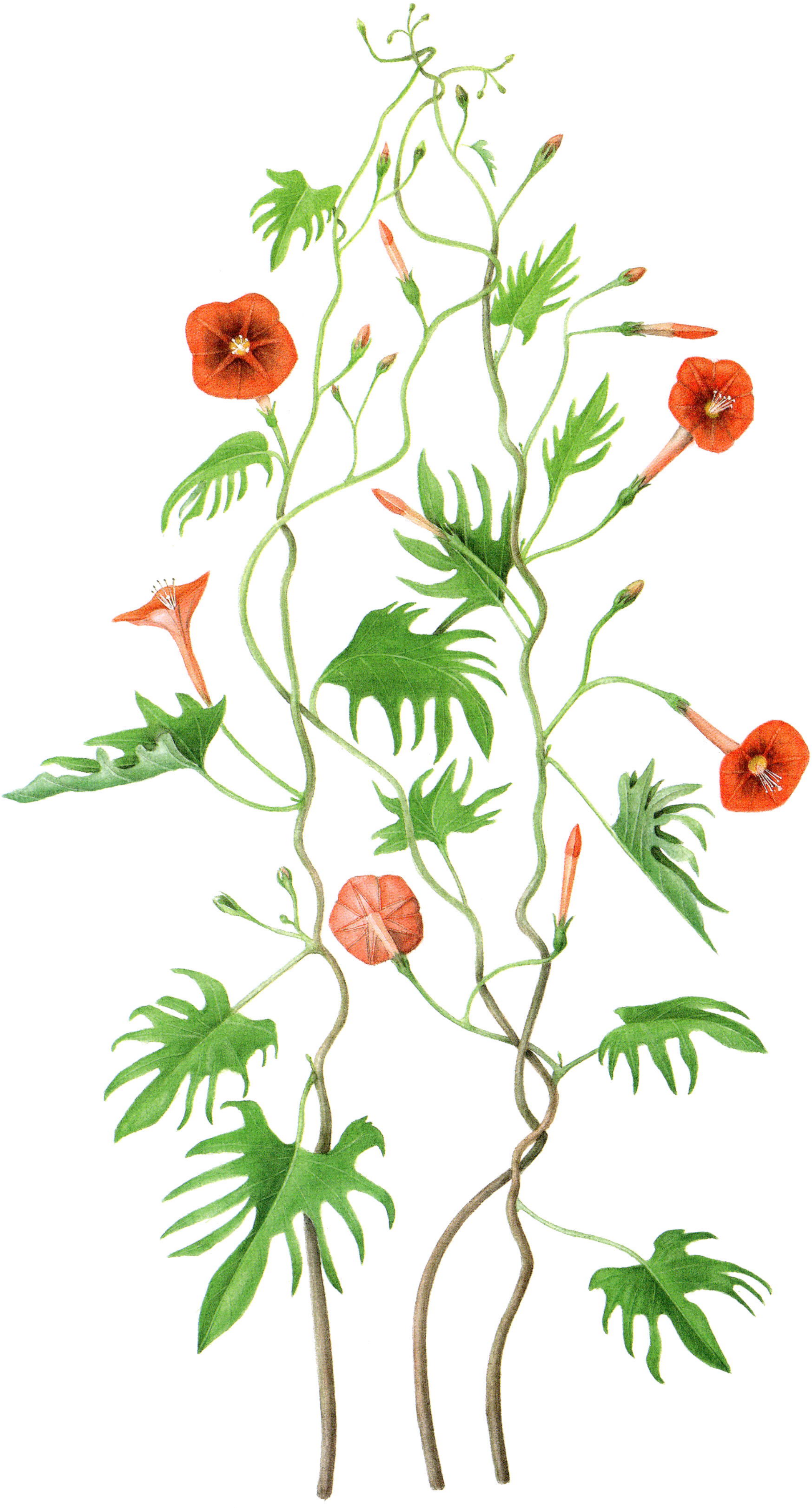

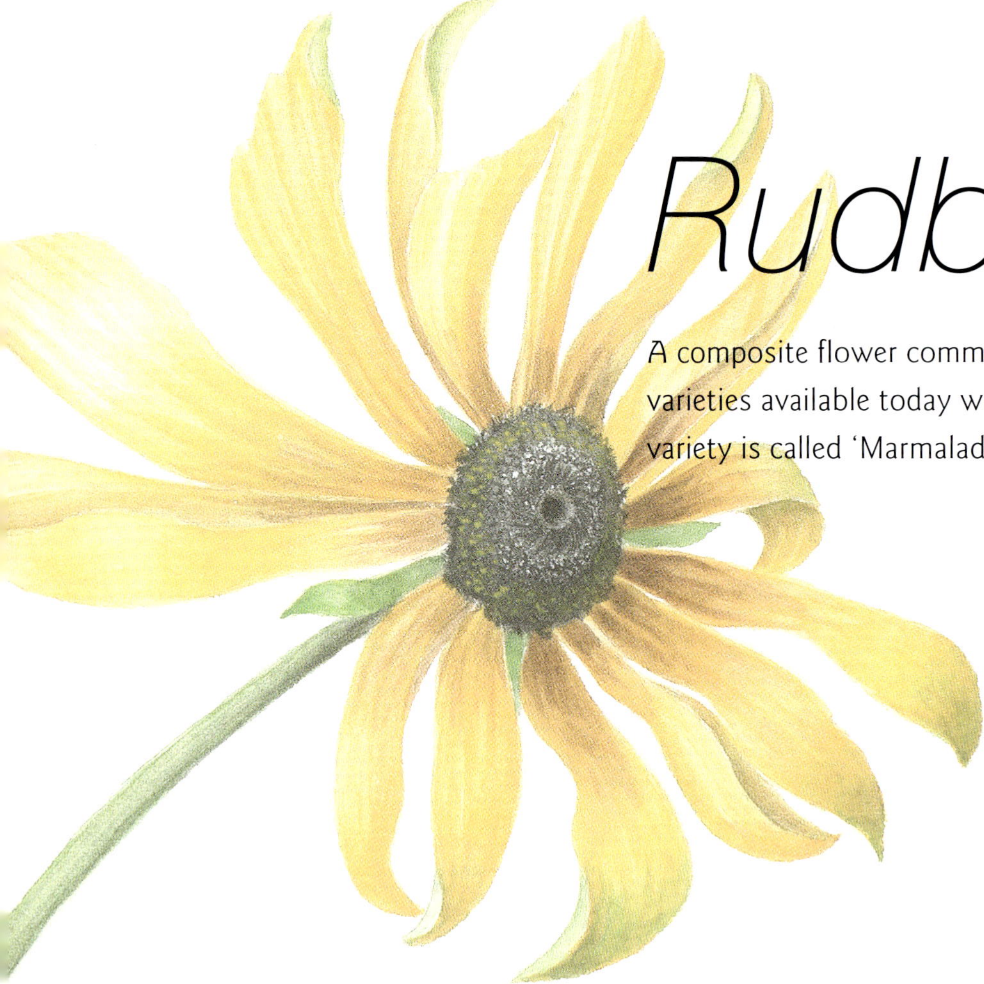

Rudbeckia

A composite flower commonly called black-eyed susan, most of the varieties available today were hybridised from the genus *Hirta*. This variety is called 'Marmalade'.

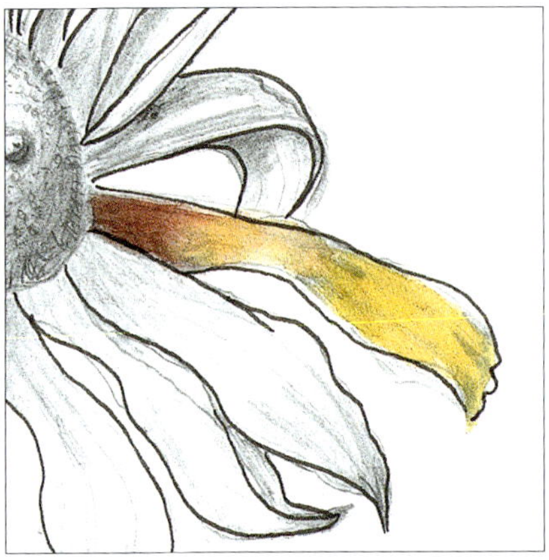

In this detail of my sketch, paint has been applied to achieve form and texture of a single petal. Preparation work in your sketchbook is vital to working out problems before starting work on your finished piece of work, but it is not necessary to do more than you need.

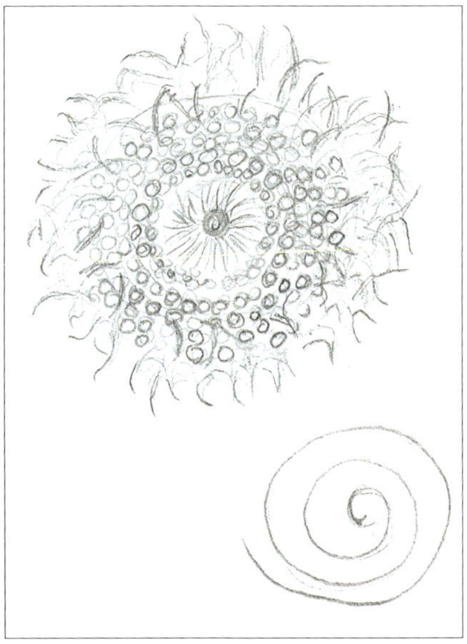

The centres of many composite flowers are very complex. This pencil drawing shows the basic spiral pattern evident in many species. Work out the patterning in your sketchbook, then paint or draw on your real painting.

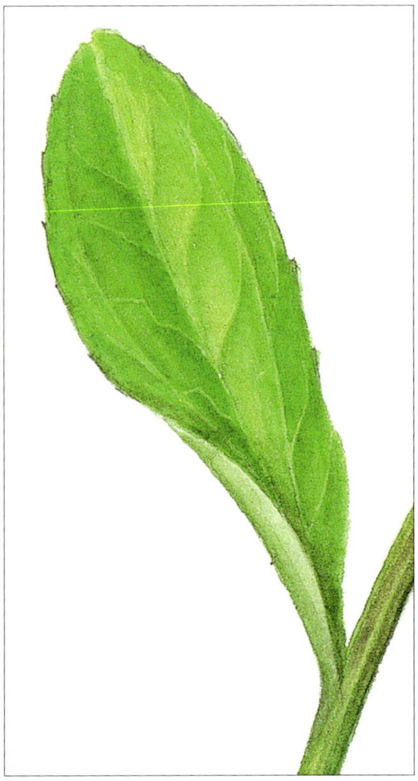

Note how the leaf stem fits to the stalk when painted. It should blend smoothly into the shape of the stalk.

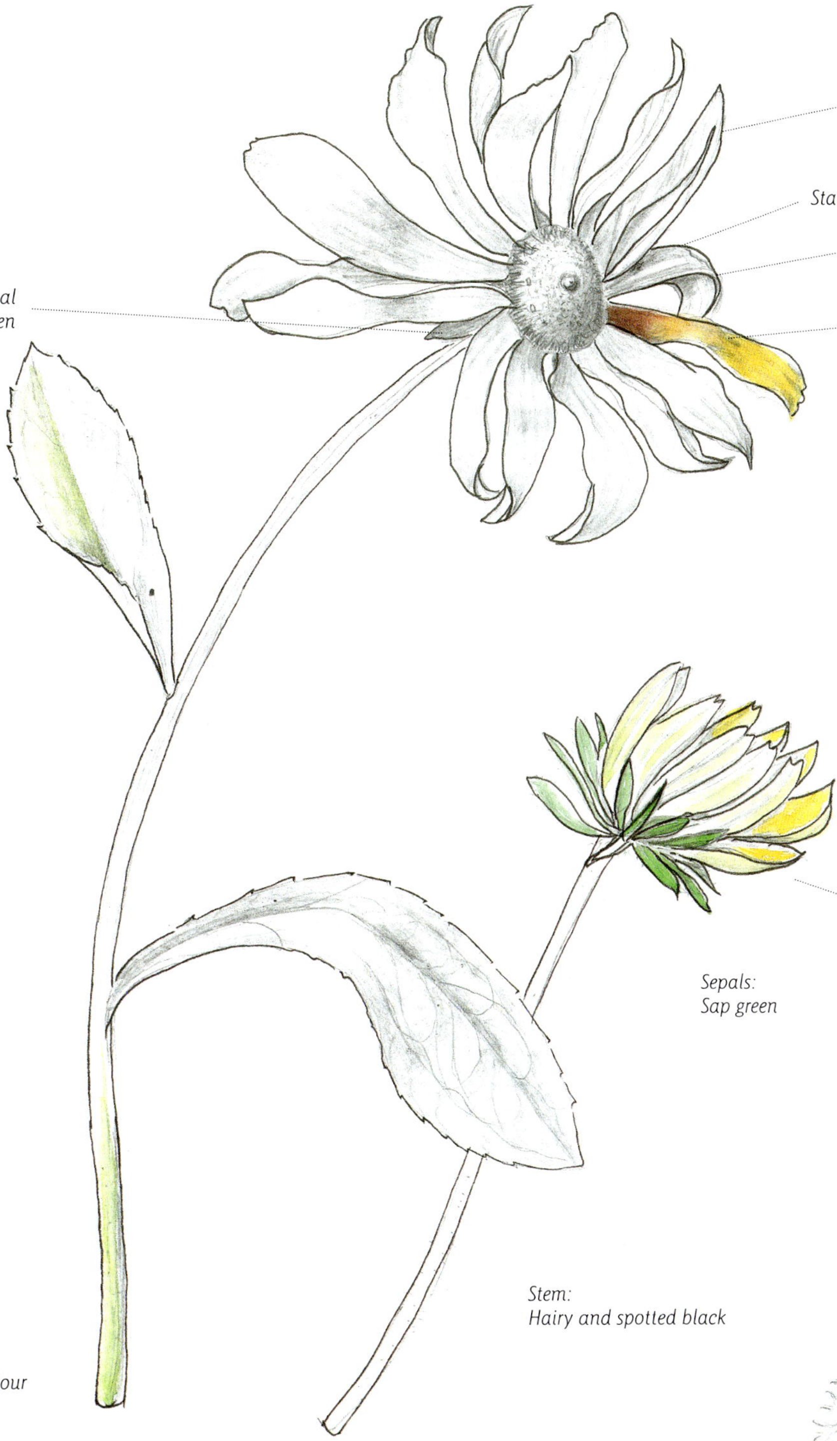

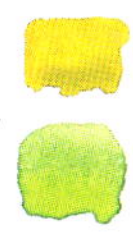

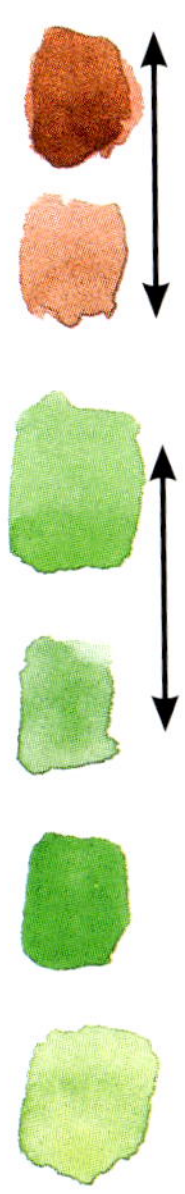

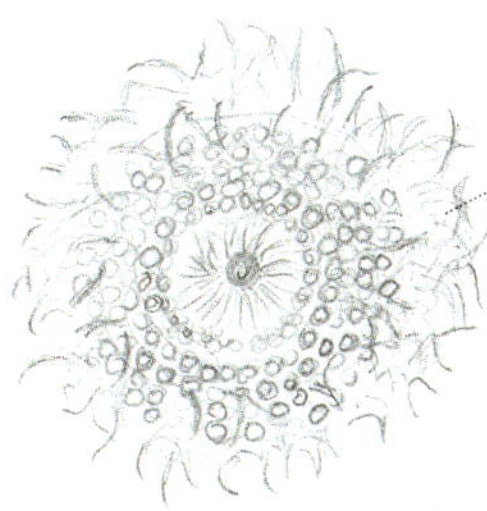

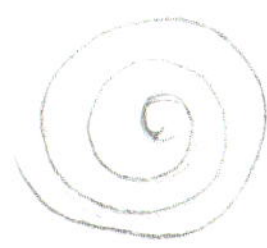

Spiral pattern

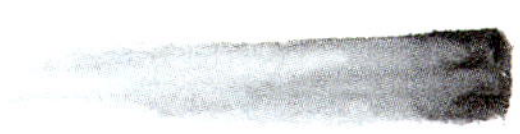

Neutral tint

Painting the *Rudbeckia*

With your sketch to hand and your colours prepared, transfer the drawing to hot-pressed watercolour paper.

First wash

1 Use a size 3 brush to glaze all of the petals with clean water. Once dry, use a dilute mix of cadmium yellow to paint the first wash on alternate petals so that the washes do not run into each other. Grade the paint from the flower centres into the highlights to create form, using strokes that follow the shape of the petals on the large flowerhead.

2 With the same brush, glaze the leaves and flower stems together with the petals on the small flowerhead and allow them to dry.

3 Use a size 2 brush and the same dilute cadmium yellow mix to paint the inside of the petals on the small flower.

4 When dry, add a little sap green to the mix and paint the outer petals, grading into the highlights.

5 Using a size 3 brush with a dilute mix of sap green and Winsor yellow, apply the first wash to the leaves, grading the paint from dark to light areas. Apply the same mix to the flower stems, grading from right to left and leaving the centres of the stems lighter in tone to create form.

6 Using a size 2 brush and a dilute mix of sap green, paint in the sepals on both the large and small flowers.

7 Still using the size 2 brush, paint in the centre of the flowers with a dilute mix of neutral tint and alizarin crimson, making sure to leave a highlight at the top left of the circle to create form and shape.

Tonal washes

1 Referring to the first wash instructions above for the brush size and colour washes to use, build up the form of all of the components with the stronger wells of the appropriate colours, making sure to grade each wash.

2 Use a size 2 brush and a dilute mix of alizarin crimson and burnt sienna to start to paint in the darker tones on the petals of the large flower. Use a dry brush technique and grade the paint into the yellow. The tips of the right-hand petals should be painted at the same time, as they are in the shadow areas.

Crossovers

1 Mix alizarin crimson and burnt sienna with a little neutral tint, and use a size 2 brush to paint in the small areas where the petals overlap on the large flower, being careful to grade out the colour.

2 Repeat this on the smaller unopened flowerhead and the sepals.

3 Paint the areas at the top of the stem under the sepals in the same way, plus any areas where the leaf overlaps the stem on the small flower, and at the base of the leaves where they are attached to the stem.

4 Repeat the washes until the tones are sufficiently dark.

Harmonisation

1 Use a size 3 brush with a mix of transparent yellow to apply a small wash to the tops of the leaves.

2 With a dilute mix of sap green, apply a small wash to the lower petals on both flowerheads.

Details

1 Using a size 1 brush and a stronger mix of alizarin crimson and neutral tint, start to paint in the stigmas and stamens on the large flowerhead, working in a clockwise spiral motion as per the magnified pencil drawing. Use lighter tones and allow to dry.

2 Switch to a size 1 brush and a stronger mix of cadmium yellow to add the pollen.

3 Lift the paint a little on the two curls on the underside of the leaves with a 2mm (⅛in) flat brush and clean water.

4 Use an HB pencil to draw the seed head scaled at twice life size, referring to your microscope to ensure you have accurate information.

Details

The use of mixed media is perfectly acceptable in botanical illustrations.

Discretionary washes

I used a size 5 brush and a dilute mix of sap green and transparent yellow to paint a wash over both leaves and both stems.

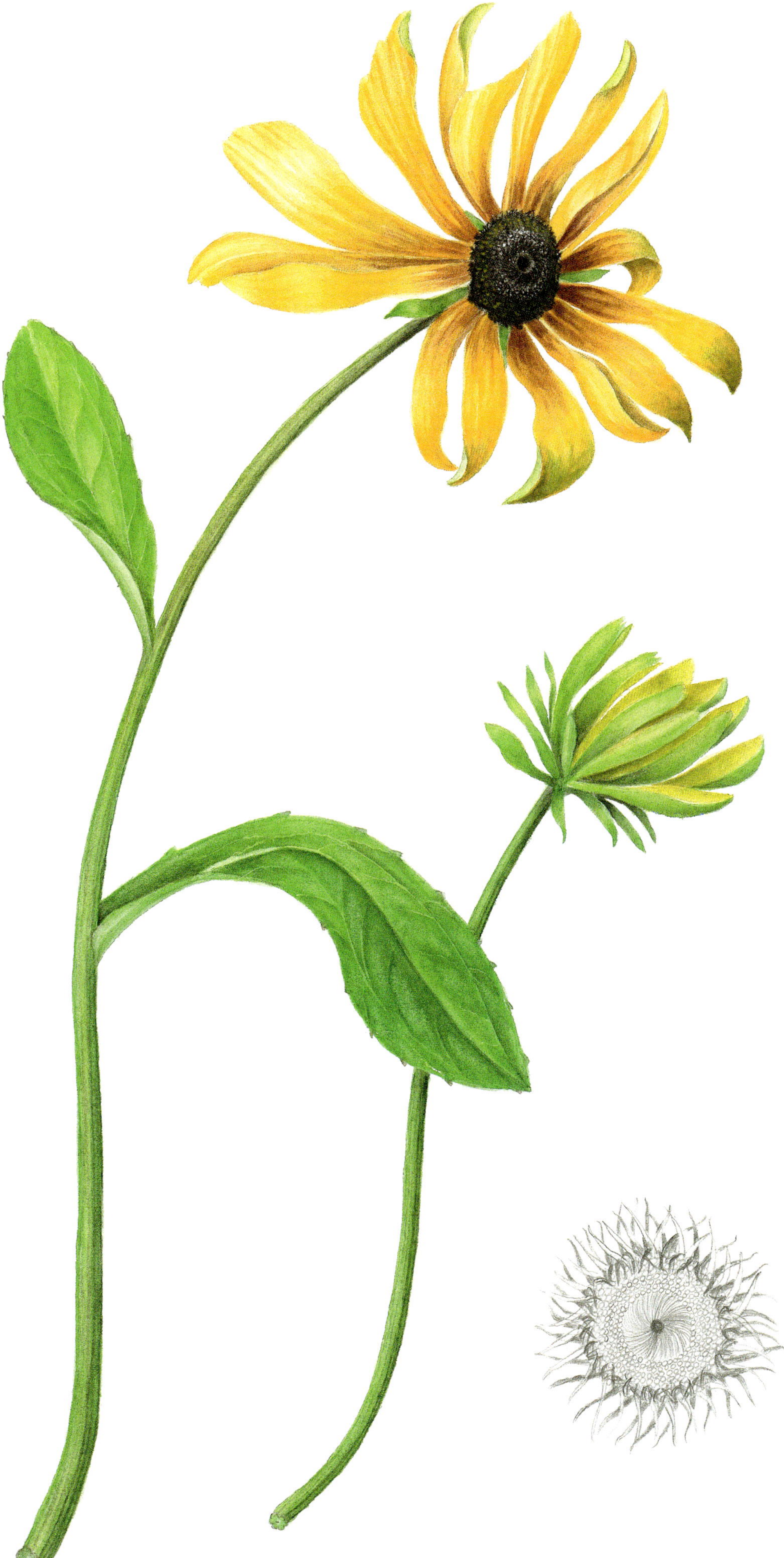

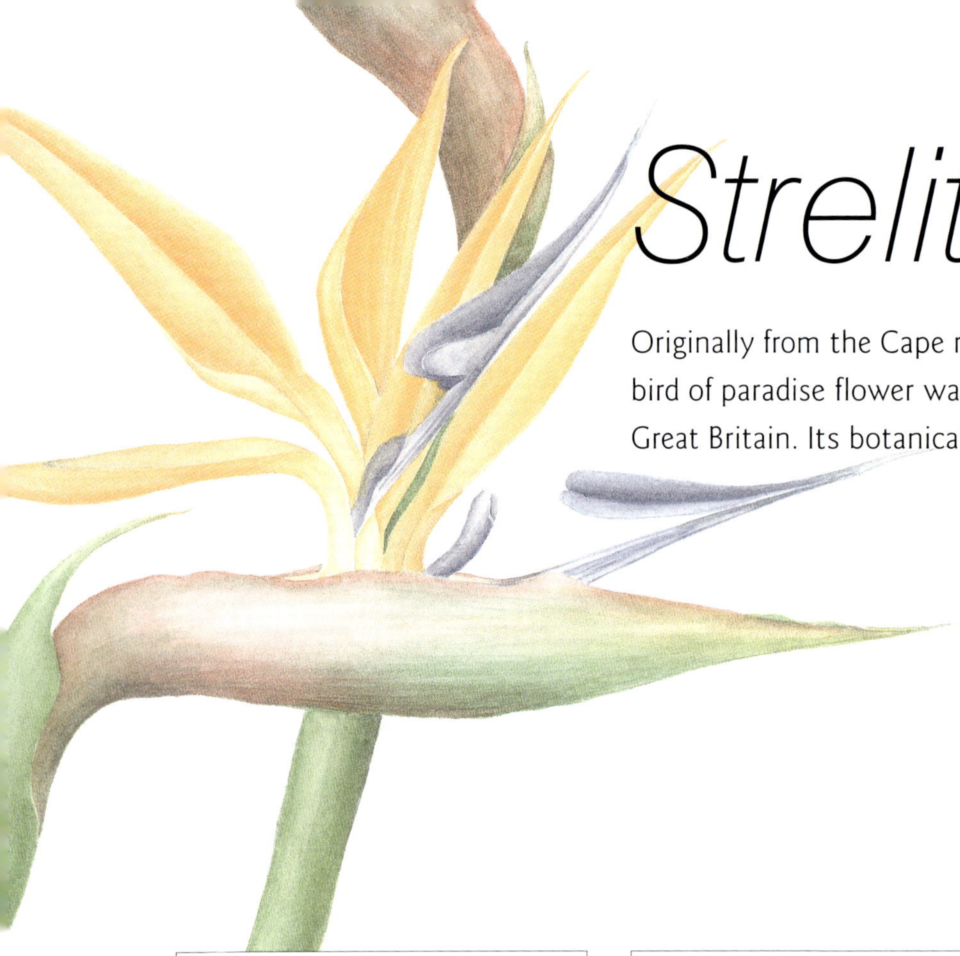

Strelitzia

Originally from the Cape region of South Africa, this exotic-looking bird of paradise flower was named in honour of Queen Charlotte of Great Britain. Its botanical name is *Strelitzia reginae*.

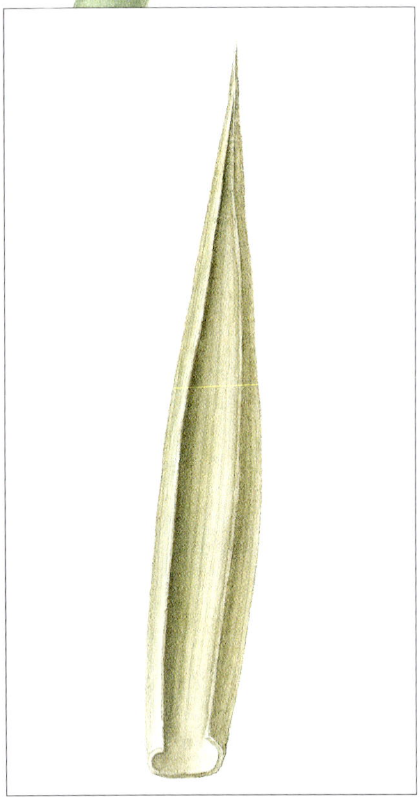

This sheath housed the main flower before becoming detatched. Plant components such as this make for interesting details on your painting, and are worth just as much time and effort as the other parts of the plant. With the light source coming from the top left, the shadow is on the left-hand side inside the sheath and the right-hand side is catching all of the light. This gives the illusion that the inside is hollow.

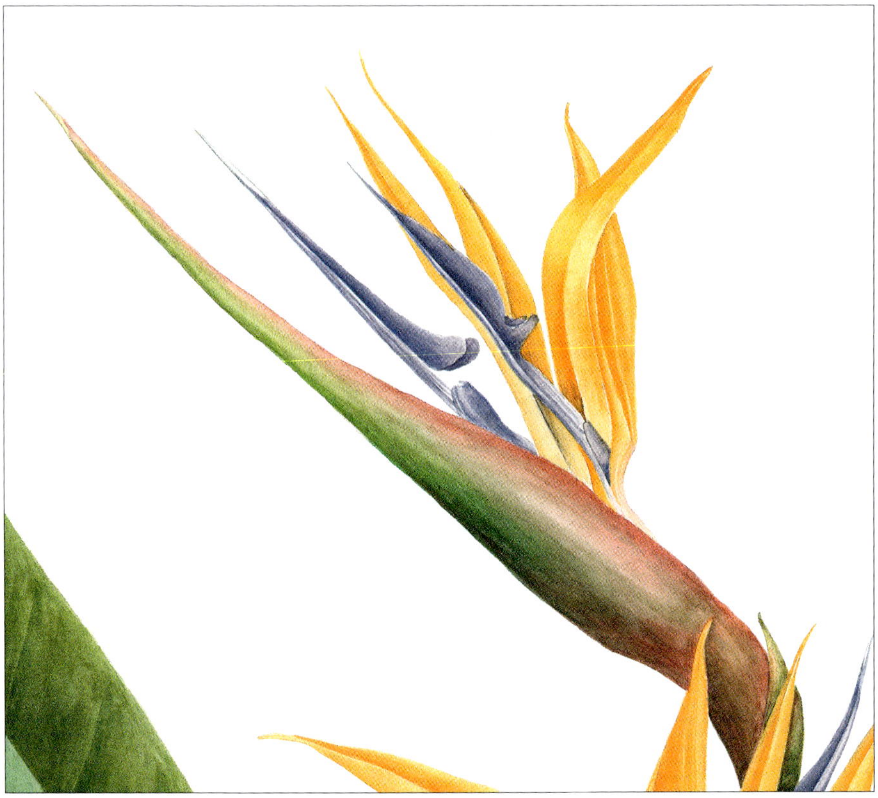

When painting the beak of the flower, care must be taken to grade each colour into the others to achieve a subtle change without hard edges. This is achieved by not using too much water in either the first wash and tonal wash stages.

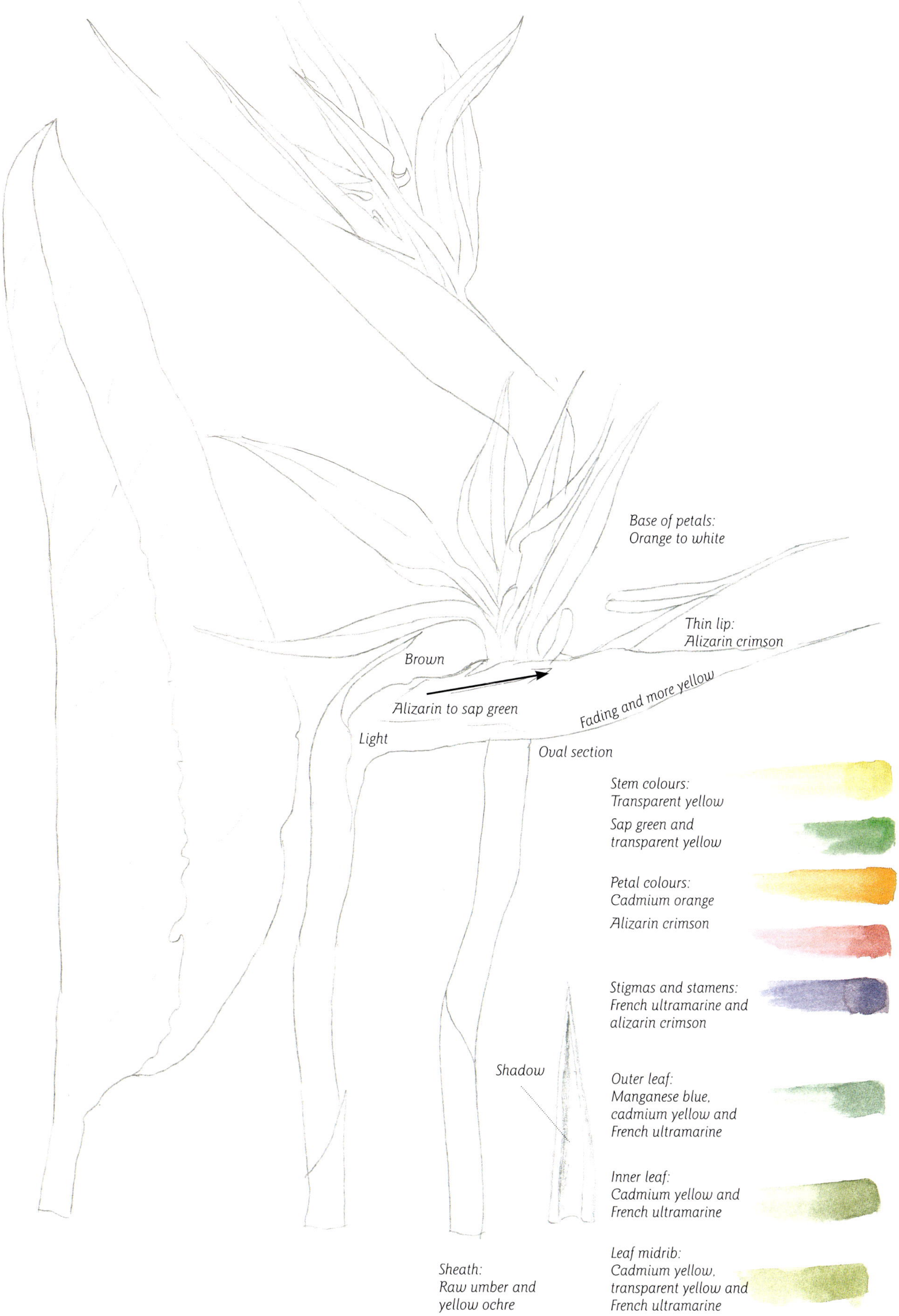
Base of petals:
Orange to white
Thin lip:
Alizarin crimson
Brown
Alizarin to sap green
Fading and more yellow
Light
Oval section
Stem colours:
Transparent yellow
Sap green and
transparent yellow
Petal colours:
Cadmium orange
Alizarin crimson
Stigmas and stamens:
French ultramarine and
alizarin crimson
Shadow
Outer leaf:
Manganese blue,
cadmium yellow and
French ultramarine
Inner leaf:
Cadmium yellow and
French ultramarine
Sheath:
Raw umber and
yellow ochre
Leaf midrib:
Cadmium yellow,
transparent yellow and
French ultramarine

Painting the *Strelitzia*

Prepare your wells of colours and place your sketch close by before transferring the drawing to hot-pressed watercolour paper.

First wash

1 Using a size 5 brush, glaze all of the flower petals, stigmas and stamen with clean water. Once dry, use a dilute mix of cadmium orange and transparent yellow to apply the first wash to the petals, grading from the shadow areas into the highlights. Repeat the process on the second flower.

2 Switch to a size 2 brush and use a dilute mix of French ultramarine and alizarin crimson to apply the first wash to the stigmas and stamens, again grading the paint to suggest the form.

3 With a size 5 brush, glaze the sheath and stems with clean water and leave them to dry, then use a dilute mix of sap green to paint the underside of the sheath grading into the centre.

4 Using the same size brush and a dilute mix of sap green and a little alizarin crimson, paint the two stems grading them from right to left and keeping the centre of each a lighter tone.

5 Use a size 6 brush to glaze the large leaf and midrib with clean water. Once dry, use a dilute mix of manganese blue, cadmium yellow and French ultramarine to paint the back of the leaf (outer – see page 111), grading from the midrib to the margin. Leave to dry.

6 Using the same brush and a dilute mix of cadmium yellow and French ultramarine, wash the inside of the leaf, grading the paint from left to right.

7 Paint in the midrib using a dilute mix of cadmium yellow, French ultramarine and a little transparent yellow, leaving the centre section a lighter tone.

8 Glaze the brown sheath using a size 2 brush and clean water. Once dry, use a dilute mix of raw umber and yellow ochre to paint the sheath, using vertical strokes and grading into the highlights.

Tonal washes

1 Using the same size brushes and stronger mixes of the colours, repeat the process in the first wash steps, making sure to leave the highlights in lighter tones.

2 When painting the sheath, use horizontal strokes to form the lines. Let each wash dry before applying another. Lift out the veins on the leaf with a 2mm (⅛in) flat brush.

Crossovers

1 With a size 1 brush, apply a dilute mix of neutral tint to the areas that overlap each other, paying particular attention to the petals over the sheath and the sheath over the stems.

2 Allowing each layer to dry before applying the next, repeat the application of the washes until the depth of colour gives the correct impression of distance between the components.

3 Using the same mix and a size 2 brush, add the shadows behind the veins to add emphasis to them.

Harmonisation

1 Use a size 3 brush and a dilute mix of sap green to paint a small wash underneath the sheath on the top flower, grading into the alizarin crimson. Apply the same wash to the underside of the lower sheath.

2 With a dilute mix of cadmium orange, apply a small wash to the top right-hand side of the inner leaf.

Details

1 Using a mix of cadmium orange and transparent yellow and a size 1 brush, sharpen up the points on the flower petals.

2 With the same brush, use French ultramarine to paint the sharp points of the stigmas.

Discretionary washes

I used a size 6 brush and a dilute mix of manganese blue to wash the underside of the leaf, then added sap green to the mix to wash the inside of the leaf. The two stems were washed over with a dilute mix of transparent yellow using the size 6 brush.

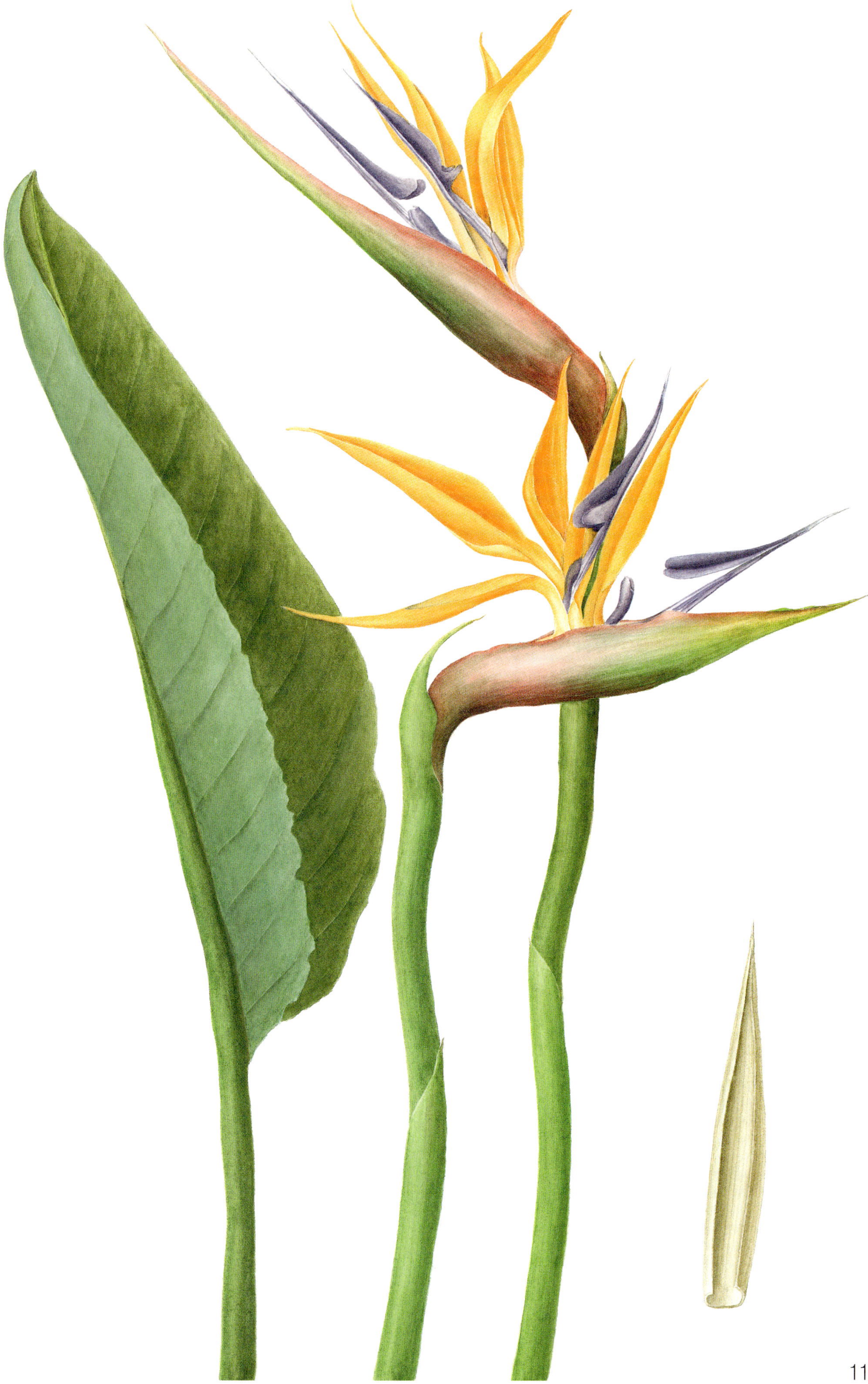

Tulipa

The tulip is now forever associated with Holland, but it originated in Turkey, and was popular in France before being introduced to the Netherlands. A craze for tulips in the seventeenth and eighteenth centuries led to particularly unusually-coloured varieties, prized specimens of which commanded extraordinary prices. This cultivar is 'Ballerina'.

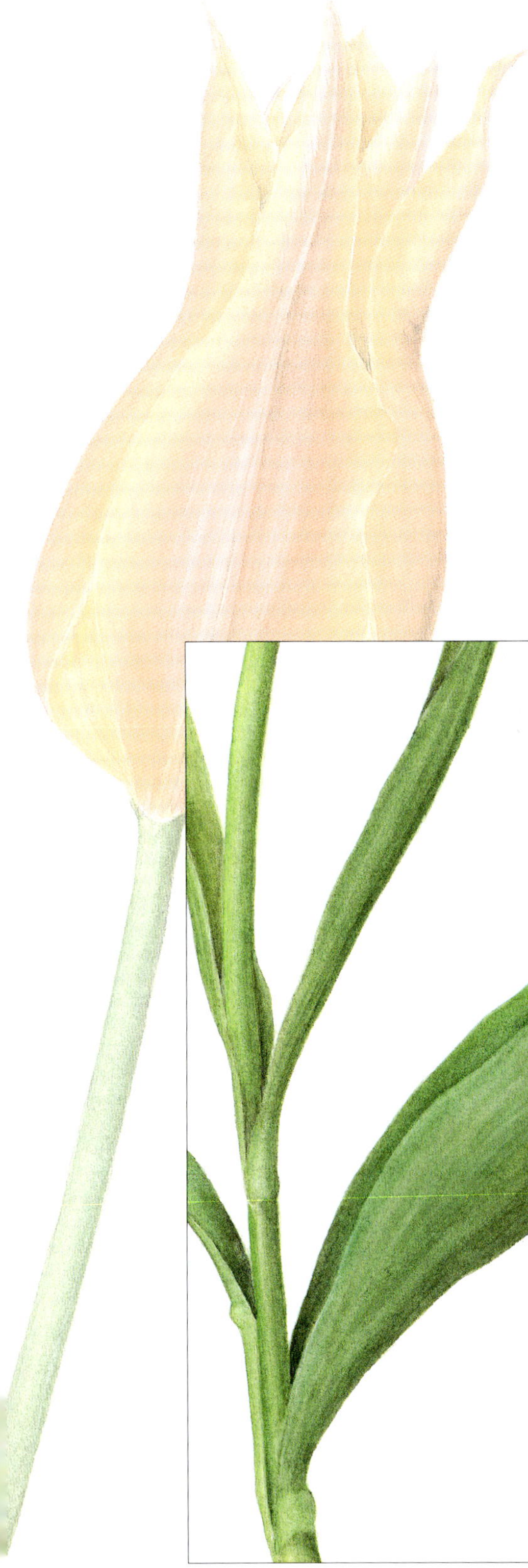

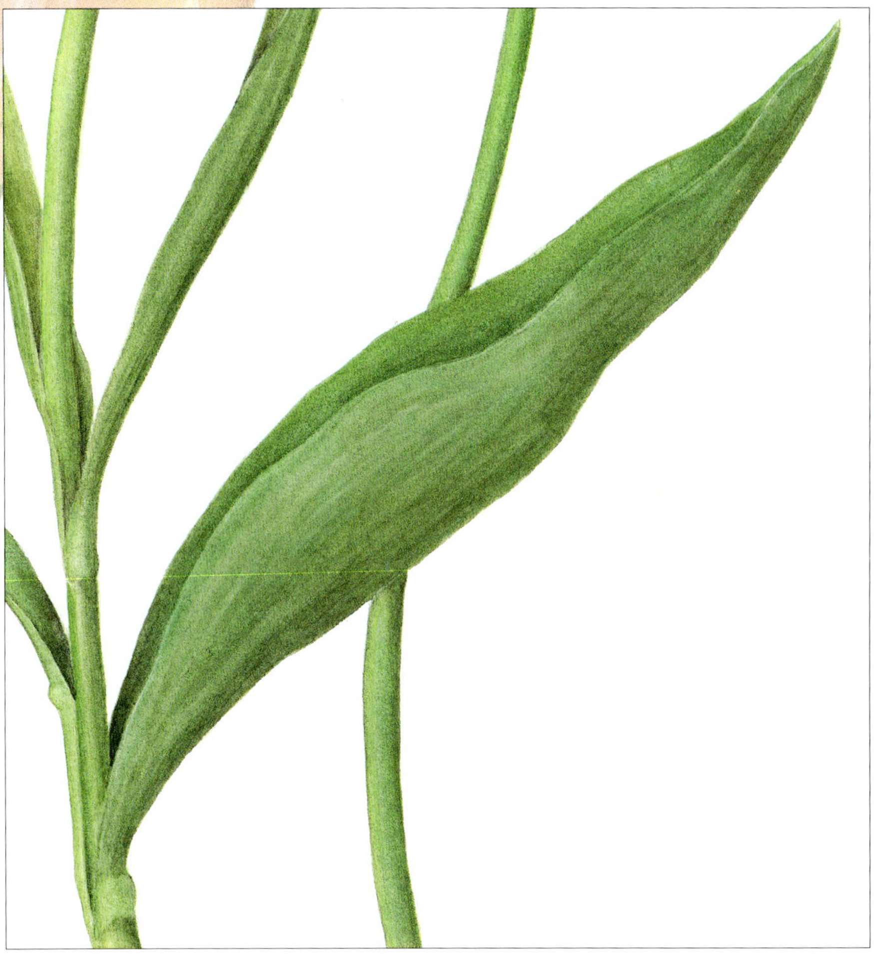

When painting the large tulip leaf it is good practice to apply the washes in vertical strokes. To achieve the narrow lines in the leaf, work with fairly dry paint. Using wetter paint will result in lines that are too wide.

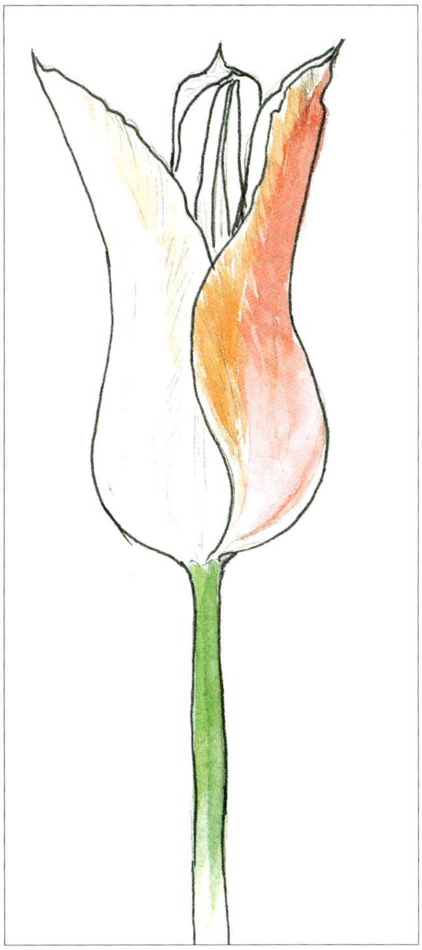

With several colours merging into each other you will have to work out the placement of each colour. This is best done in your sketchbook beforehand: apply the various colours to your sketch until you are confident enough to proceed with the finished piece.

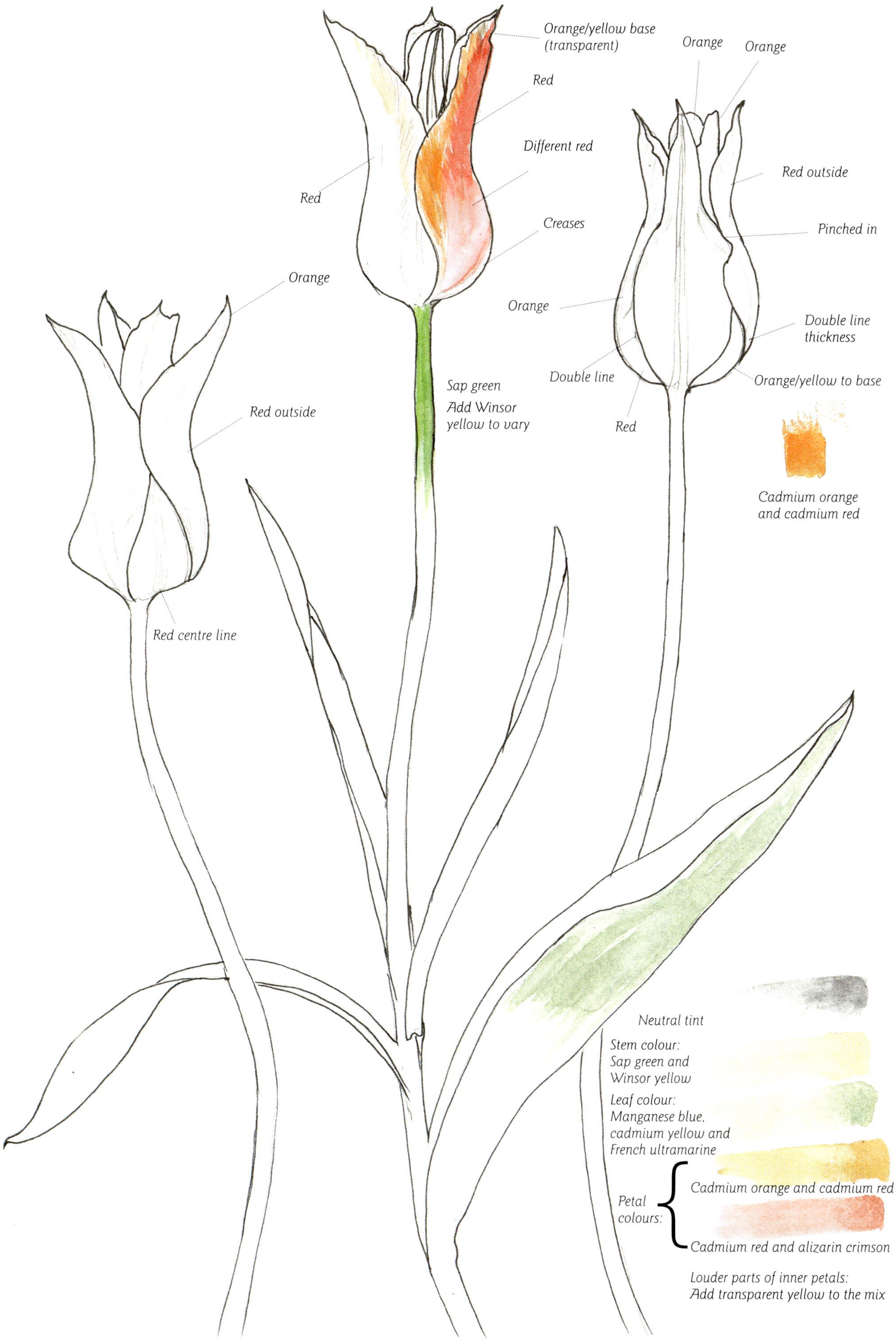

Orange/yellow base (transparent)
Orange
Orange
Red
Red
Different red
Red outside
Pinched in
Creases
Orange
Orange
Double line thickness
Red outside
Sap green
Add Winsor yellow to vary
Double line
Orange/yellow to base
Red
Cadmium orange and cadmium red
Red centre line
Neutral tint
Stem colour:
Sap green and Winsor yellow
Leaf colour:
Manganese blue, cadmium yellow and French ultramarine
Petal colours:
Cadmium orange and cadmium red
Cadmium red and alizarin crimson
Louder parts of inner petals:
Add transparent yellow to the mix

Painting the *Tulipa*

With your sketch to hand and your colours prepared, transfer the drawing to hot-pressed watercolour paper.

First wash

1 Using a size 3 brush and clean water, glaze over all of the petals and leave them to dry. With a dilute mix of cadmium orange and cadmium red, grade from the outer, lighter parts of the petals.

2 Glaze all of the leaves with clean water. Once dry, use a dilute mix of manganese blue, cadmium yellow and a little French ultramarine to paint the leaves, grading into the highlights.

3 Glaze the stems with clean water and, when dry, apply a mix of sap green and Winsor yellow, starting on the right-hand side and grading to the left.

4 Add transparent yellow to the petal mix (cadmium orange and cadmium red) and apply it to the lower inner petals, leaving the midrib unpainted.

Tonal washes

1 With a size 3 brush and a slightly thicker mix of cadmium orange and cadmium red, grade from the outer lighter parts of the petals.

2 Once dry, use a mix of cadmium red and alizarin crimson, paint the darker red parts of the petals, avoiding the midribs. Leave the portrait to dry.

3 Apply several washes in the same way to build up the tone and form, blending the cadmium orange and cadmium red mix with dry brushwork to give the petals texture.

4 Use a size 5 brush and a stronger mix of the leaf colour (manganese blue, cadmium yellow and a little French ultramarine) to paint the larger leaf with long strokes to give the leaf its striped texture. Repeat this on the underside of the remaining three leaves.

5 Add transparent yellow to the leaf mix to paint the inner parts of the leaves, grading into the highlights. Build up the form of all of the stems using a size 3 brush and the mix as above.

Crossovers

1 With a size 2 brush and neutral tint added to the outer leaf mix (manganese blue, cadmium yellow and a little French ultramarine), shade the stems where they cross the leaves, painting in a small triangle of the mix and grading out to the lighter areas.

2 Use the same mix at the base of the leaves to give them distance from the stems.

3 Add neutral tint to the alizarin crimson and cadmium red mix to darken the areas of the petals in shadow, especially on the right-hand side of the three blooms and to the right of the petal midribs.

Harmonisation

1 Use a size 3 brush with a dilute mix of cadmium orange and cadmium red to wash a thin layer on to the tops of the leaves at the point where they are closest to the flowerheads.

2 Make a dilute mix of sap green and Winsor yellow and wash the lower petals of the left-hand flower.

Details

1 Sharpen the points of all of the flower petals with a size 1 brush and a mix of cadmium red and cadmium orange.

2 Use the same mix to paint in the centre lines in the middle of the midribs on the petals, and to tidy up the lines at the base of the flowerheads where they met the stems.

Discretionary washes

I used a size 5 brush and a dilute mix of transparent yellow to wash all of the leaves including the highlights. I then used the same mix to wash over all of the flowerheads, keeping accurately to the edges of the flowers and leaves.

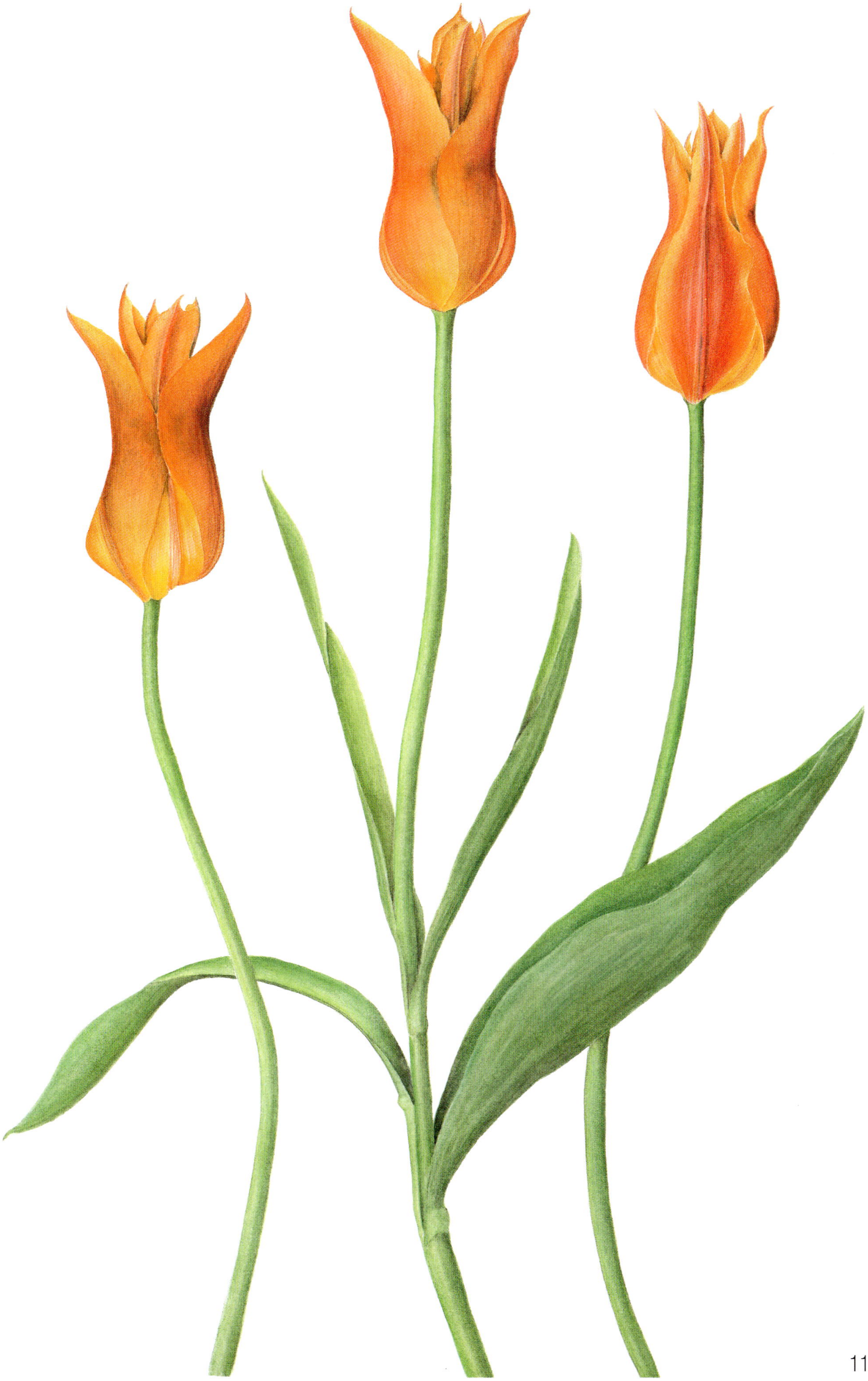

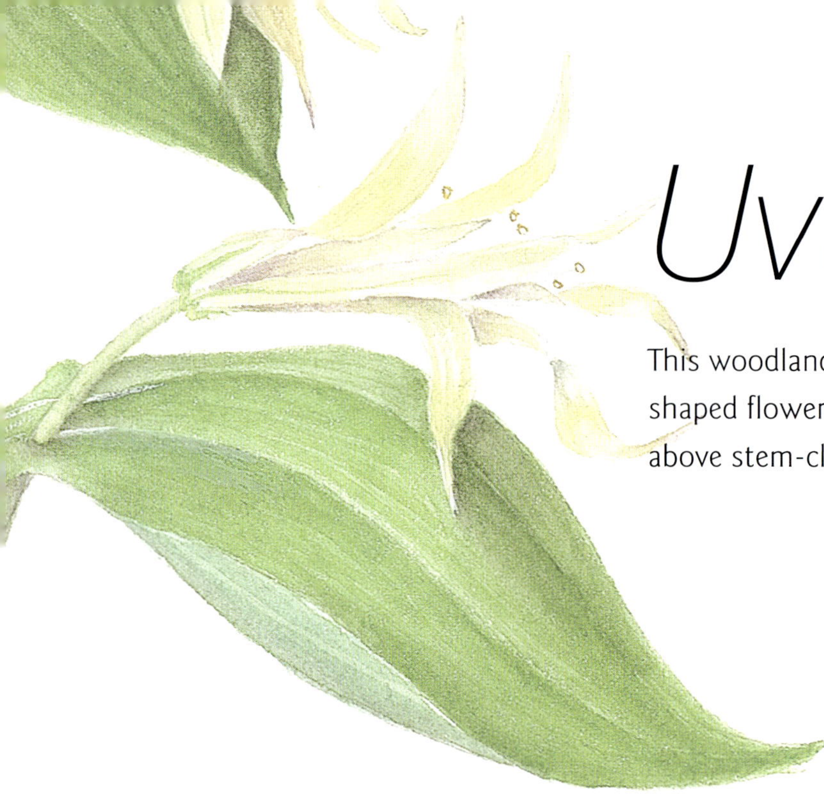

Uvularia

This woodland plant, *Uvularia perfoliata*, has creamy yellow bell-shaped flowers which appear in spring on numerous slender stems above stem-clasping narrow oval leaves.

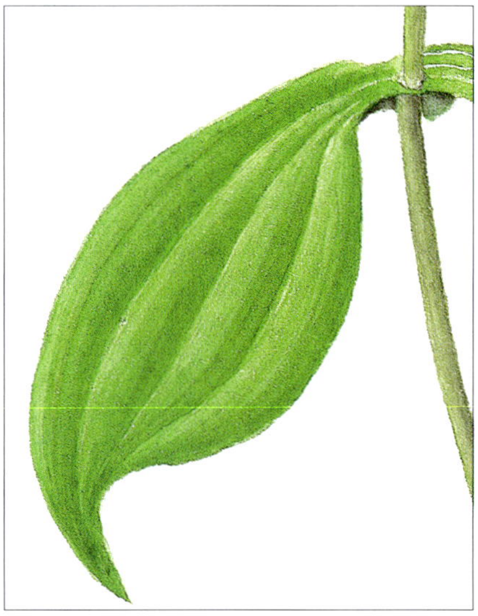

The leaves of Uvularia perfoliata *are ribbed. To achieve this effect, apply your first dilute washes to the right-hand side of each vein and grade to the centre of the rib. As you apply more washes the ribs will become more promenent. Note the unusual stem-clasping of the leaves.*

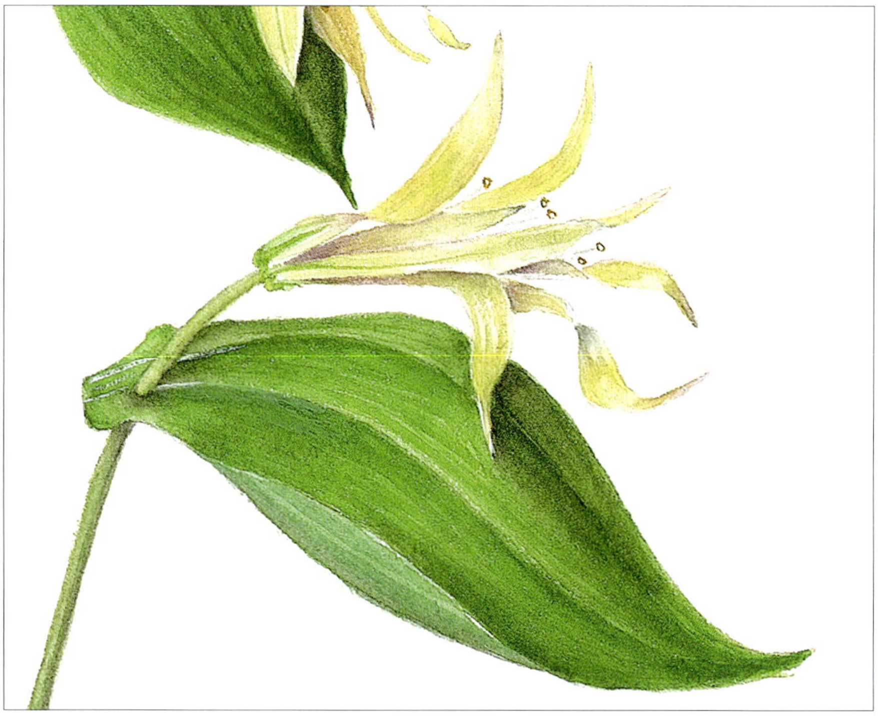

The flower stems are most unusual in the way in which they emerge through the leaves. Fortunately this is a bonus to the botanical artist as the leaf forms a natural backdrop for the much lighter-toned flower.

Sketching

The stem clasping of Uvularia perfoliata *is quite unusual, so make a note of 'Us' for the underside of the leaves and 'T' for the top sides on your sketch. Refer to it regularly when painting to avoid painting the different areas with the wrong mix.*

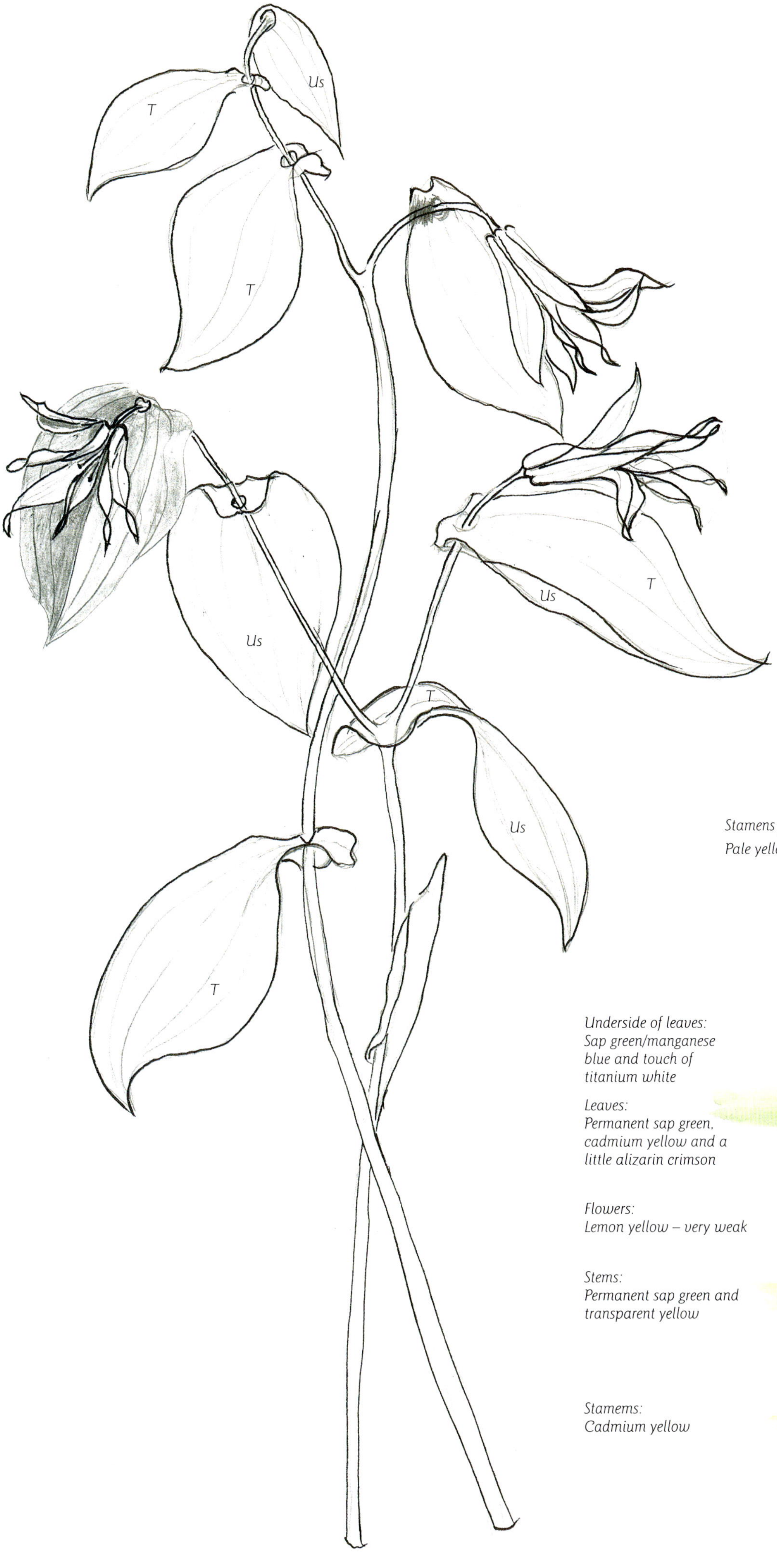

Underside of leaves:
Sap green/manganese blue and touch of titanium white

Leaves:
Permanent sap green, cadmium yellow and a little alizarin crimson

Flowers:
Lemon yellow – very weak

Stems:
Permanent sap green and transparent yellow

Stamems:
Cadmium yellow

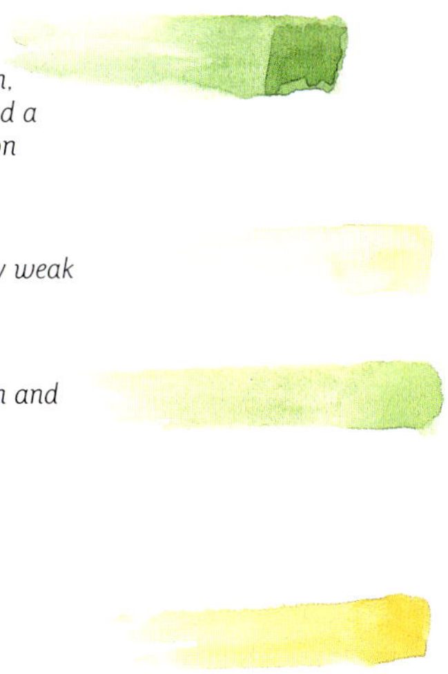

Painting the *Uvularia*

With your sketch to hand and your colours prepared, transfer the drawing to hot-pressed watercolour paper.

First wash

1 Use a size 1 brush to glaze all of the petals with clear water and leave them to dry. With a dilute wash of lemon yellow, paint in the petals, grading the colour to keep the highlights unpainted and to suggest form.

2 Swap to a size 3 brush and glaze all of the leaves – both top and underside – with clean water. Once dry, make a dilute wash of sap green and cadmium yellow with a little alizarin crimson and wash the leaves, grading from right to left between the veins to create surface modelling.

3 Glaze the stems with clean water and leave them to dry, then use a dilute wash of sap green and transparent yellow to paint them. Apply the wash to the right-hand side and grade it into the highlight.

4 With a mix of sap green, manganese blue and titanium white, paint the underside of the leaves.

Tonal washes

1 Using a size 1 brush and the stronger wells of lemon yellow, continue to paint the petals, starting with the darker areas and grading into the highlights.

2 Change to a size 3 brush and a slightly thicker top side leaf mix (sap green and cadmium yellow with a little alizarin crimson), starting with the top of the leaf. Continue to darken and build up the form and tone, leaving the veins unpainted.

3 Repeat the process on the underside of the leaves using the stronger wells of the underside mix (sap green, manganese blue and titanium white).

4 With a size 1 brush and the stronger mix of sap green and transparent yellow, paint the stems until the form looks correct.

Crossovers

1 Using a size 2 brush and a dilute mix of sap green and neutral tint, shadow the right-hand side of the flower petal at the point where the petals are on top of the leaves. This helps to make the flowers stand out from the darker leaves.

2 Shadow the petals at the point where they overlap each other, to make the petals look more individual, using a size 1 brush and a dilute mix of neutral tint.

3 With the same mix and brush, shadow the veins on the underside of the leaves, applying the paint to the right-hand side of the veins.

4 Shadow the stems at the point where they cross and in the centre of the lower young leaf, again using the same mix.

Harmonisation

1 Using a size 2 brush and a dilute mix of transparent yellow, wash over all of the leaves that are behind the flowers.

2 Add a little sap green to the mix and wash over the petals.

Details

1 With a size 0 brush and a little white gouache, paint in the styles and stamens, then sharpen up the areas where the stems meet the leaves.

Discretionary washes

Using a size 3 brush and a dilute mix of transparent yellow and sap green, I washed over all of the leaves including the undersides, and the stems.

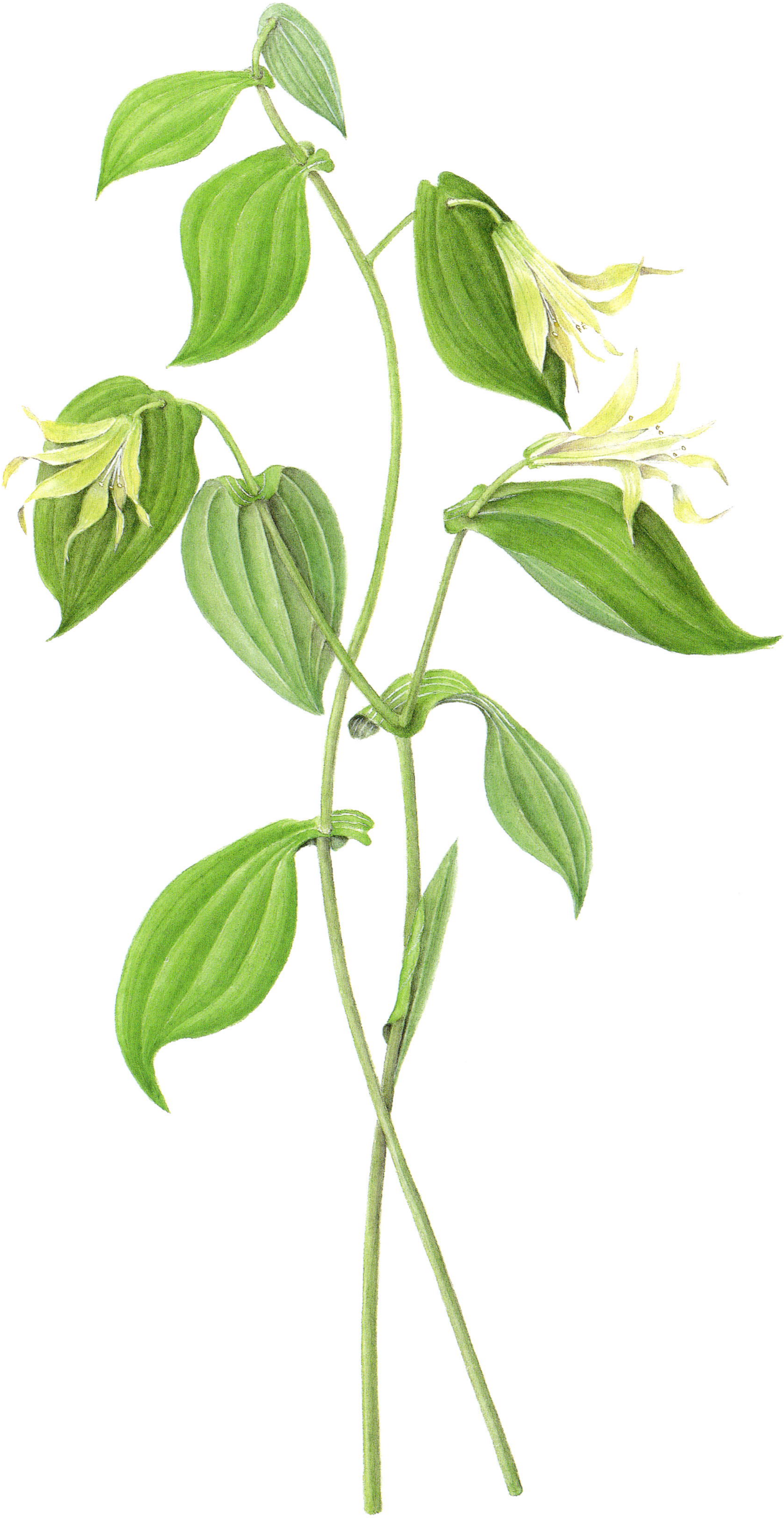

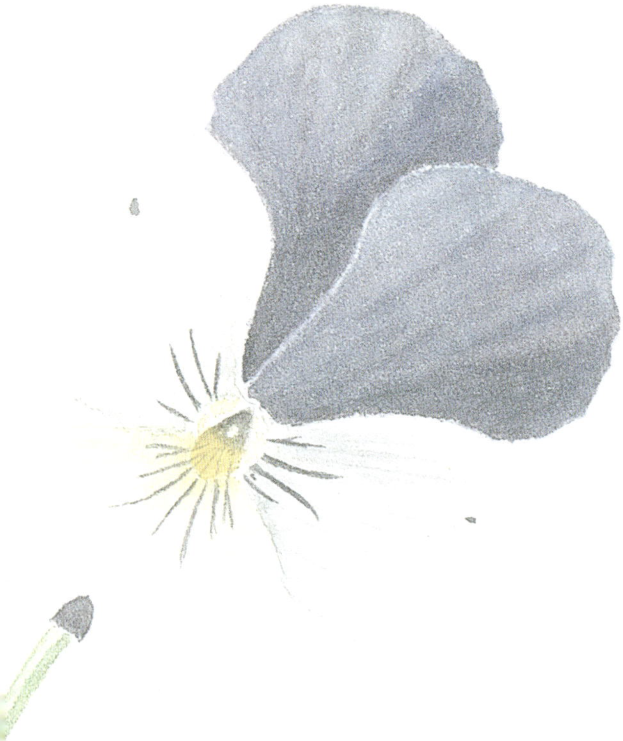

Viola

Still a cottage garden favourite, *Viola tricolor* is the wild forerunner of modern garden pansies. It is known as heartsease in its native England, and as johnny jump-up in the USA. Since the early nineteenth century, many hybrids have been cultivated, with great variety in colour and size.

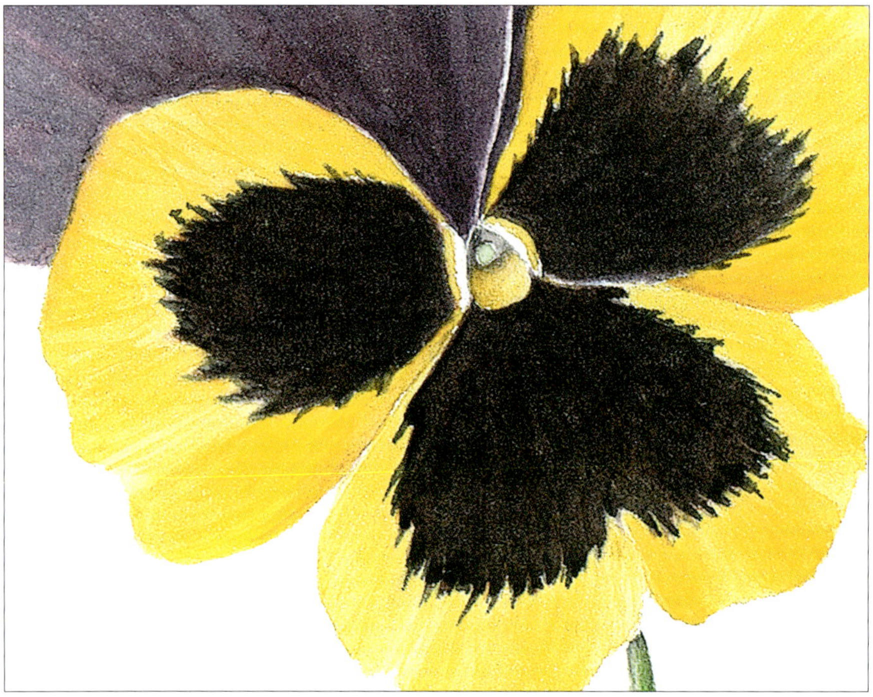

The dark areas of the three lower petals are not mixed as one colour. Instead, separate washes are applied sequentially on to the yellow base colour to give the rich velvet effect.

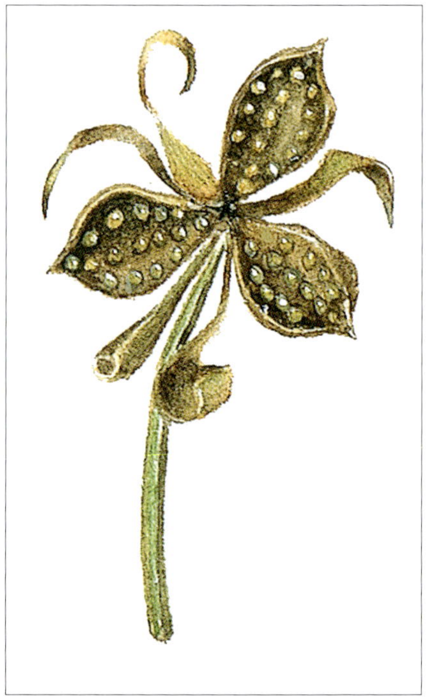

Each separate seed inside each pod should be painted individually. Leave a highlight on each seed then add a shadow to the background to give more form to the seeds.

Winter flowering
Large flower: pansy yellow/purple wing
Small top: orange-magenta ('Orange Duet')
Bottom: magenta-violet ('Coconut Duet')

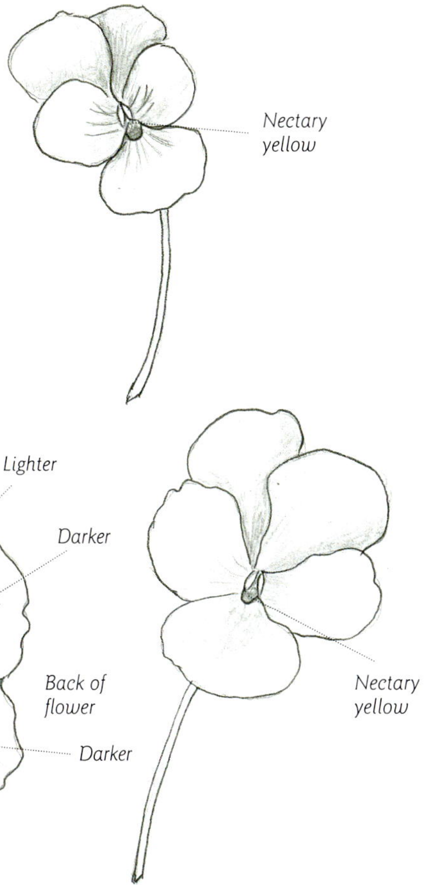

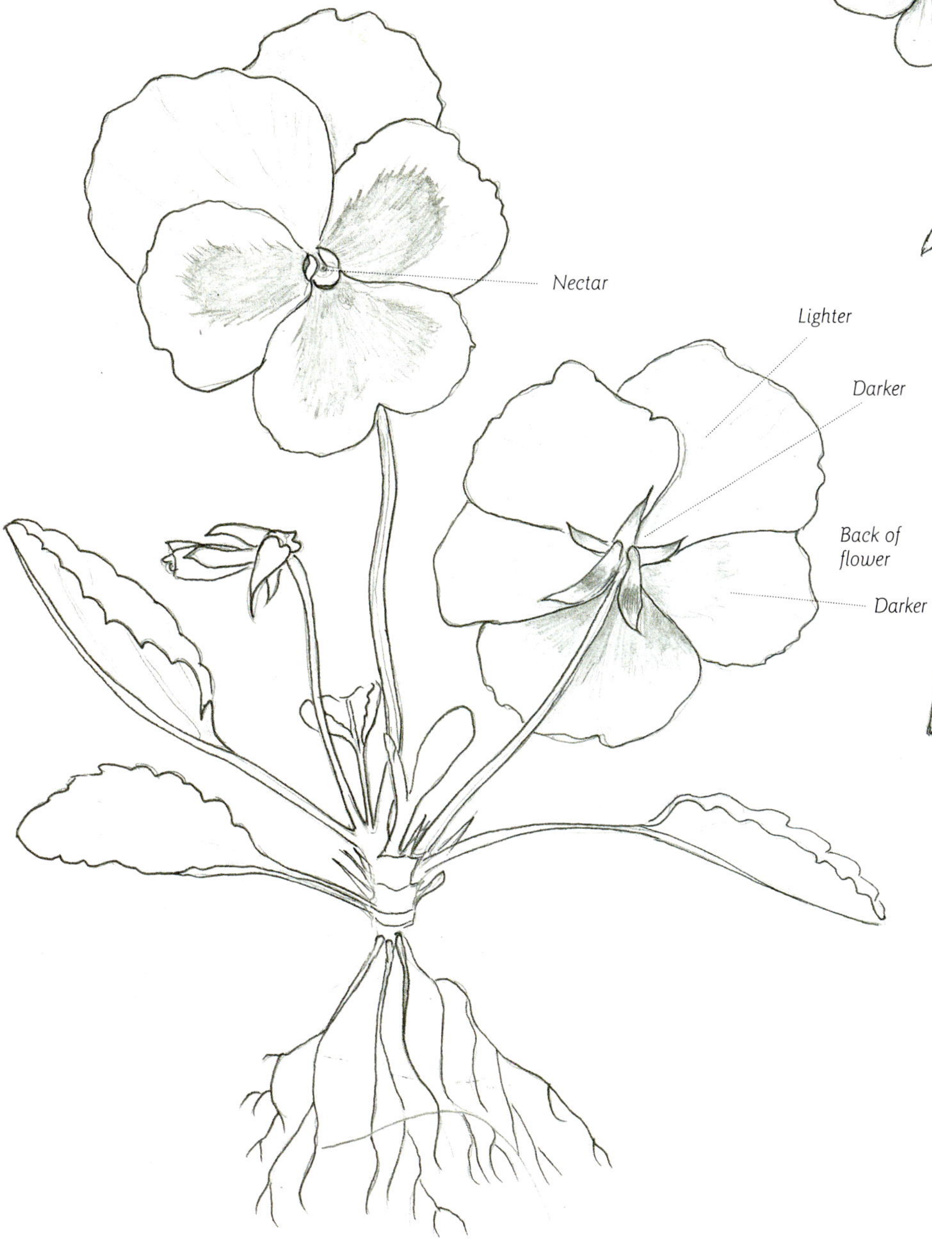

Yellow ochre

Raw umber

Seeds and seed pod

Stems:
Sap green and transparent yellow

Leaves:
Sap green and alizarin crimson

Wings of 'Coconut Duet':
Permanent magenta and
Winsor blue (red shade)

Underside of leaves (back):
Sap green, alizarin crimson
and a touch of titanium white

Large flower:

Permanent magenta
French ultramarine — *Two wings*

Winsor yellow — *Three petals*

Winsor yellow
French ultramarine
Permanent magenta
Alizarin crimson — *Three centres of petals*

'Orange Duet':

Alizarin crimson
French ultramarine — *Wings*

Winsor orange

Neutral tint for white petals
Winsor yellow patterning detail with same colour as wings for 'Coconut Duet'.

Painting the Viola

With your sketch to hand and your colours prepared, transfer the drawing to hot-pressed watercolour paper.

First wash

1 Using a size 3 brush, glaze all of the flower petals and allow them to dry. With a dilute mix of permanent magenta and French ultramarine, start to paint the top two petals, starting at the darker base and grading out to leave the highlights much lighter.

2 Paint in the small petals of the opening flower with the same mix and brush, then add a little alizarin crimson and apply the dilute mix to the two back petals, grading from the centre upwards into the lighter areas.

3 Once dry, use the size 3 brush with a dilute mix of Winsor yellow to start to paint the three other petals on the forward-facing flower. Again, start at the base. Ensure the stamens and nectary areas are left unpainted and grade the mix out towards the larger of the flower petals, leaving the highlights unpainted but grading into them.

4 Paint the back of the petals on the lower larger flower in the same way, leaving the highlights as before.

5 Using a size 2 brush and a dilute mix of alizarin crimson and French ultramarine, apply the first wash to the top two petals of the smaller 'Orange Duet' flower (top right), leaving the highlights as before.

6 With the same brush and a dilute mix of permanent magenta and Winsor blue (red shade), paint the top two petals of the 'Coconut Duet' flower (bottom left) using the same procedure as before.

7 Once both are dry, use the same size 2 brush and a dilute mix of Winsor orange to paint the three lower petals of the 'Orange Duet' making sure to leave the nectarines, stigma and stamens unpainted. Still using the same brush, but with a dilute mix of neutral tint, shadow the three lower petals of the 'Coconut Duet', leaving the white areas unpainted.

8 With the size 3 brush and clear water, glaze all of the stems and leaves. Once dry, use a dilute mix of sap green and transparent yellow to paint in the stems. These are square in section to make sure that the right-hand sides are darker and not graded.

9 Use the same dilute mix of sap green and transparent yellow to paint the sepals on the opening bud, the larger right-hand flower and the younger leaves.

10 With a mix of sap green and alizarin crimson, apply the first wash to the tops of the leaves and allow them to dry.

11 Add a little white gouache to the mix, and paint the underside (i.e. the back) of the leaves, leaving the veins unpainted.

12 Using a dilute mix of permanent magenta, alizarin crimson, French ultramarine and a little Winsor yellow, apply the first wash to the darker centre areas of the large main flower, starting from the centre and painting the pattern carefully as shown. Use a slightly dilute mix on the back of the other flower, creating the pattern as you work.

Tonal washes

1 Referring to the first wash steps for the appropriate brush size and mixes, repeat the steps above, building up the tone and form by using slightly stronger mixes.

Crossovers

1 Using a slightly stronger mix of neutral tint and a size 1 brush, paint in the small areas where the petals and sepals overlap.

2 Paint in the crossovers on the stems and leaves in the same way.

3 Repeat the steps until the individual components look correctly distanced and separate from each other.

Harmonisation

1 Use a size 2 brush and a dilute mix of sap green and transparent yellow to apply a small wash to the base of the petals on both of the large flowerheads.

Details

1 With a size 1 brush and a slightly stronger mix of permanent magenta and Winsor blue (red shade), add the patterning to the 'Coconut Duet' petals.

2 Using a stronger mix of alizarin crimson, French ultramarine and neutral tint, add the patterning to the 'Orange Duet'.

3 Change to the size 0 brush and use a dilute mix of yellow ochre to paint the seeds in the seed pod, leaving a highlight on each seed.

4 Once the seeds have dried, paint the pods and sepals using raw umber for the shadows. Add a little neutral tint to darken the tone until it is correct.

5 Still using the size 0 brush, paint the fine lines on all of the darker petals with a stronger mix of permanent magenta and alizarin crimson, and painting from the centre outwards.

6 Using a size 1 brush and a dilute mix of neutral tint, start to paint in the root system, grading into the highlight areas and darkening the areas in the background, keeping the front roots much lighter.

7 Once the roots have dried, follow the crossover instructions above to put the roots in position.

8 With the same brush and a dilute mix of raw umber, paint in the basal plate where the roots emerge.

9 With a size 0 brush and a mix of Winsor yellow, paint the stamens and stigmas on all of the flowers, adding a little sap green to the mix where necessary.

First wash

When painting the pattern on the main flower, refer to your sketch and the original flower if possible.

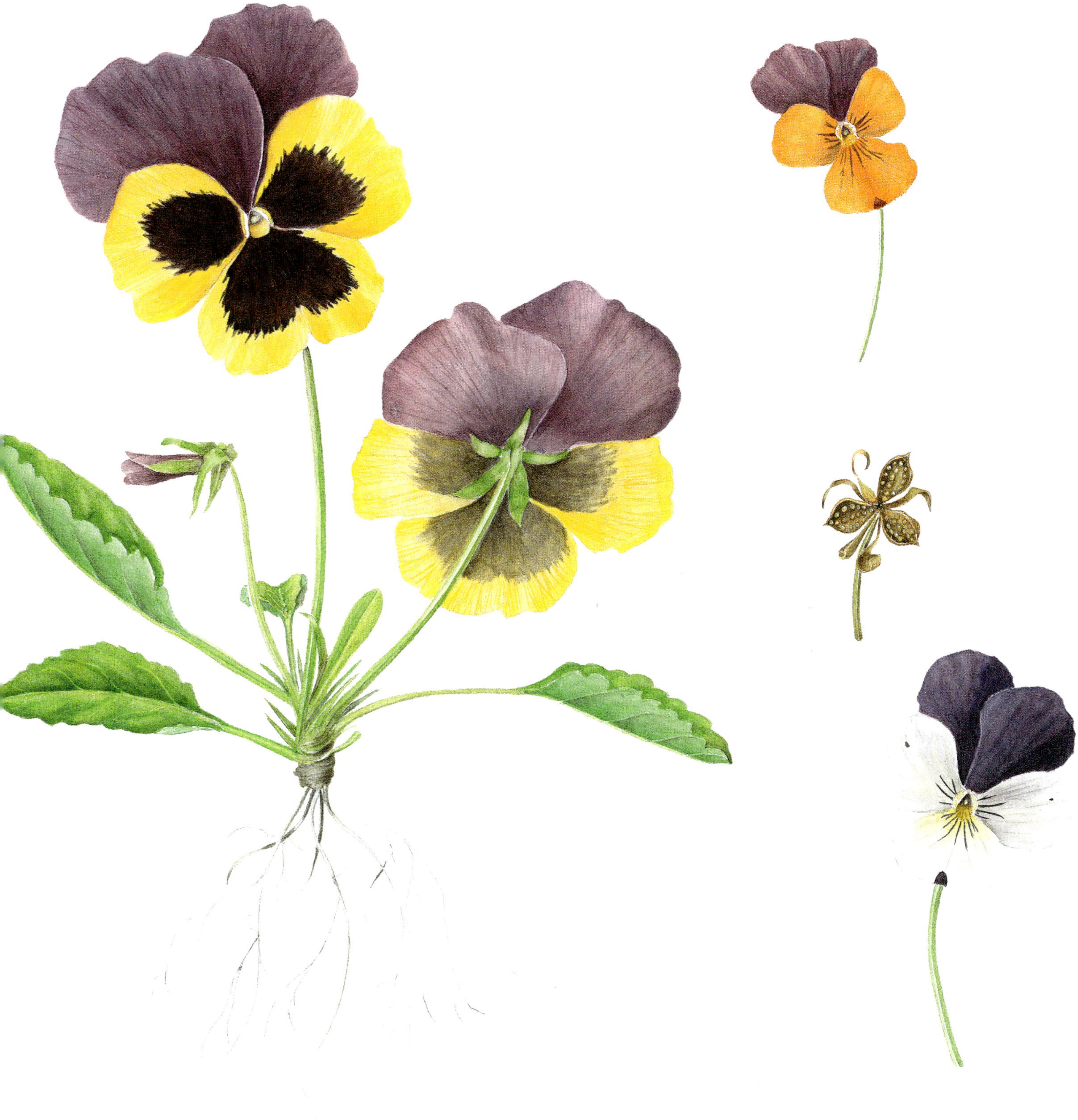

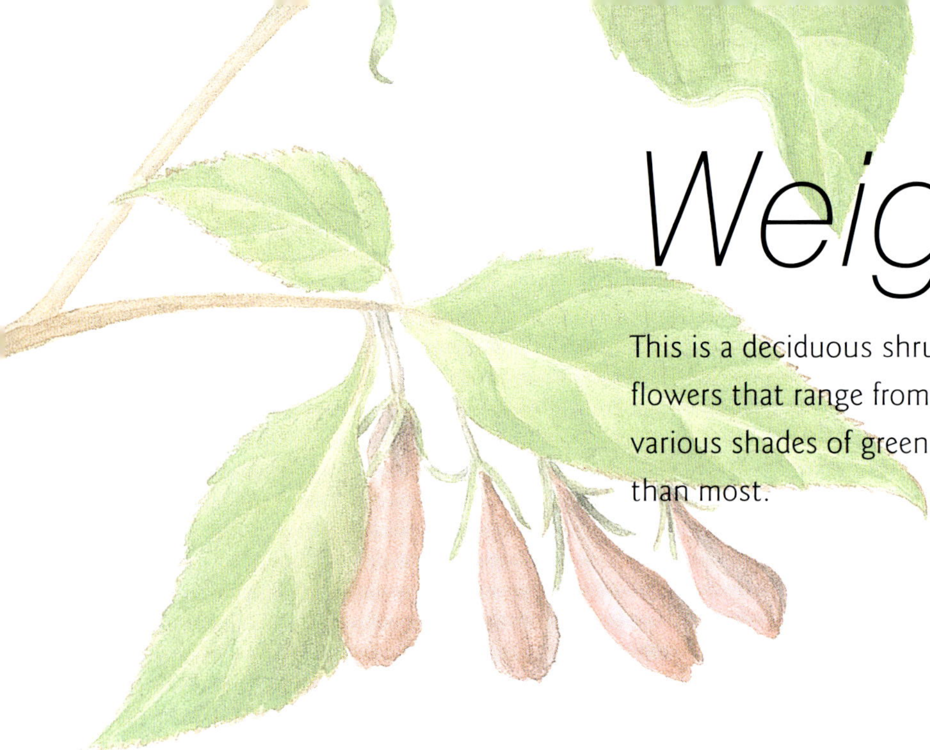

Weigela

This is a deciduous shrub found in the summer with foxglove-like flowers that range from white to pink and ruby red. The leaves are various shades of green, this particular variety being a lighter tone than most.

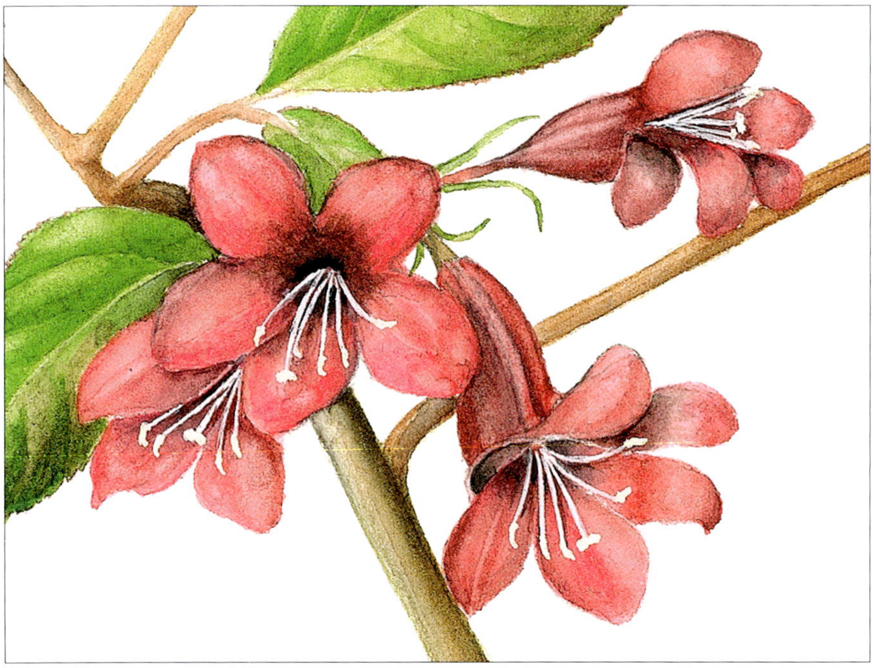

To obtain the highlights on each petal you will need to lift off using a little water and a small brush. The stigmas and stamens, meanwhile, can be painted in with a little white gouache.

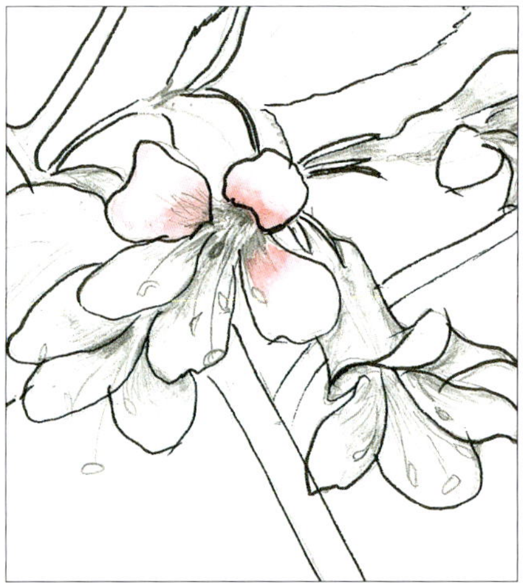

After drawing each flower in the sketchbook, a dilute wash of the appropriate colour was applied to suggest the form of one of them. This will give you invaluable practice before you begin the final painting of these complex areas.

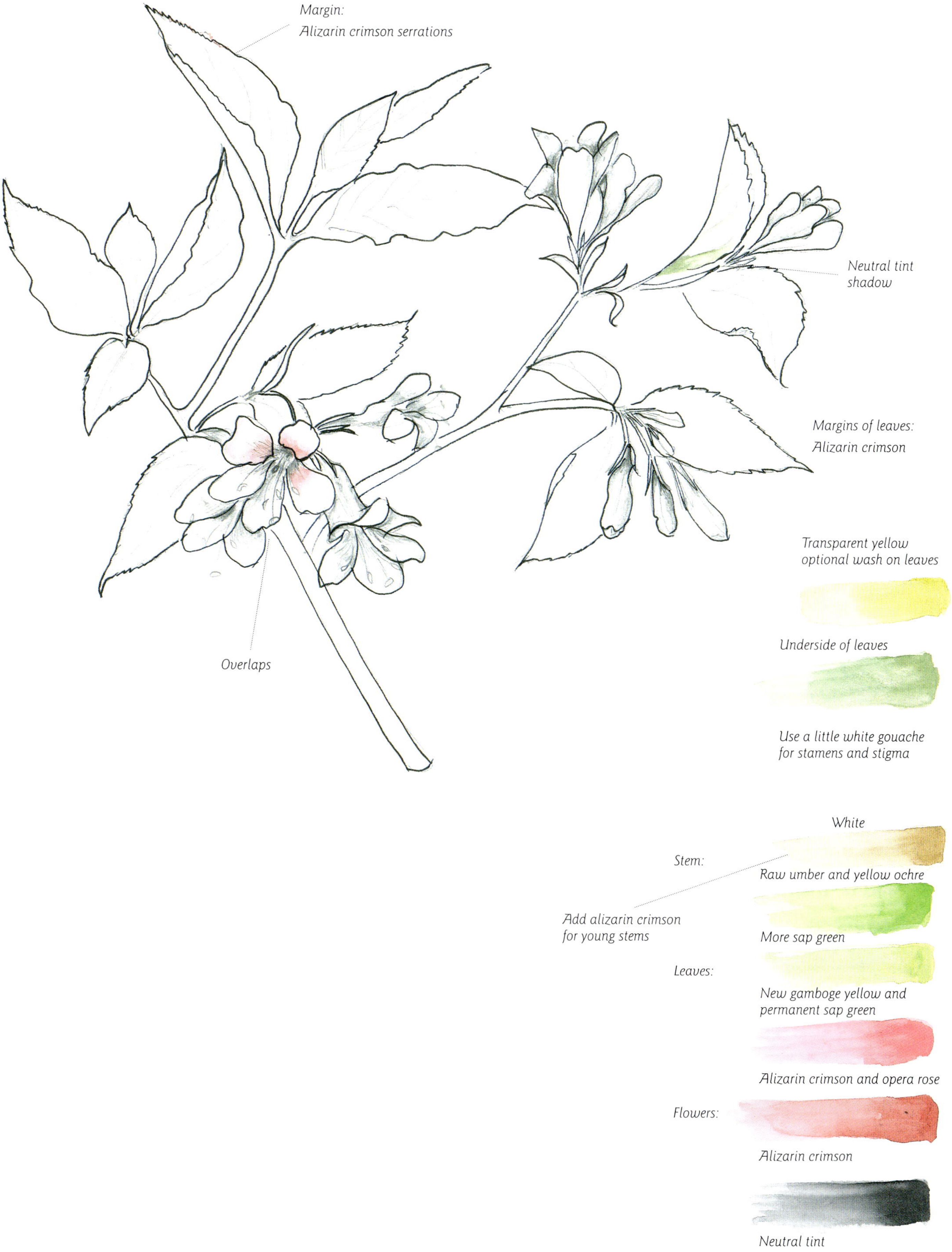

Margin:
Alizarin crimson serrations
Neutral tint shadow
Margins of leaves:
Alizarin crimson
Overlaps
Transparent yellow optional wash on leaves
Underside of leaves
Use a little white gouache for stamens and stigma
White
Stem:
Raw umber and yellow ochre
Add alizarin crimson for young stems
More sap green
Leaves:
New gamboge yellow and permanent sap green
Alizarin crimson and opera rose
Flowers:
Alizarin crimson
Neutral tint

Painting the *Weigela*

With your sketch to hand and your colours prepared, transfer the drawing to hot-pressed watercolour paper.

First wash

1 Use a size 3 brush to glaze all of the flower petals with clean water. With the same brush and a dilute mix of alizarin crimson and opera rose, paint the petals individually, starting in the centre of each flower and leaving the highlights unpainted at this stage.

2 Still using a size 3 brush, glaze all of the leaves with water and leave to dry. Using the same brush and a dilute mix of sap green and new gamboge yellow, paint the top side of the leaves, grading into the highlights but leaving them unpainted.

3 Switch to a size 2 brush and glaze all of the stems with clear water. Once dry, use a dilute mix of raw umber and yellow ochre to paint the stems, grading from right to left. Allow them to dry.

4 With the same brush and a mix of sap green, manganese blue and a little new gamboge yellow, paint the undersides of the leaves, leaving the veins unpainted.

Tonal washes

1 Repeat the washes on the flower petals using a size 2 brush and a stronger mix of alizarin crimson and opera rose. Make sure to grade into the throat of each flower and grade out to the highlights to shape and give form to the flowers.

2 Using the same brush and a mix of alizarin crimson, paint the buds, again grading into the highlights. Once this is dry, paint the flower stems and the sepals.

3 With a size 3 brush and a stronger mix of sap green and a little new gamboge yellow, build up the form and texture on all of the older larger, leaves. Add more new gamboge yellow to the mix for the younger, smaller leaves.

4 Using a size 2 brush and a stronger mix of raw umber and yellow ochre with a little neutral tint added, build up the form of the stems until the correct tone has been achieved and the portrait looks three-dimensional.

Crossovers

1 Use a size 1 brush and a mixture of neutral tint to shade behind each flower petal that is behind another, and also to shade flower stems or leaves behind the flowerheads.

2 Using the same brush and mix, shade behind the veins on the underside of the leaves to make them stand out and become convex.

Harmonisation

1 Using a size 2 brush and a dilute mix of alizarin crimson and opera rose, paint a small wash on to the leaves that are behind the flowers and buds.

2 With a dilute mix of the leaf colour, wash the flower petals closest to the leaves to harmonise the tones.

Details

1 Using a size 0000 brush and a little white gouache, paint the styles, stamens and the centre stigma.

2 With the same size brush and alizarin crimson, carefully paint in the serrations on the leaves and also the small veins.

Discretionary washes

I used a size 3 brush and a dilute mix of transparent yellow to wash over all of the leaves to enhance the greens.

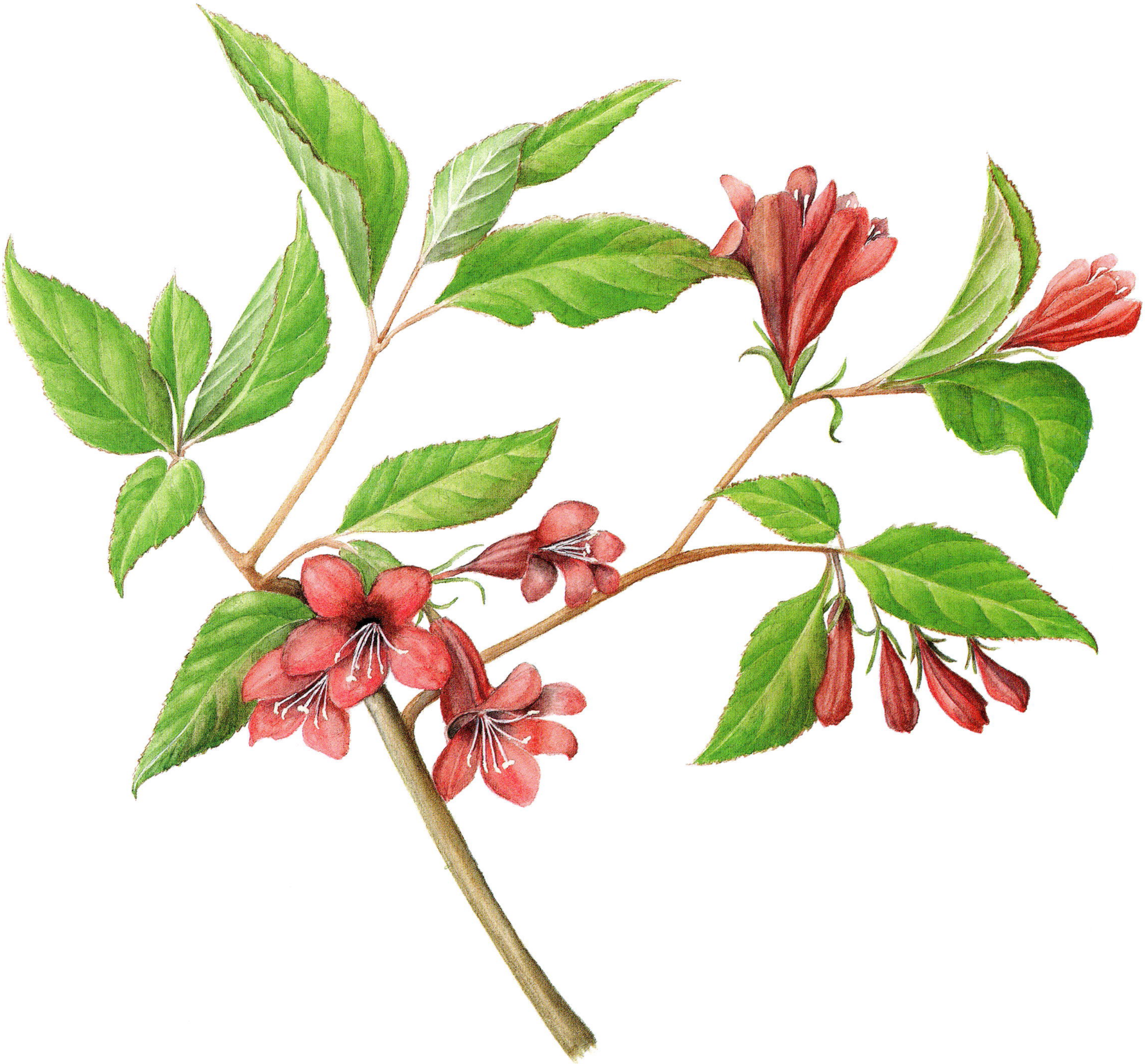

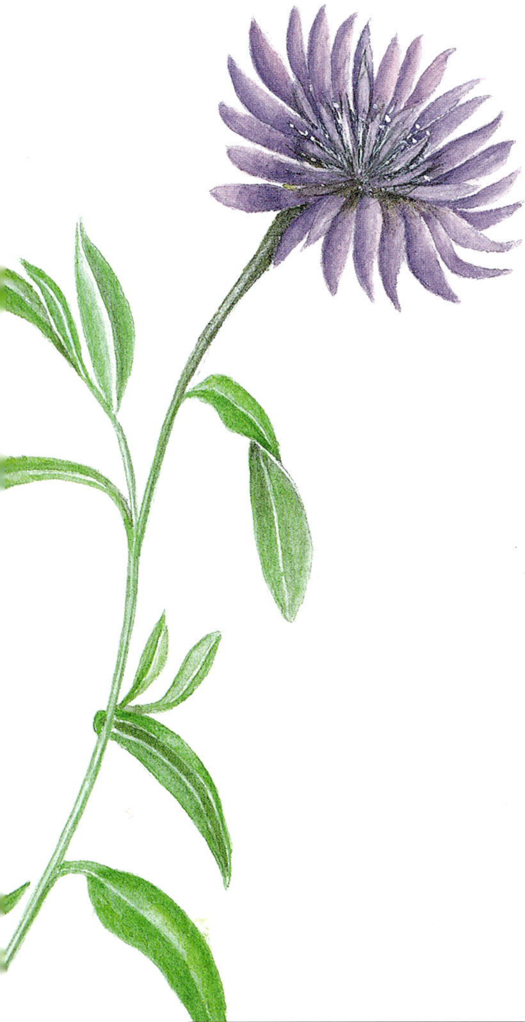

Xeranthemum

Named the everlasting flower, owing to its papery texture, the daisy-like purple flowers of *Xeranthemum annuum* can be dried and preserved with little to no loss of colour or form. This flower was very popular in the Victorian era as a cut flower.

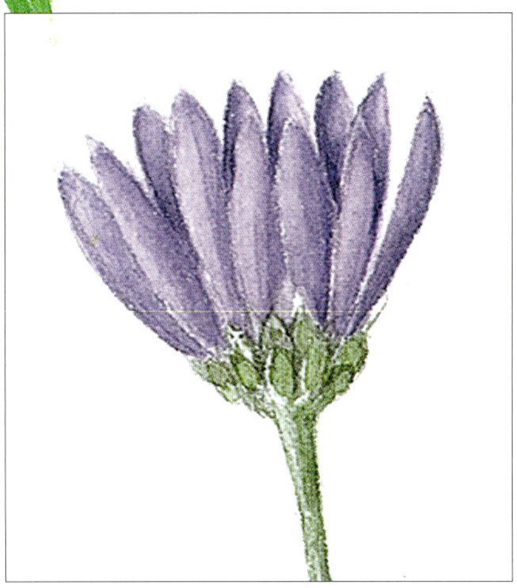

Note how dark the inner petals are compared to the outer ones. This helps to separate the individual petals while retaining the form of the flowerhead as a whole.

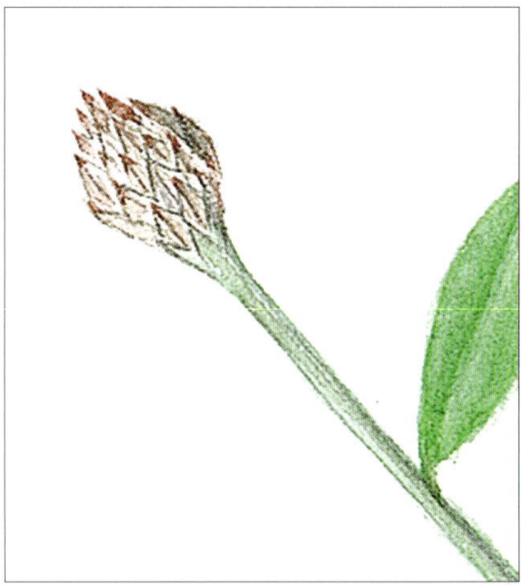

The closed buds are a completely different colour to the open flowers. This should be observed and noted on your sketch.

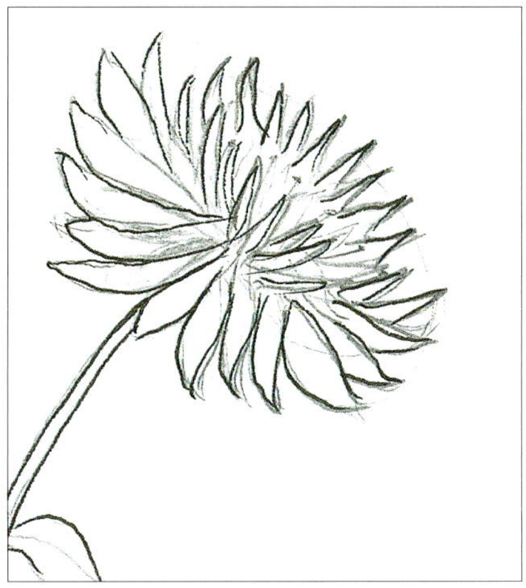

The composite flower has many petals, so care must be taken to observe and note the various angles in your sketchbook before painting. The small white stamens should also be noted.

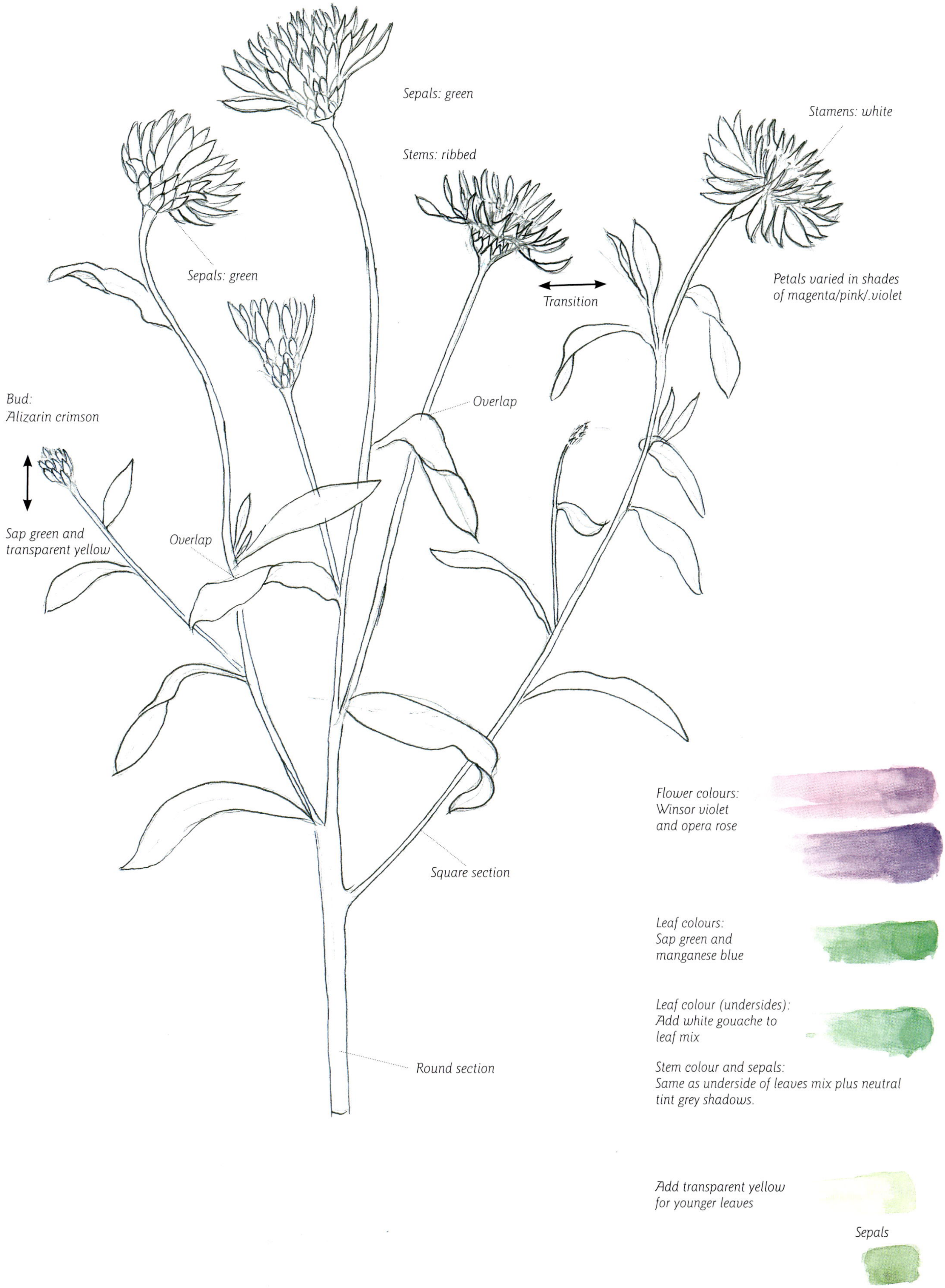
Sepals: green
Stamens: white
Stems: ribbed
Sepals: green
Transition
Petals varied in shades of magenta/pink/.violet
Overlap
Bud:
Alizarin crimson
Sap green and transparent yellow
Overlap
Square section
Round section
Flower colours:
Winsor violet
and opera rose
Leaf colours:
Sap green and
manganese blue
Leaf colour (undersides):
Add white gouache to
leaf mix
Stem colour and sepals:
Same as underside of leaves mix plus neutral
tint grey shadows.
Add transparent yellow
for younger leaves
Sepals

Painting the *Xeranthemum*

With your sketch to hand and your colours prepared, transfer the drawing to hot-pressed watercolour paper.

First wash

1 Use a size 2 brush to glaze the petals of each of the flowerheads with clean water. Once dry, use a dilute wash of Winsor violet and opera rose to paint the individual petals, leaving the highlights unpainted.

2 Paint the remaining flowerheads in this way. Create the effect of a three-dimensional image by painting the petals on the right-hand side darker and graded into the lighter areas.

3 Glaze the leaves and stems with clean water and allow to dry. With the same brush and a dilute mix of sap green and manganese blue, wash the top side of the leaves, grading from dark to light and ensuring the midrib is left unpainted.

4 Apply a thin wash of the leaf colour with a little white gouache added to paint the underside of the leaves and sepals. Allow the washes to dry completely.

Tonal washes

1 With a slightly thicker mix of the same colours and a size 2 brush, repeat the first wash stages until the correct depth of colour has developed. Add a little transparent yellow to the original mix for the topside of the younger leaves.

Tonal washes

Remember to leave the highlights unpainted by grading the paint out with water. It is still important to grade all the way over the area to avoid 'tidemarks' where the pigment settles.

Crossovers

1 With a size 1 brush and a dilute mix of neutral tint, darken the areas where the leaves overlap the stems. Repeat until the leaves are properly separated from the stems.

2 Darken the shadow areas between the flower petals with the same mix. Repeat this process until the correct tone is achieved.

Harmonisation

1 Use a size 2 brush to apply a small wash of a dilute mix of Winsor violet and opera rose to the upper leaves closest to the flowers.

2 Apply another small wash of the same mix to the upper stems.

3 With the same size brush and a mix of sap green and manganese blue, apply a small wash to the flower petals and sepals closest to the leaves. Allow to dry.

Details

1 Paint in the small sepal shapes using a size 0 brush and a mix of sap green and transparent yellow, adding alizarin crimson to the mix towards the top of the bud.

2 Repeat this process for the smaller bud.

3 Use the same size brush and a little white gouache to paint in the styles and stamens on the two right-hand flowerheads.

4 Still using the size 0 brush, paint in the shadows on the stigmas and styles with neutral tint.

Discretionary washes

Using a size 1 brush I washed a dilute mix of manganese blue and sap green over all of the leaves including the midribs. Once dry, I applied a second wash but this time stippled the paint to give a mottled look to the leaves. I left this to dry and then applied a dilute wash of transparent yellow over all of the tops of leaves and left to dry.

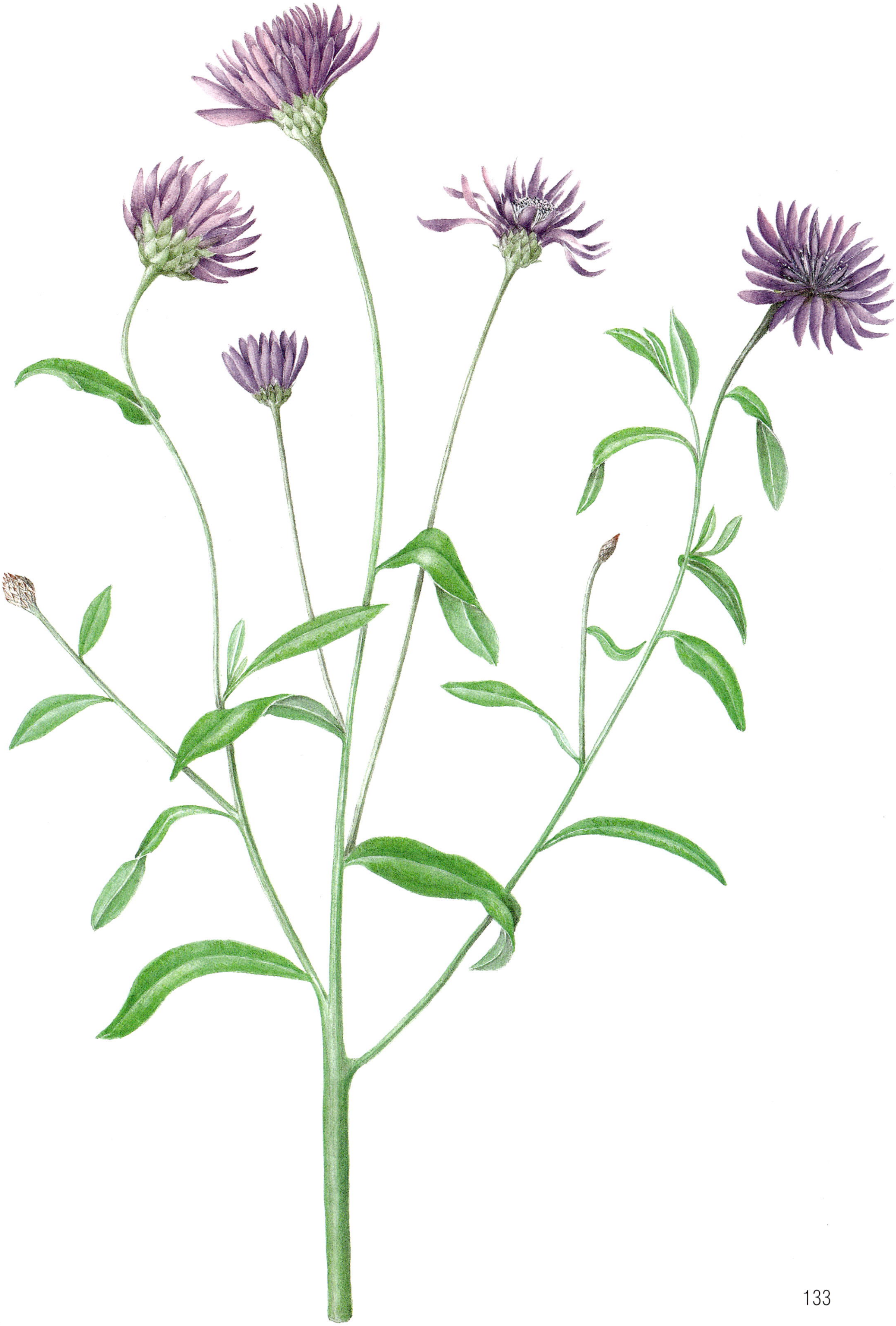

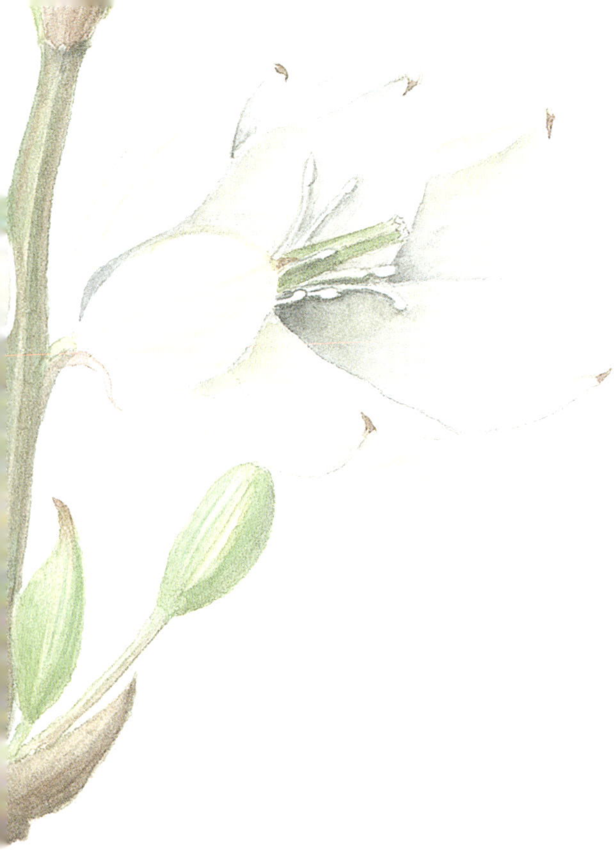

Yucca

Yucca flaccida is an evergreen short-stemmed shrub that produces tufts of narrow dark green leaves alongside long attractive panicles of bell-shaped creamy-white flowers.

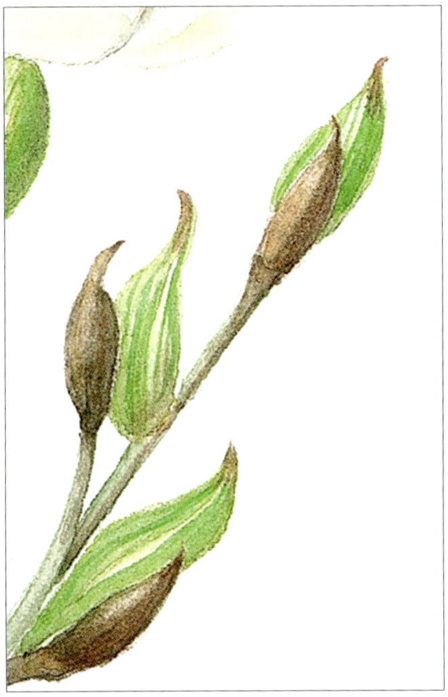

When closed, the buds are light green with much lighter veins. These must be left unpainted, which is best achieved by working your brush in long strokes alongside the veins that run the length of the leaf.

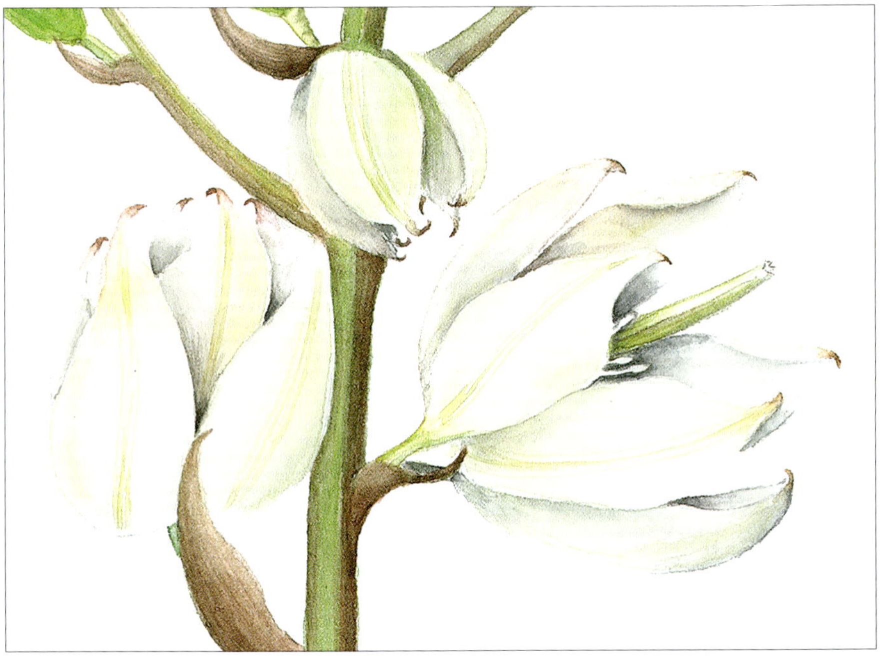

Dilute washes of neutral tint applied to the shaded areas of this creamy-white flower help to give the petals form and structure. This is best done at an early stage before the light greens are applied, as otherwise the petals can appear flat and uninteresting.

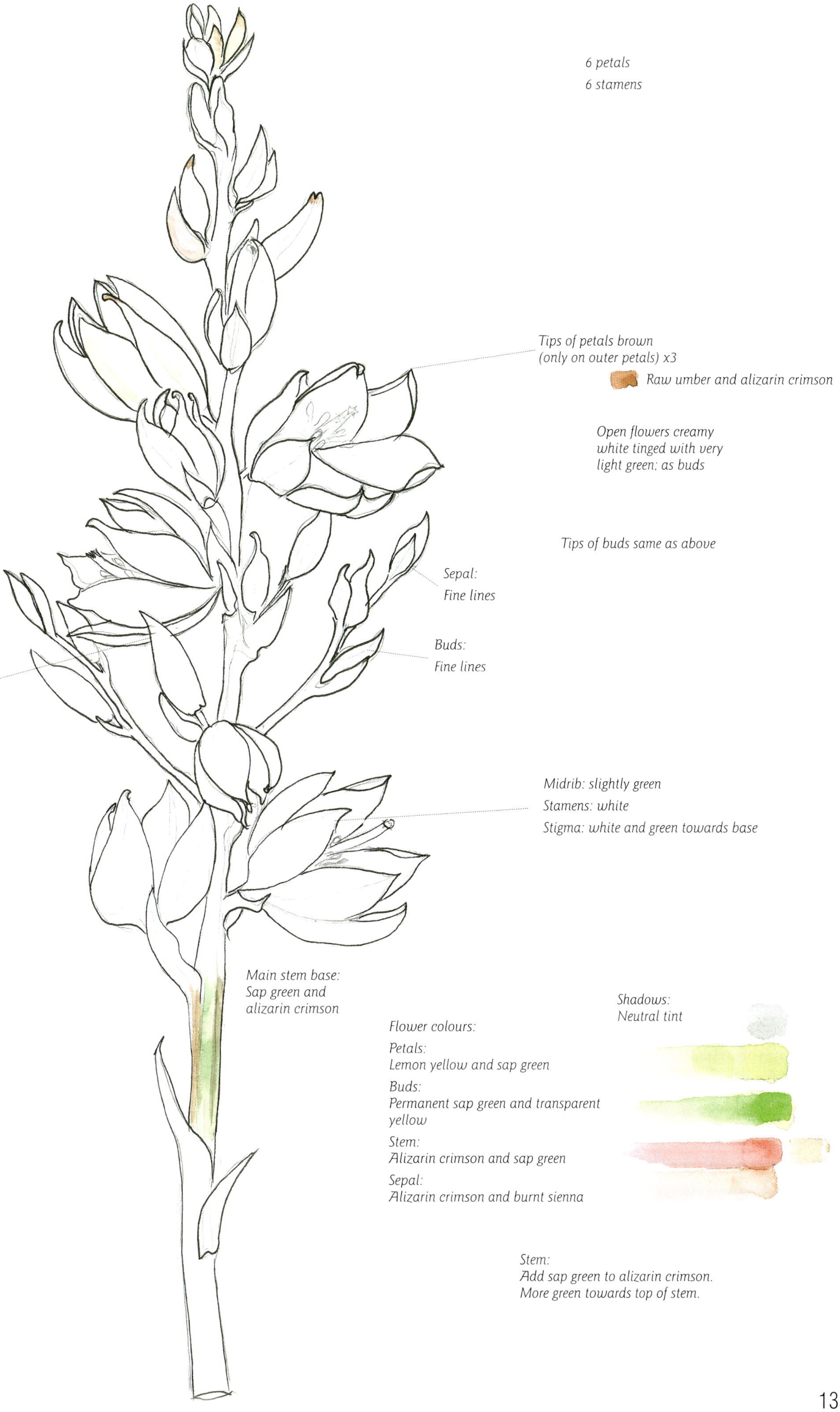
6 petals
6 stamens
Tips of petals brown
(only on outer petals) x3
Raw umber and alizarin crimson
Open flowers creamy
white tinged with very
light green; as buds
Tips of buds same as above
Sepal:
Fine lines
Buds:
Fine lines
Overlap
Midrib: slightly green
Stamens: white
Stigma: white and green towards base
Main stem base:
Sap green and
alizarin crimson
Shadows:
Neutral tint
Flower colours:
Petals:
Lemon yellow and sap green
Buds:
Permanent sap green and transparent
yellow
Stem:
Alizarin crimson and sap green
Sepal:
Alizarin crimson and burnt sienna
Stem:
Add sap green to alizarin crimson.
More green towards top of stem.

Painting the *Yucca*

With your sketch to hand and your colours prepared, transfer the drawing to hot-pressed watercolour paper.

First wash

1 With a size 2 brush and clean water, glaze all of the petals and stem and allow them to dry. As the flower is predominantly white, use a dilute mix of neutral tint to paint the flowerheads and each of the petals and buds by applying the mix to the shadow areas to create form and depth.

2 Use the same brush with a dilute mix of sap green and transparent yellow to paint in the buds, grading each from right to left and leaving the highlights unpainted.

3 With a dilute mix of alizarin crimson and burnt sienna, paint the sepals in the same way as the buds.

4 Use a dilute mix of alizarin crimson and sap green to paint the stem. As the stem is almost square in cross-section, with strong angles, paint it to leave a line showing the shape of the section, adding more sap green towards the top of the stem.

Tonal washes

1 Use a size 2 brush to build up the shadow areas of the flowerheads with neutral tint. Once dry, use a dilute mix of lemon yellow and sap green to paint from the centre midrib of the outer petals and shadow areas. Be careful not to use too much of this mix or the white flower will look too green.

2 With a size 2 brush and the alizarin crimson and sap green mix, darken the stem on the right-hand side keeping the square section.

3 Use a thicker mix of transparent yellow and sap green to build up the buds.

4 Build up the sepals using a thicker mix of alizarin crimson and burnt sienna.

Crossovers

1 Use a size 1 brush and a dilute mix of neutral tint to paint in the small areas where the petals, sepals and buds overlap each other, ensuring that you darken the areas in the distance a little more.

Harmonisation

1 Use a size 2 brush with a dilute mix of Winsor yellow and sap green to wash the sepals and buds closest to each other. This creates the effect of light reflecting a little of the colour from the sepals to the buds and vice versa.

2 With a dilute mix of alizarin crimson and burnt sienna, wash the petals closest to the buds and sepals to harmonise the colours.

Details

1 With a size 1 brush and a slightly thicker mix of alizarin crimson and raw umber, paint the tips of the outer petals and buds.

2 Use a mix of sap green and transparent yellow to paint in the stigmas, grading from dark to light, then use the same mix to paint the lines on the buds and stem.

3 Paint the lines of the sepals with a mix of alizarin crimson.

4 Switch to a size 00 brush and use white gouache to paint in the styles and stamens.

Discretionary washes

I used a size 2 brush and a dilute mix of transparent yellow to wash over the stems and green buds.

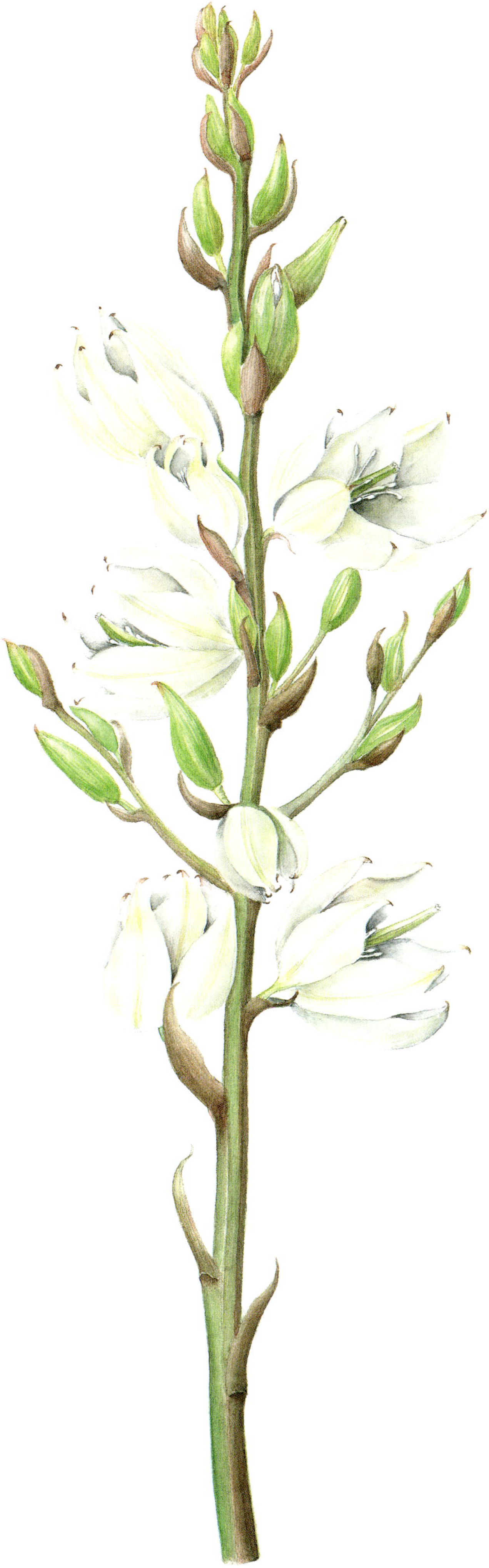

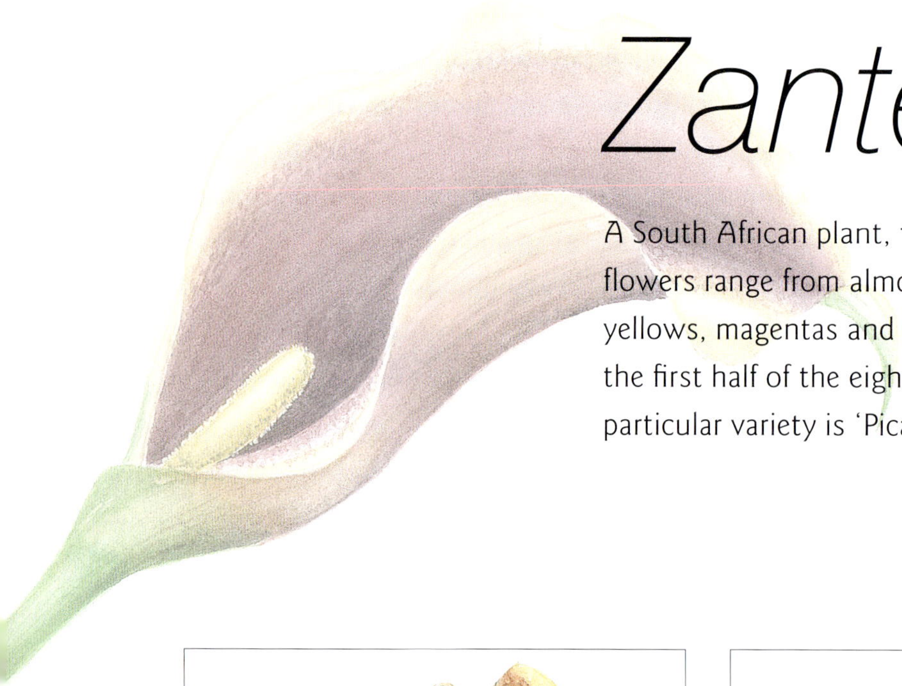

Zantedeschia

A South African plant, the calla lily comes in many colours. The flowers range from almost black to nearly pure white, and include yellows, magentas and pinks. The flower was brought to Europe in the first half of the eighteenth century and to England in 1731. This particular variety is 'Picasso'.

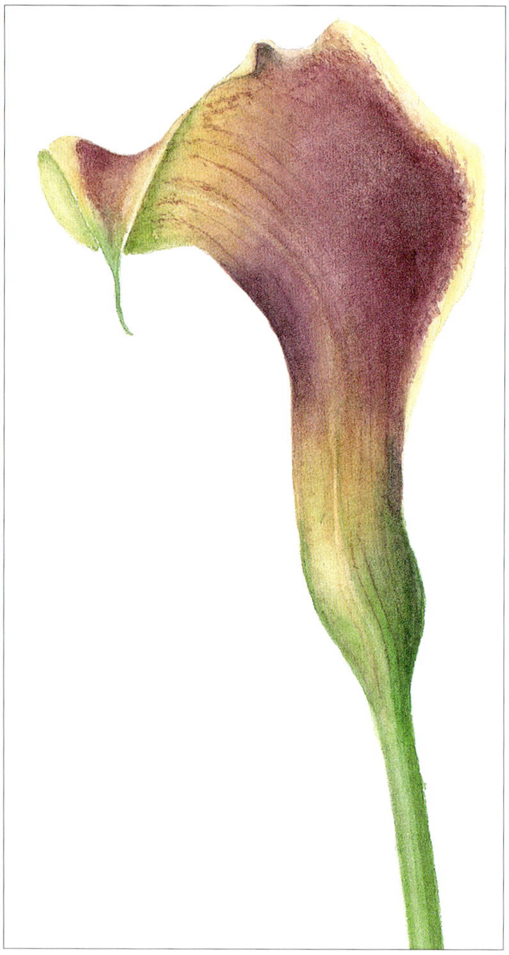

When grading strong colours such as permanent magenta and alizarin crimson into much lighter colours, grading should start early so as not to lose the highlights and form.

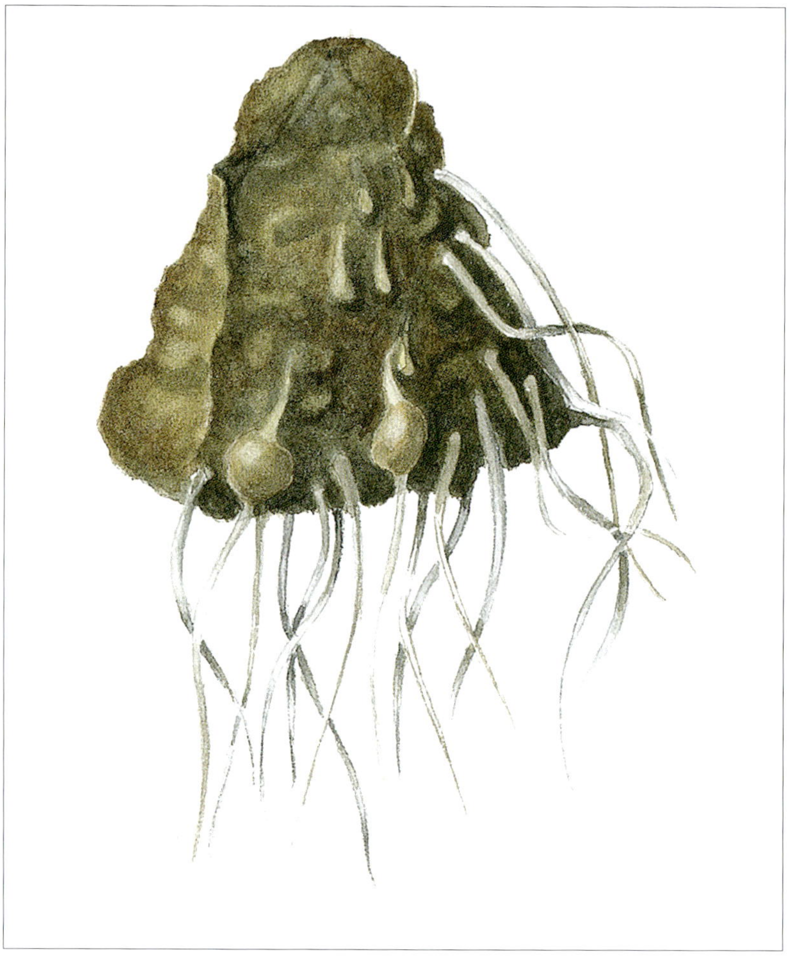

The rhizomes on the calla lily come in all shapes and sizes, with small baby rhizomes attached to them. These can be safely removed and grown on to form larger ones. However, when painting the plant, these can make an interesting addition to the portrait, so you should include the rhizomes.

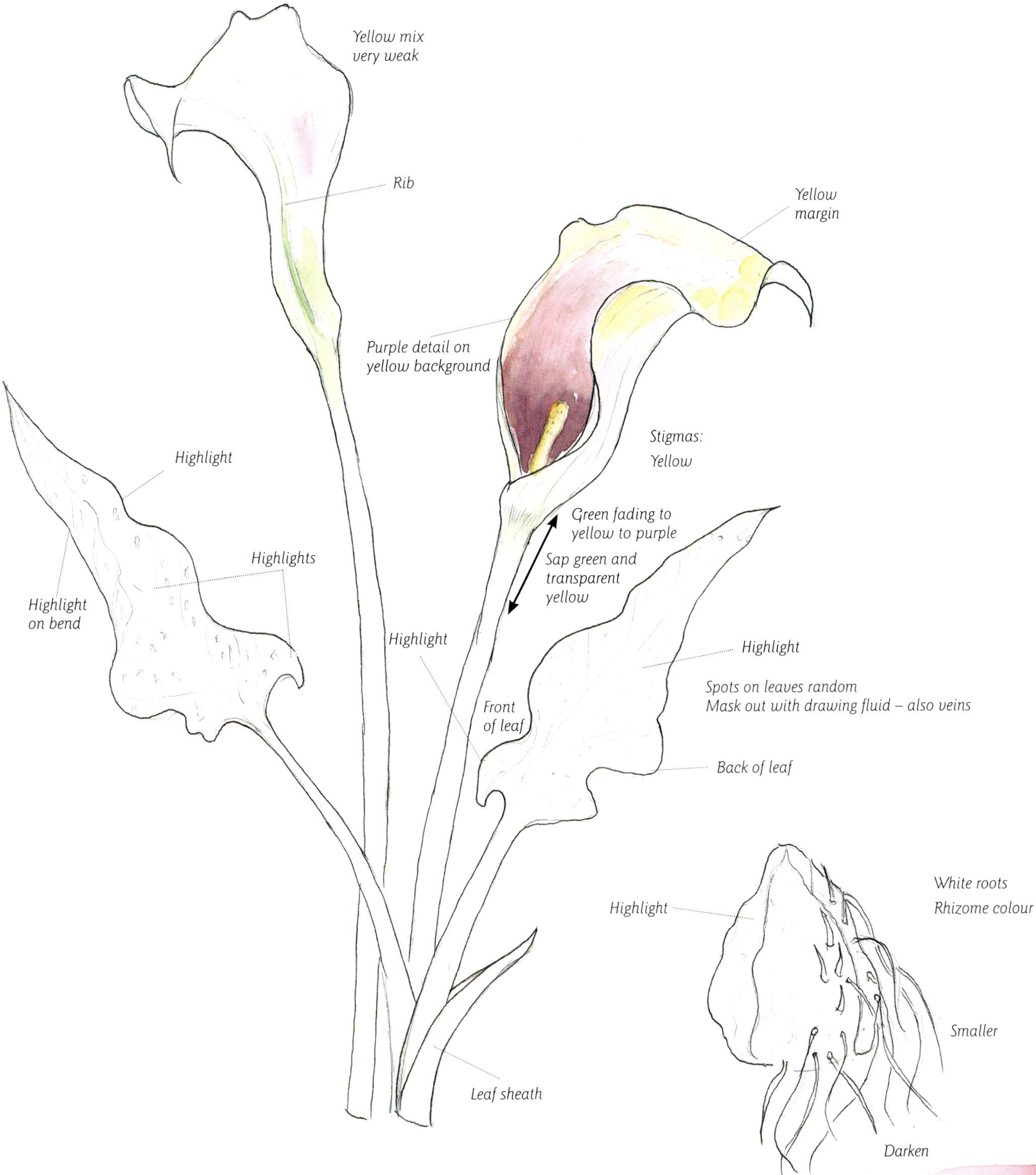

Flower patterning and stems:
Permanent magenta and
Prussian blue

Flower stems:
Sap green and transparent yellow

Flower petal:
Lemon yellow

Roots:
Thin neutral tint

Corm:
Grey/light brown

Front of leaf:
Permanent sap green and alizarin crimson

Back of leaf:
Sap green and transparent yellow

Painting the *Zantedeschia*

With your sketch to hand and your colours prepared, transfer the drawing to hot-pressed watercolour paper.

First wash

1 Glaze all of the flowerheads using a size 3 brush and clean water. Once dry, apply a dilute mix of lemon yellow as a wash, grading into the highlights to form the base colour.

2 Apply a very dilute mix of permanent magenta, starting with the throat of the flower and grading into the highlight. Whilst waiting for this to dry, grade a dilute mix of sap green and transparent yellow down the stem into the white of the stem.

3 Mask out the light spots on the leaves. When the masking fluid is completely dry, glaze the leaves with water using a size 3 brush and allow to dry.

4 Apply a dilute mix of Sennelier sap green with a touch of alizarin crimson to the top of the leaves, grading the paint into the highlights.

5 Using a dilute mix of transparent yellow and sap green, paint the undersides of the leaves.

6 Glaze the stems with clean water and use the transparent yellow and sap green mix to paint in the stems, grading into the highlight areas. Paint the small leaf sheath in the same way.

7 Glaze the rhizome with clean water and allow to dry before applying a dilute wash of raw umber, grading into the highlight.

Tonal washes

1 Using the size 3 brush, repeat the first wash steps using the slightly stronger wells of paint to darken and create a three-dimensional image, including the rhizome.

2 When the leaves are looking lifelike with form and tonal value, remove the masking fluid by gently rubbing it away with a clean finger.

3 Use a size 3 brush with a thicker mix of permanent magenta and Prussian blue to darken the throat of the right-hand flower, grading upwards to the lighter magenta.

4 Build up the rhizome using yellow ochre added to the initial wash colour.

Crossovers

1 Using a size 2 brush and neutral tint, shadow the areas where the stems, leaves and flowers cross, grading out to blend in with the base colours.

2 Repeat as necessary until the stems and leaves look the correct distance from each other.

3 With the same brush and mix, shadow the right-hand side of the stigma, grading the colour into the magenta of the flower throat.

4 Using a size 1 brush, shadow the roots of the rhizome at the points where they cross and add shadows to the new shoots on the rhizome.

Harmonisation

1 Using a size 3 brush and a very dilute mix of permanent magenta, wash the top half of the right-hand leaf and grade into the green avoiding the white patterning.

2 With a dilute mix of sap green and transparent yellow, wash the lower halves of both flowers and allow to dry before continuing.

Details

1 Using a size 1 brush with a mix of permanent magenta, paint in the vertical lines on the flowers, keeping them thin and neat.

2 Add the stamens to the stigma using the same mix and brush.

3 Add a dilute wash of neutral tint to the right-hand side of the root, carefully blending into the white paper.

Discretionary washes

Using a size 3 brush with a dilute mix of sap green and transparent yellow, I washed both leaves, including the white patterning marks previously masked out. This diffused them and gave a more natural look.

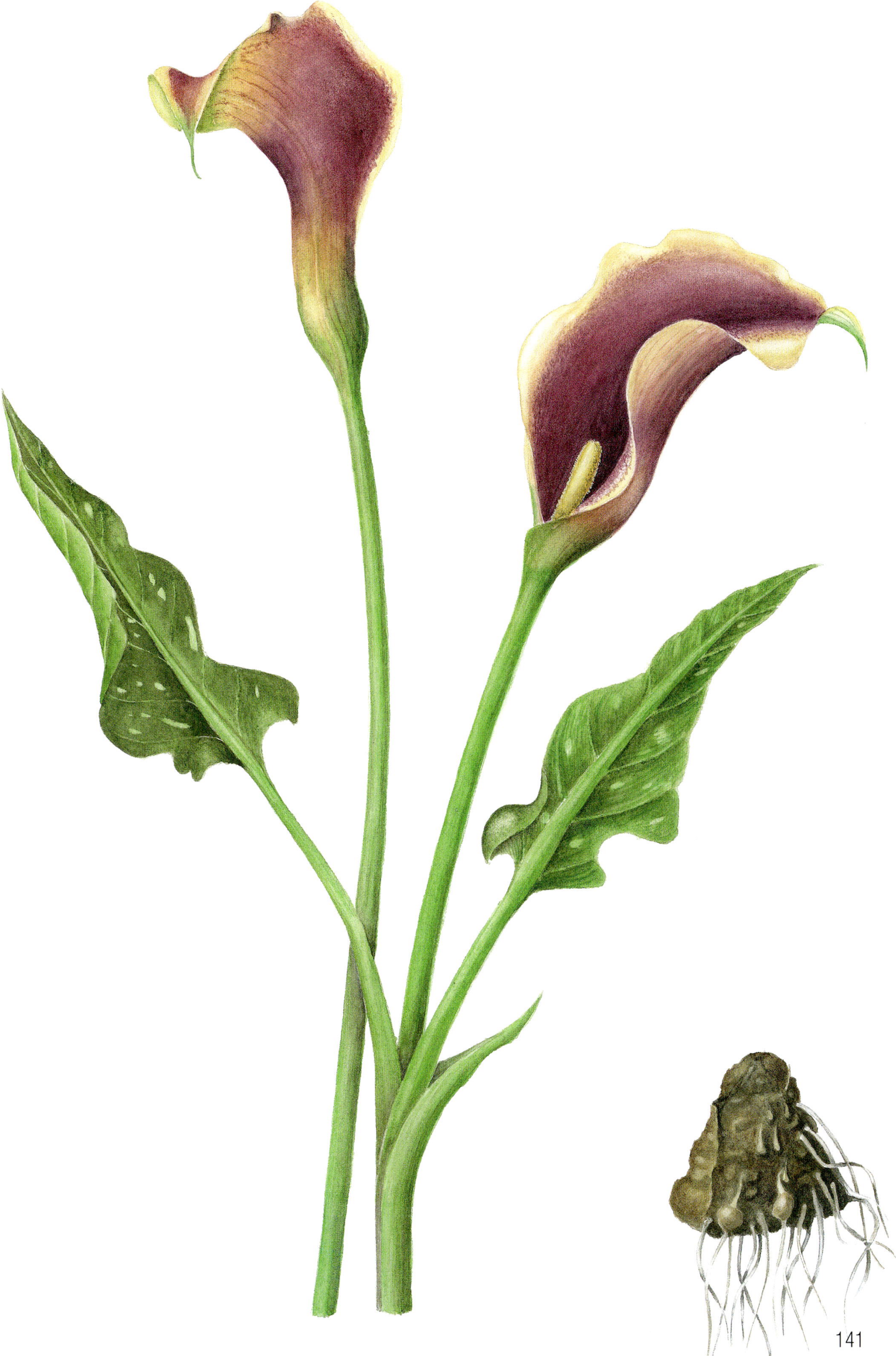

Finishing your work

When you think you have finished your work, leave it for a day or two, then scrutinise your painting to ensure your edges are neat and crisp. If necessary, remove any pencil marks with an eraser, and clean any other untidiness

I find that another artist's critique of the work is always useful before you declare the painting finished.

Tip

If you have had the misfortune to make errant marks with your paint, you can use a sharp scalpel to gently scrape them away from the surface. Once removed, smooth the paper using the back of a spoon.

Naming your work

The naming of plants follows an international system, to ensure the plant has a name recognisable in any part of the world in addition to its regional, common name.

Plant names have two parts, which is why the system is called binomial nomenclature. The first part of the name is the genus, and this is always capitalised. This is followed by the species, which is not capitalised. Both of these parts are italicised.

Some plants are grown for specific purposes, and while they remain the same species as one another, are distinct. These include different garden varieties of flowers, where the colour, shape or size may vary; and are known as cultivars. Cultivars are distinguished by the addition of a third name, which has an initial capital letter, is not italicised, and is enclosed by single quotation marks.

An example of naming

Camelia	*japonica*	'Jupiter'
Genus	*Species*	*Cultivar/ variety*

Mounting and framing your work

The mount you use needs to be of good quality. I would recommend archival quality mounts, which are acid-free and will not discolour with age. Off-white tones usually set off botanical paintings best, and you might like to experiment with double or triple mounts.

Make sure you (or your framer) uses acid-free tape on your work. I also recommend ultraviolet glass to help protect your work from fading.

Like the mount, the frame you use for your work is a personal choice, but I find simple, plain mounts best for botanical work, whether they be dark wood or natural oak or ash.

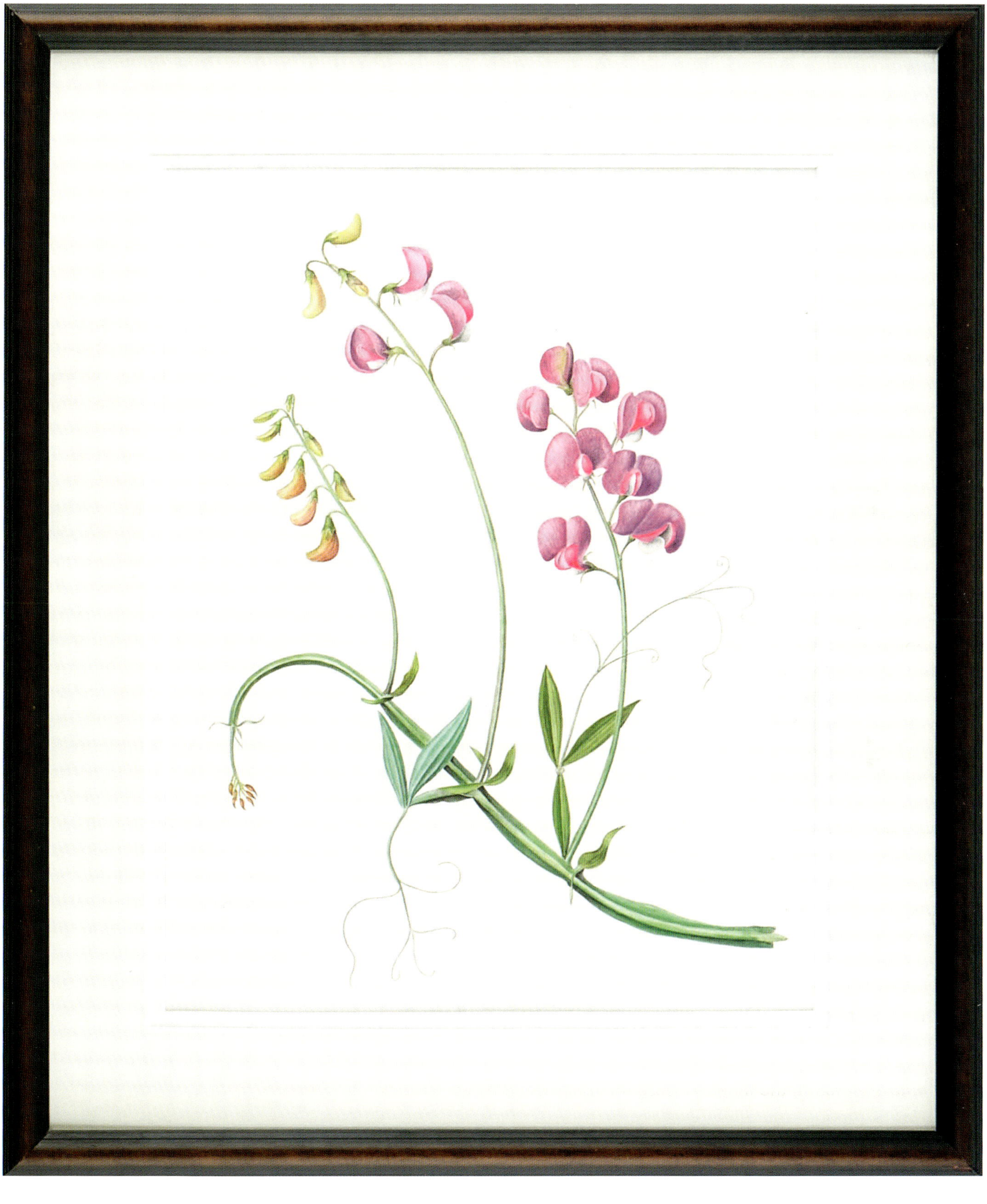

Index

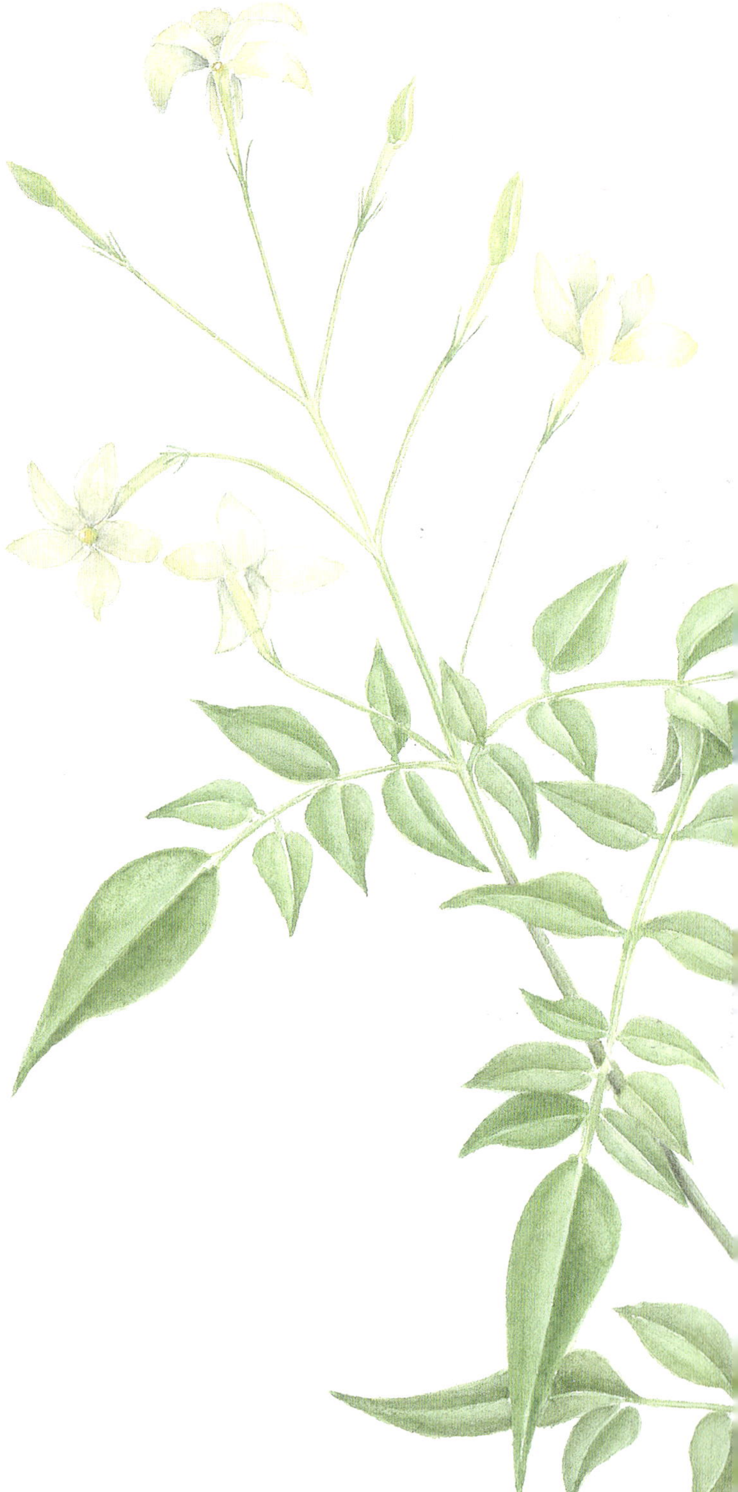